GET READY FOR SCHOOL: SECOND GRADE

421 ACTIVITIES & 1,834 ILLUSTRATIONS

GET READY FOR SCHOOL: SECOND GRADE

HEATHER STELLA

421 ACTIVITIES & 1,834 ILLUSTRATIONS

BLACK DOG
& LEVENTHAL
PUBLISHERS
NEW YORK

Black Dog & Leventhal Publishers
Hachette Book Group
1290 Avenue of the Americas
New York, NY 10104
www.hachettebookgroup.com
www.blackdogandleventhal.com

First Edition: May 2016
First Revised Edition: April 2021

Black Dog & Leventhal Publishers is an imprint of Perseus Books, LLC, a subsidiary of Hachette Book Group, Inc. The Black Dog & Leventhal Publishers name and logo are trademarks of Hachette Book Group, Inc.

Interior design by Clea Chmela

LCCN: 2020939149

ISBNs: 978-0-7624-7240-6 (spiral bound)

Printed in China

APS

10 9 8 7 6 5 4 3 2 1

CONTENTS

A NOTE TO PARENTS

GET READY FOR SCHOOL: SECOND GRADE is an indispensable educational companion for your child. It builds on skills learned in first grade and introduces your child to new concepts, including reading, writing complete sentences, counting by 2s, 5s, and 10s, adding and subtracting, shapes and measurements, time and money, weather, basic world geography, the solar system, and more. In addition, there are plenty of fun word games, mazes, and coloring activities that are designed to entertain and amuse your child while boosting his or her basic skills.

We recommend setting aside some time each day to read with your child. The more your child reads, the faster he or she will acquire other skills. We also suggest that you have your child complete a portion of this book each day. You and your child can sit down and discuss what the goals for each day will be, and perhaps even choose a reward to be given upon completion of the whole book—such as a trip to the park, a special playdate, or something else that seems appropriate to you.

While you want to help your child set educational goals, be sure to offer lots of encouragement along the way. These activities are not meant as a test. By making them fun and rewarding, you will help your child look forward to completing them, and he or she will be especially eager to tackle the educational challenges ahead!

Hey, kids!
Remember to have
a pencil and some crayons
handy when playing
with your
Get Ready book!

Sight Words: BECAUSE

Read, Trace, and Write It

because

Fill in the Missing Letter

___ecause

be___ause

becau___e

beca___se

Find and Circle It

because	became	become
behave	because	between
become	before	because
became	because	before
because	between	behave

Read and Copy

Please hurry because I am late!

Box It: Tall, Small, or Fall?

b e c a u s e

Clap It: because

How Many Syllables?

1 2 3

Sight Word: BEFORE

Read, Trace, and Write It

before

Fill in the Missing Letter

befo__e

be__ore

b__fore

befor__

Find and Circle It

become	became	before
became	before	behave
between	behave	before
before	between	below
below	before	become

Read and Copy

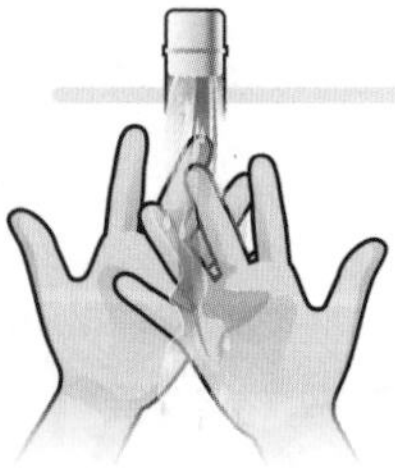

Wash your hands before you eat!

Box It: Tall, Small, or Fall?

b e f o r e

Clap It: before

How Many Syllables?

1 2 3

Sight Word: DOES

Read, Trace, and Write It

does

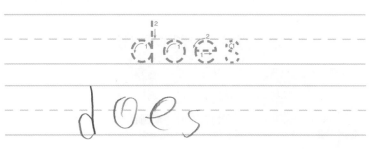

Fill in the Missing Letter

doe___

do___s

___oes

d___es

Find and Circle It

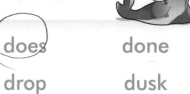

dose	does	done
does	drop	dusk
drop	dose	days
does	dusk	does
days	does	done

Read and Copy

He does not look happy.

Box It: Tall, Small, or Fall?

Clap It: does

How Many Syllables?

1 2 3

Sight Word: FOUND

Read, Trace, and Write It

found

Fill in the Missing Letter

f___und

foun___

fo___nd

fou___d

Find and Circle It

find	found	fought
fond	find	found
sound	found	sound
fought	four	four
found	fond	found

Read and Copy

I found a ball.

Box It: Tall, Small, or Fall?

Clap It: found

How Many Syllables?

1 2 3

Sight Word: GOES

Read, Trace, and Write It

goes

Fill in the Missing Letter

g___es

___oes

goe___

go___s

Find and Circle It

goes	nose	toes
toes	goes	goes
goat	does	goal
goal	nose	does
goes	goes	goat

Read and Copy

The car goes fast.

Box It: Tall, Small, or Fall?

Clap It: goes

How Many Syllables?

1 2 3

Sight Word: MADE

Read, Trace, and Write It

made

Fill in the Missing Letter

m___de

mad___

___ade

ma___e

Find and Circle It

mane	made	raid
made	paid	made
paid	laid	said
laid	said	mane
raid	made	made

Read and Copy

I made you a cake.

Box It: Tall, Small, or Fall?

Clap It: made

How Many Syllables?

1 2 3

Sight Word: MANY

Read, Trace, and Write It

many

Fill in the Missing Letter

m___ny

___any

man___

ma___y

Find and Circle It

mane	man	nanny
many	mane	many
mail	man	pony
pony	many	many
many	nanny	mail

Read and Copy

There are many presents.

Box It: Tall, Small, or Fall?

Clap It: many

How Many Syllables?

1 2 3

Sight Word: READ

Read, Trace, and Write It

read

Fill in the Missing Letter

re___d

r___ad

rea___

___ead

Find and Circle It

read	reed	read
reed	read	dead
bread	head	lead
dead	read	head
read	lead	bread

Read and Copy

I like to read books.

Box It: Tall, Small, or Fall?

Clap It: read

How Many Syllables?

1 2 3

Sight Word: SLEEP

Read, Trace, and Write It

sleep

Fill in the Missing Letter

sl___ep

slee___

s___eep

___leep

Find and Circle It

slip	sleep	steep
slide	slip	sleep
sleet	sleep	slide
sleek	steep	sleet
sleep	sleek	sleep

Read and Copy

I go to sleep early.

Box It: Tall, Small, or Fall?

Clap It: sleep

How Many Syllables?

1 2 3

Sight Word: THEIR

Read, Trace, and Write It

their

Fill in the Missing Letter

the___r

t___eir

thei___

th___ir

Find and Circle It

there	their	that
their	tear	this
that	their	them
tear	them	their
this	their	there

Read and Copy

They colored with their crayons.

Box It: Tall, Small, or Fall?

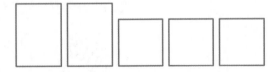

Clap It: their

How Many Syllables?

1 2 3

Sight Word: THESE

Read, Trace, and Write It

these

Fill in the Missing Letter

the___e

thes___

t___ese

___hese

Find and Circle It

there	these	please
trees	there	these
please	these	trees
this	them	these
these	this	them

Read and Copy

These are my friends.

Box It: Tall, Small, or Fall?

Clap It: these

How Many Syllables?

1 2 3

Sight Word: UPON

Read, Trace, and Write It

upon

Fill in the Missing Letter

upo___

u___on

___pon

up___n

Find and Circle It

open	opal	upon
upon	open	used
udon	upon	udon
undo	used	opal
upon	undo	upon

Read and Copy

Once upon a time, there was a queen.

Box It: Tall, Small, or Fall?

Clap It: upon

How Many Syllables?

1 2 3

Sight Word: USE

Read, Trace, and Write It

use

Fill in the Missing Letter

___se

us___

u___e

us___

Find and Circle It

fuse	upon	use
use	fuse	us
upon	use	use
us	used	lose
used	lose	use

Read and Copy

I use a spoon to eat.

Box It: Tall, Small, or Fall?

Clap It: use

How Many Syllables?

1 2 3

Sight Word: VERY

Read, Trace, and Write It

very

Fill in the Missing Letter

ver___

___ery

ve___y

v___ry

Find and Circle It

very	valley	way
merry	why	very
very	very	merry
valley	veil	very
way	why	veil

Read and Copy

I am very strong.

Box It: Tall, Small, or Fall?

Clap It: very

How Many Syllables?

1 2 3

Sight Word: WHICH

Read, Trace, and Write It

which

Fill in the Missing Letter

wh___ch

___hich

whi___h

whic___

Find and Circle It

witch	which	when
which	with	witch
with	which	which
where	while	where
while	when	which

Read and Copy

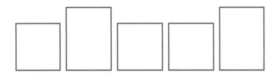

Which color do you like best?

Box It: Tall, Small, or Fall?

Clap It: which

How Many Syllables?

1 2 3

Sight Word: WORK

Read, Trace, and Write It

work

Fill in the Missing Letter

w___rk

___ork

wor___

wo___k

Find and Circle It

work	fork	wired
word	work	fork
walk	wired	work
wood	walk	word
work	wood	work

Read and Copy

A garden is a lot of work.

Box It: Tall, Small, or Fall?

Clap It: work

How Many Syllables?

1 2 3

Sight Word: WOULD

Read, Trace, and Write It

would

Fill in the Missing Letter

w___uld

___ould

woul___

wou___d

Find and Circle It

could	where	would
should	would	wood
where	could	would
would	word	should
wood	would	word

Read and Copy

Would you like some fruit?

Box It: Tall, Small, or Fall?

Clap It: would

How Many Syllables?

1 2 3

Sight Word: WRITE

Read, Trace, and Write It

write

Fill in the Missing Letter

wr___te

___rite

wri___e

writ___

Find and Circle It

write	wrote	write
wrote	write	written
site	right	wrap
write	wrap	written
right	write	site

Read and Copy

I can write my name.

Box It: Tall, Small, or Fall?

Clap It: write

How Many Syllables?

1 2 3

Sight Word: YOUR

Read, Trace, and Write It

your

Fill in the Missing Letter

y___ur

you___

___our

yo___r

Find and Circle It

you	four	your
your	you	more
our	out	your
four	more	our
your	your	out

Read and Copy

Can you write your ABCs?

Box It: Tall, Small, or Fall?

Clap It: your

How Many Syllables?

1 2 3

Sight Word Activities

Sight Word Kaboom

Need: 12 Popsicle sticks, pen, jar

Write ten sight words on Popsicle sticks. Then write the word **dynamite** on two sticks. Put all of the sticks in a jar. Pull them out one at a time and read the word. If you pull a **dynamite** stick, you have to put all of the sticks back and start over.

The goal of the game is to read all of the sight words without pulling a **dynamite** stick.

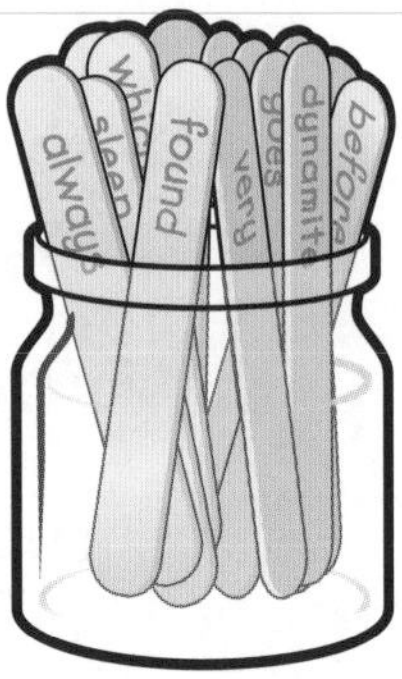

Target Practice

Need: 10 paper plates, pen, tape, soft ball

Write ten sight words on paper plates. Tape the plates to the wall at different heights. Call out the word you are going to hit. Then throw a soft ball at the plate with that word. If you hit it, you get a point. The goal is to hit all of the plates. Play by yourself or compete against a friend.

Shaving Cream

Need: shaving cream

When you take a bath, spread a thin layer of shaving cream on the wall. Practice writing your sight words with your finger in the shaving cream.

Toss the Balloon

Need: balloon, marker

Write six sight words at different spots on a balloon after you've blown it up. Take turns hitting the balloon back and forth with a partner or against a wall. When you catch it, read the closest sight word.

Beginning Consonant Blends S

Look at each picture and read the word out loud. Then write new words by adding the **st** or **sp** blend before each set of letters in the letter bank. The first one has been done for you.

arfish **op** ory ing ep

starfish

st

oon **ider** ade ell ark

spoon

sp

Beginning Consonant Blends S

Fill in the missing letters with the correct **consonant blends**.

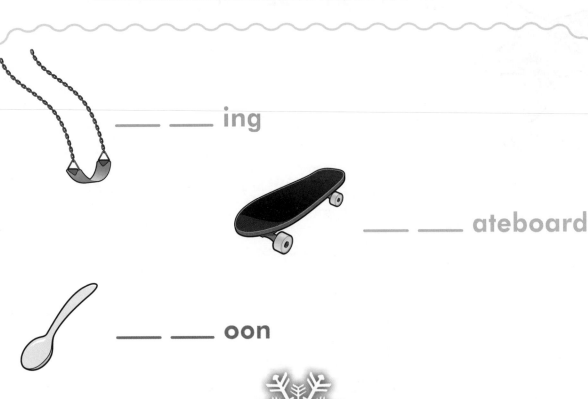

sn sp sk **sw**

___ ___ ing

___ ___ ateboard

___ ___ oon

___ ___ owflake

___ ___ irt

___ ___ ider

Beginning Consonant Blends R

Two consonants together that can both be heard are called a **consonant blend**.

Example:
t + r = tr   tree

Common S blends: sc, sk, sn, st, sp, sw
Common R blends: br, dr, pr, cr, fr, tr
Common L blends: pl, cl, bl, gl, fl

Circle the things below that begin with **cr**, **dr**, or **tr**.

Beginning Consonant Blends R

Look at each picture and read the word out loud. Then write new words by adding the **tr** or **dr** blend before each set of letters in the letter bank. The first one has been done for you.

ain ack ap ick iangle

train

tr

um eam aw ag ip

drum

dr

Beginning Consonant Blends R

Say the picture name out loud.
Circle the correct **r** blend that the picture begins with.

dr

fr

br

cr

pr

tr

dr

fr

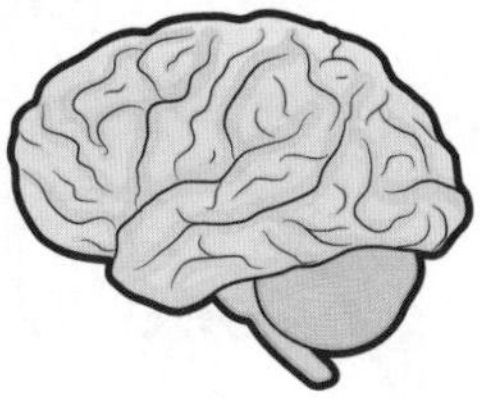

cr

br

dr

fr

pr

cr

pr

tr

Beginning Consonant Blends R

Color each **fr**og **br**own that has a word in it that begins with either **br** or **fr**.

Beginning Consonant Blends L

Look at each picture and read the word out loud. Then write new words by adding the **fl** or **bl** blend before each set of letters in the letter bank. The first one has been done for you.

ag ower oat ap y

flag

fl

block

ock ank oom ast ack

bl

Beginning Consonant Blends L

Color the spaces with the letters below
to see what begins with an **fl**.

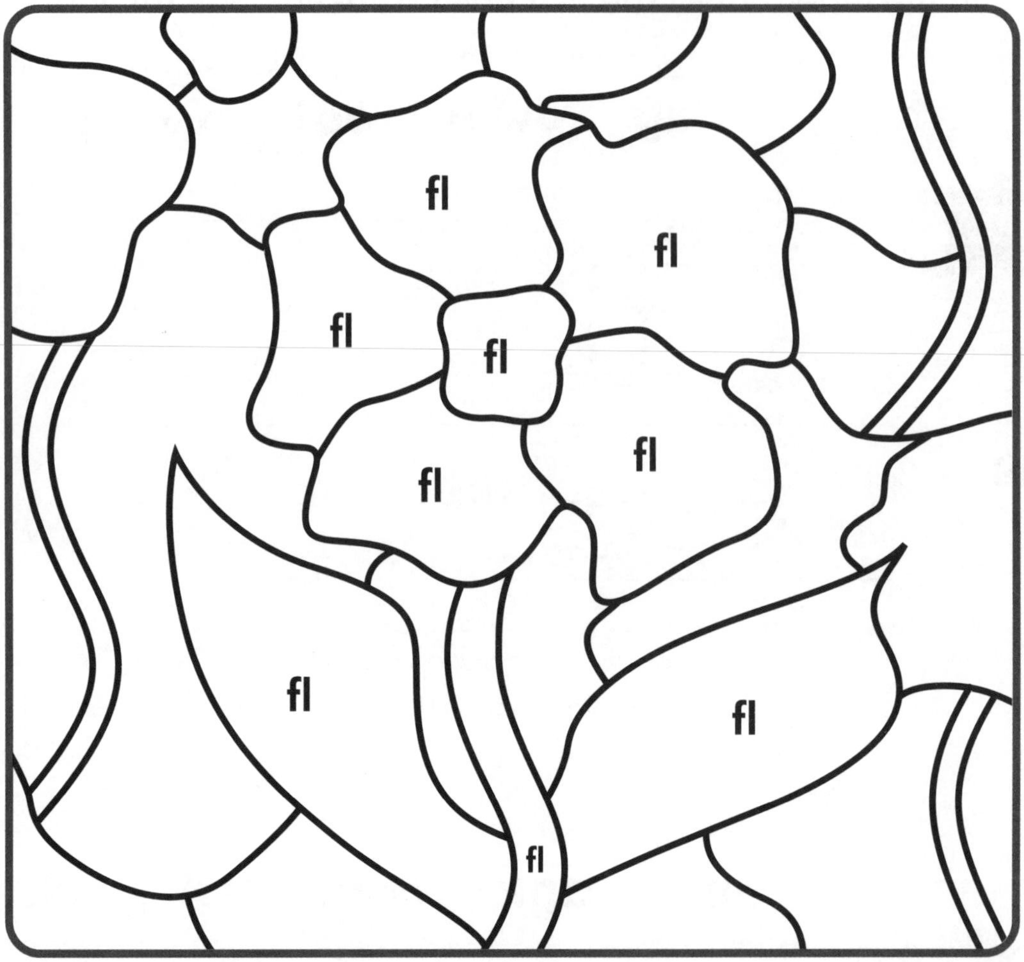

Riddle

What kind of flowers are on your face?

___ ___ ___ ___ ___ ___
2 4 1 5 3 6

1 = l 2 = t 3 = p 4 = u 5 = i 6 = s

Beginning Consonant Blends L

Fill in the missing letters with the correct **consonant blends**.

pl **cl** **gl** **bl**

___ ___ oud

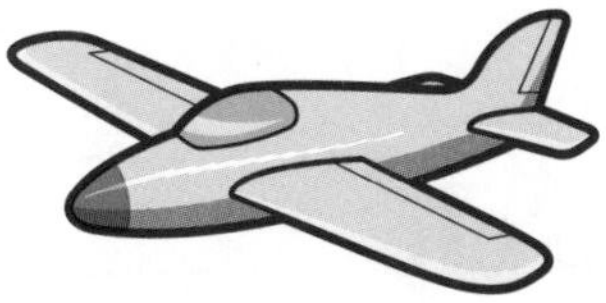

___ ___ ane

___ ___ ock

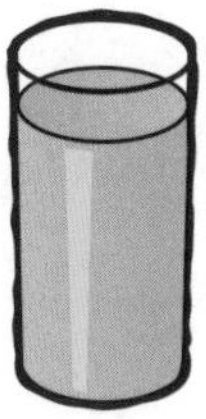

___ ___ ass

___ ___ own

___ ___ ayground

Word Families ock

Choose the letter or letters from the letter bank to complete the words ending in **ock**. Then write each word on the line.

bl l s r cl

________ **ock** ________________

________ **ock** ________________

________ **ock** ________________

________ **ock** ________________

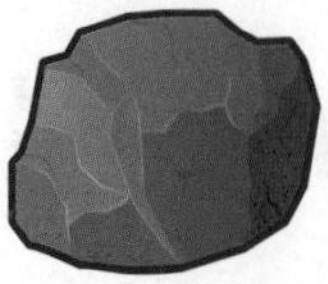
________ **ock** ________________

Word Families ack

Word Jumble: Unscramble the letters to form words that end in **ack**.

ckabl ____________

rccka ____________

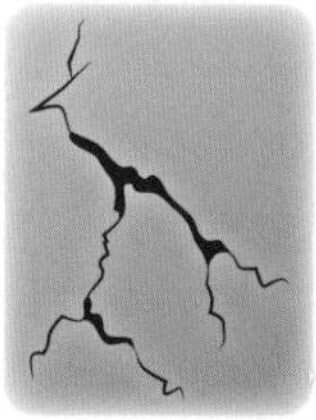

qckua ____________

kcas ____________

rtack ____________

Word Families ain

Look at each picture below. If it ends in **ain**, color the picture and then write the word on the line.

____

____

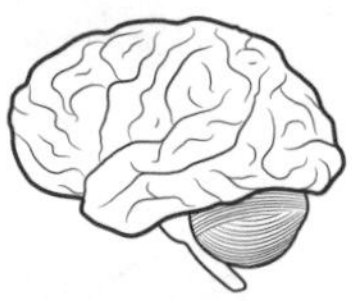

____

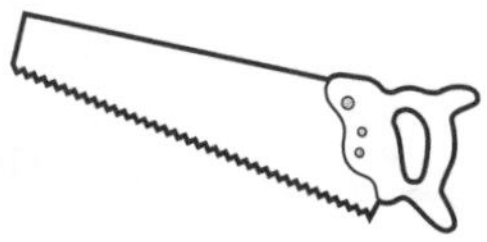

____

____

____

____

Word Families ail

WORDS

Write the missing letters to the **ail** words below.

___ ___ **ail**

___ **ail**

___ **ail**

___ **ail**

___ ___ **ail**

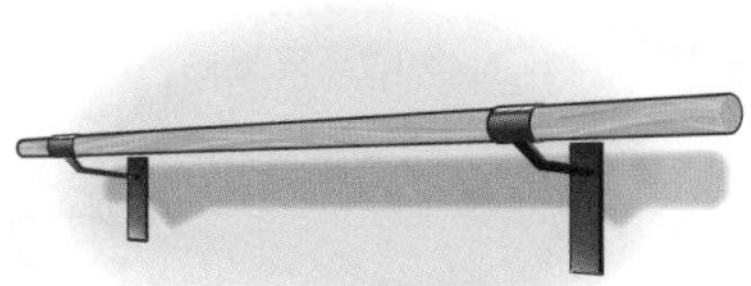

___ **ail**

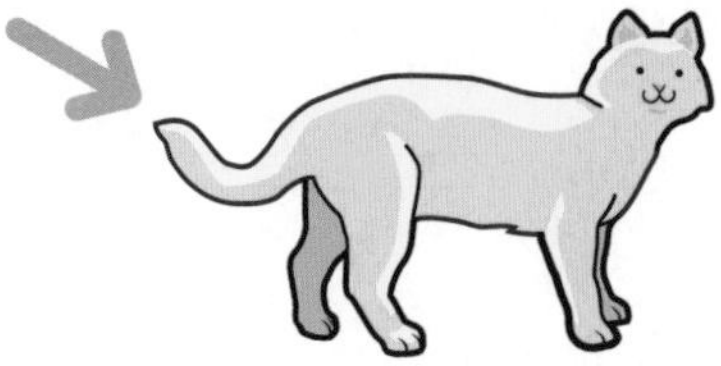

___ **ail**

___ **ail**

Word Families

Choose a **word family** ending to complete each word.

uck ake ice unk

chipm ___ ___ ___

tr ___ ___ ___

c ___ ___ ___

m ___ ___ ___

r ___ ___ ___

p ___ ___ ___

Adding ing

If a word ends with a vowel and a consonant, like **hop**, you should double the consonant before adding **-ing**.

Example:
hop + ing = hopping

Draw a line between the beginning and ending of each word.

shop	ting
hug	ning
run	ting
sit	ping
bat	ging

Adding ing to ie

When adding **-ing** to words that end in **ie**, you must change the **ie** to **y** and then add **-ing**.

Example:
I don't know how to tie my shoes.
Soon I will be tying my own shoes!

Add **-ing** to each word below. Don't forget to change the **ie** to **y** before adding the **-ing.**

die + ing = ____________________

lie + ing = ____________________

untie + ing = ____________________

Find the new **-ing** words in the word search below. Words can go up, down, across, or diagonally.

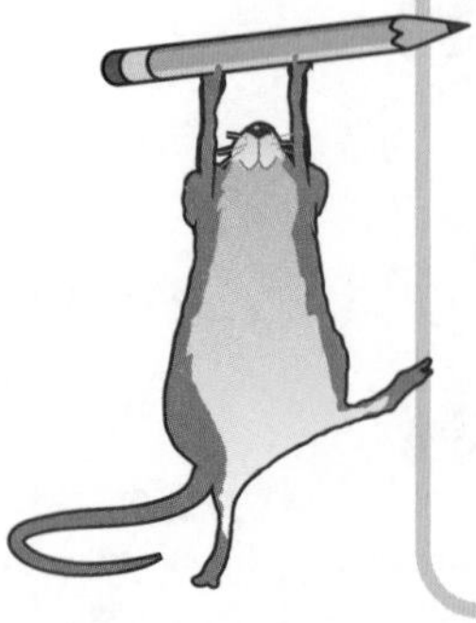

D	E	V	B	I	L	S	L	U	T
N	A	F	J	U	Y	O	Y	N	C
G	H	X	Q	N	I	R	D	T	I
E	M	E	W	I	N	G	C	Y	E
C	D	Y	I	N	G	O	E	I	H
I	L	R	B	G	F	A	D	N	Z
N	A	A	P	E	E	K	Y	G	N

Adding ing to ee

For words that end in **ee**, you just add the **-ing**.

Example:
I see a car.
I can't believe I am seeing
an alligator in a car!

Read each sentence. Then take the underlined word that ends in **ee** and add **-ing** for the second sentence.

The animals want to run free.

I want to run when they are ____________________
the animals from their cages!

We just can't seem to agree.

I am happy when we are ____________________
with each other.

The worm wants to flee from the bird.

But the bird is too busy ____________________
from the cat!

Adding ing

If a word ends with a **-y**, like **play**, just add **-ing**.

Example: play + ing = playing

Add **-ing** to the base word below and write the new word on the line.

play + ing = ______________________

stay + ing = ______________________

try + ing = ______________________

carry + ing = ______________________

enjoy + ing = ______________________

spy + ing = ______________________

Adding ing

If a word ends with an **-e**, like the word **come**, take off the **-e** and add **-ing**.

Example: come + ing = coming

Read each word out loud. Put an X through the **e**.
Then rewrite the word adding **-ing**. Write the new word on the line.

share + ing

____

skate + ing

____

slide + ing

____

wave + ing

____

Adding ing to words ending in e

Remember, when a word ends in an **e**, drop the **e** and then add your **-ing**. The first one has been done for you.

	Word	+ ing	New Word
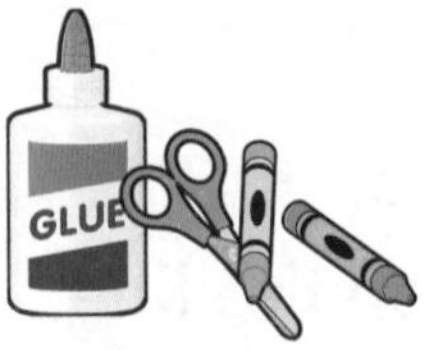	make	+ ing	making
	hope	+ ing	
	write	+ ing	
	bake	+ ing	
	drive	+ ing	
	tune	+ ing	

Verbs + ing

Add **-ing** to the base word below and write the new word on the line. Remember to follow the rules!

y + ing = ying

study + ing = ______________

cry + ing = ______________

try + ing = ______________

e + ing = ~~e~~ing

whine + ing = ______________

bake + ing = ______________

time + ing = ______________

ee + ing = eeing

free + ing = ______________

see + ing = ______________

agree + ing = ______________

ie + ing = ~~ie~~ ying

die + ing = ______________

lie + ing = ______________

tie + ing = ______________

p/t/n + ing = pping

hop + ing = ______________

hit + ing = ______________

begin + ing = ______________

Past Tense Verb Sounds ed

When you add **-ed** to verbs to make them past tense, they can take on three different sounds.

They can make the sound **t** such as in the word **picked**. Can you hear the **t** sound at the end?

They can make the sound **d** such as in the word **called**. Can you hear the **d** sound at the end?

They can make the sound **ed** such as in the word **folded**. Can you hear the **ed** sound at the end?

Sort the words from the word bank into the boxes below based on the ending sound they make.

dressed	handed	talked	looked	visited	rushed
tied	greeted	turned	loved	added	hugged

t	d	ed

Adding ed

For words that end with **-e**, like **dance**, just drop the **e** and add **-ed**.

Example: dance + ed = danced

Drop the **e** and add **-ed** to the base word and write the new word on the line.

chase + ed = ______________________

dive + ed = ______________________

graze + ed = ______________________

sneeze + ed = ______________________

Adding ed

For words that end with **-y**, like **bury**, change the **y** to an **i** and then add **-ed**.

Example: bury + ed = buried

Add **-ed** to the base word and write the new word on the line.

try + ed = ____________________

study + ed = ____________________

hurry + ed = ____________________

carry + ed = ____________________

Adding ed

For words that end with a short vowel and a consonant, like **stop**, double the final consonant before adding **-ed**.

Example: stop + ed = stopped

Add **-ed** to the base word, after doubling the final consonant, and write the new word on the line.

grab + ed = ______________________

skip + ed = ______________________

trip + ed = ______________________

slam + ed = ______________________

WORDS

Adding ed

For most other words, just add **-ed**.
Example: jump + ed = jumped

Add **-ed** to each word and write the new word on the line.

paint + ed = ____________________

rain + ed = ____________________

kick + ed = ____________________

play + ed = ____________________

Contractions

A **contraction** is a shortened form of two words. In a contraction, an apostrophe takes the place of the missing letter or letters.

Examples:

I + will = I'll **did + not = didn't** **she + is = she's**

Look at each pair of words. Write the **contraction** of the two words on the space provided.

they + are = ____________________

we + are = ____________________

you + will = ____________________

he + is = ____________________

Contractions

Draw a line from the words on the left to their correct **contraction**.

we have	it's
I am	he's
we are	we've
he is	I'm
it is	don't
do not	we're
I will	I'll

Contractions

Pick a **contraction** from the word bank below to take the place of the underlined words. Write that contraction on the line.

didn't couldn't We'll weren't She's

I could not ____________ go outside to play because it was raining.

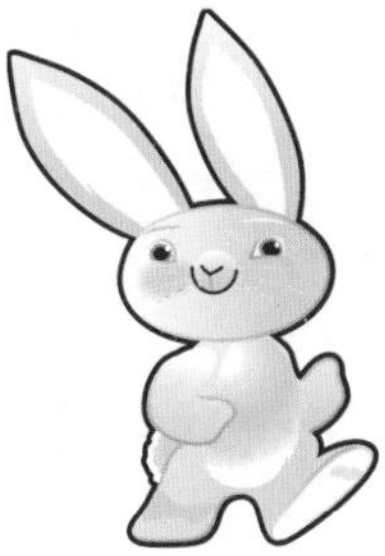

We will ____________ take a walk after dinner.

We were not ____________ given homework by our teacher over the weekend.

You did not ____________ clean your room.

She is ____________ my best friend.

Contractions

Read the words below. Circle the correct **contraction** to go with the words.

we are

we've **we're**

I will

I'd **I'll**

I have

I'm **I've**

you are

you're **you'd**

it will

it's **it'll**

you have

you're **you've**

she is

she'd **she's**

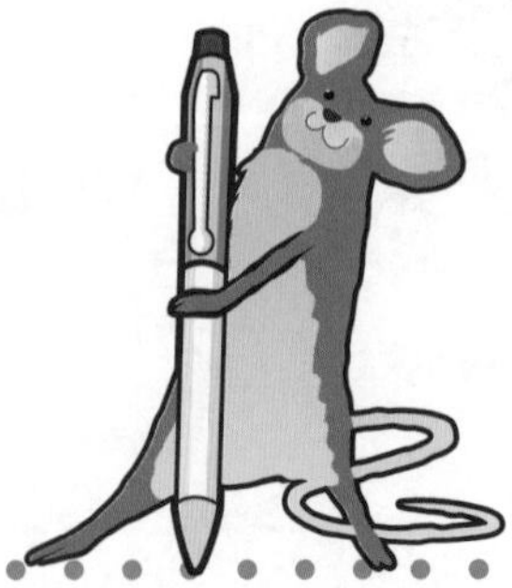

Contractions

Write the correct **contraction** for the underlined words.
Remember, an apostrophe goes where a letter or letters are missing.

Example: I am = I'm

A fish would not be able to live out of water.

____

I would not like a muffin for breakfast.

____

You will not have to take turns on the slide.

____

I am getting popcorn at the movie theater.

____

Contractions

How many **contractions** can you think of?
Write them in the bubbles below. One has been done for you.

I will

I'll

Compound Words

A **compound word** is made up of two words that are combined to form a new word.

Example:
dog + house = doghouse

Combine the words below to make a **compound word**. Write the word on the line.

skate + board = ____________________

sun + shine = ____________________

foot + prints = ____________________

after + noon = ____________________

air + port = ____________________

chalk + board = ____________________

Compound Words

Draw a line from one word to another to make a **compound word**. The first one has been done for you.

pop	bird	
lady	bug	
sail	fly	
base	corn	
bath	boat	
blue	tub	
butter	ball	

Compound Words

Use a word from the word bank to make a **compound word**.
Use the pictures as clues.

fighter	flake	snake	melon
way	bowl	house	

snow + ____________ = ________________ 

water + ____________ = ________________ 

fire + ____________ = ________________ 

fish + ____________ = ________________ 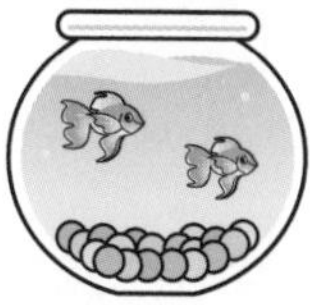

dog + ____________ = ________________ 

rattle + ____________ = ________________ 

high + ____________ = ________________ 

Synonyms

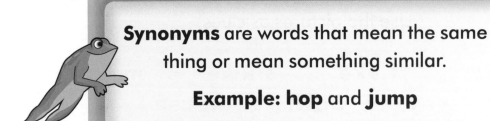

Synonyms are words that mean the same thing or mean something similar.

Example: hop and **jump**

Read each sentence. Then circle the **synonym** to the underlined word.

My mom likes me to keep my room <u>clean</u>.

neat dirty

It is starting to <u>rain</u>.

drizzle snow

My favorite season is <u>autumn</u>.

summer fall

Apple pie is <u>delicious</u>.

tasteless tasty

I like to <u>smell</u> the flowers.

sniff taste

Synonyms

Look at the two words below each picture.
Write **same** if they mean the same thing or **different** if they mean different things.

house home

____

full empty

____

stop go

____

thin skinny

____

fruit vegetable

____

present gift

____

Antonyms

Antonyms are words that mean the opposite of each other.

Example: asleep and **awake**

Draw a line from the word on the left to its **antonym**, or opposite, on the right.

sad	good
hot	hard
easy	early
smile	cold
late	small
messy	frown
big	happy
bad	neat
win	lose
day	night

Antonyms

Choose a word from the word bank that means the **opposite** of the word to the right of the line in parentheses.

beautiful closed sweet
fast love good hot stay

I had a ________________ day at school. (bad)

I like my soup to be

________________. (cold)

I am a very ________________ runner. (slow)

Keep the door ________________. (open)

I ________________ my present. (hate)

Roses are ________________ flowers. (ugly)

I'm having so much fun,

I want to ________________. (go)

Strawberries are really

________________. (sour)

Homonyms

Homonyms are pairs of words that are pronounced like one another but have a different meaning and are usually spelled differently.

Example: be and **bee**

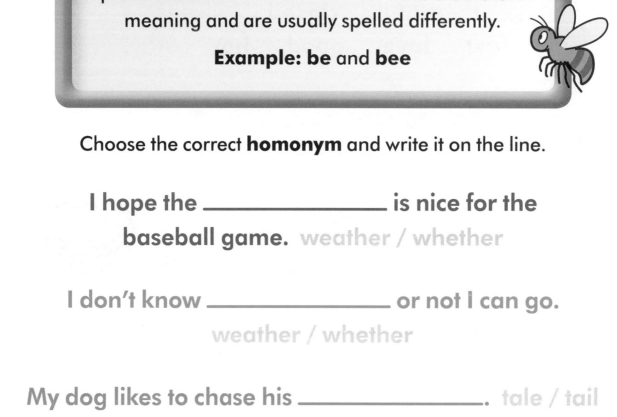

Choose the correct **homonym** and write it on the line.

I hope the ______________ is nice for the baseball game. weather / whether

I don't know ______________ or not I can go. weather / whether

My dog likes to chase his ______________. tale / tail

"Cinderella" is my favorite fairy ______________. tale / tail

My dog always ______________ at me. stares / stairs

Be careful running up the ______________. stares / stairs

I need to use milk, eggs, and ______________ to bake a cake. flour/flower

The ______________ smells so pretty! flour/flower

Homonyms

Draw a line connecting the **homonyms**.

die	dear
fair	eight
deer	daze
brake	bare
days	hare
bear	sell
cell	for
ate	dye
hair	fare
four	break

Prefixes

A **prefix** is a group of letters added to the beginning of a word. When you add a prefix to a word, its meaning changes.

Prefix	Meaning	Example
mis	wrongly	misunderstood (to understand wrongly)
un	not	unclear (not clear)
re	again	redo (do again)

Add the prefix to each word below to make a new word. Write each new word on the line.

Prefix		Base Word		New Word
re	+	appear	=	______
un	+	do	=	______
mis	+	place	=	______
re	+	paint	=	______
un	+	healthy	=	______

Prefixes

Un- means not.

She is unlucky. This means she is not lucky.

Mis- means wrong.

There is a misprint in the book.

This means something was printed wrong.

Fill in the correct prefix, **mis-** or **un-** to finish the word.

You shouldn't

______behave
(not behave)

at school.

You should never

______treat
(treat wrong)

animals!

It is very

______usual
(not usual)

to see a chipmunk jumping rope!

I always

______spell
(spell wrong)

the word "beautiful."

Prefixes

Add the prefix **re-** to make a new word that means **again**.

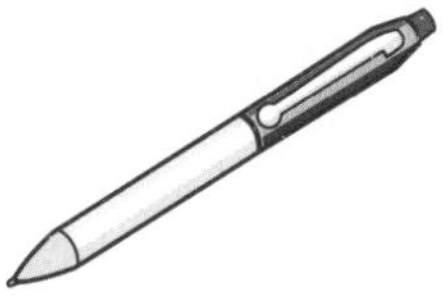

write again

___ ___ ___ ___ ___ ___ ___

read again

___ ___ ___ ___ ___ ___

plant again

___ ___ ___ ___ ___ ___ ___

build again

___ ___ ___ ___ ___ ___ ___

trace again

___ ___ ___ ___ ___ ___ ___

paint again

___ ___ ___ ___ ___ ___ ___

Suffixes

A **suffix** is a group of letters added to the end of a word. Adding a suffix to the end of a word changes its meaning.

Suffix	Meaning	Example
ness	state of	brightness (state of being bright)
less	without	painless (without pain)
er	person who	teacher (person who teaches)
est	most	tallest (most tall)
ful	full of	careful (full of care)

Add the suffixes to the following words:

Word	-er	-est
tall	______________	______________
small	______________	______________
strong	______________	______________
weak	______________	______________
smart	______________	______________
loud	______________	______________
quiet	______________	______________

Suffixes

Read the sentences below. Look and listen for words with the suffixes **-ness**, **-less**, or **-ful**. Circle these words. Then write the base word and the suffix on the lines connected by a (+) sign. For example, for **wonderful**, you would write **wonder+ful**.

I am clueless when it comes to directions.

________________ + ________

The darkness at night is sometimes scary.

________________ + ________

She asked for her friend's forgiveness.

________________ + ________

I was surprised by the lightness of the feather.

________________ + ________

The dancer's moves were graceful.

________________ + ________

Suffixes

Read each sentence. Choose the word that best completes the sentence by circling the answer.

The star shone with great ________.

brightness brightly

A mouse is ________ than a cat.

smaller smallest

My mother said my work was very ________.

helpless helpful

I am the ________ student in my class.

tallest taller

An ant is ________.

harmful harmless

A dog is ________ than a turtle.

faster fastest

I am not afraid of ghosts; I am ________.

fearless fearful

Singular and Plural Nouns

When a noun is **singular**, it names **one** person, place, or thing. When a noun is **plural**, it names **more than one** person, place, or thing. Adding an **-s** to most nouns will make them plural, or more than one.

Examples:

I have **a dog** named Spot.

I have **two dogs** named Spot and Buddy.

Circle all the words below that are **plural**.

cars

oranges

hat

banana

dogs

ant

balls

pencil

flowers

friends

games

Singular and Plural Nouns

Look at each picture. Circle the word that is either **singular** or **plural**, according to the picture. Write the word on the line at right.

frog frogs ______________________

crayon crayons ______________________

shoe shoes ______________________

egg eggs ______________________

pig pigs ______________________

student students ______________________

candle candles ______________________

Plural Nouns

Add **-es** to words ending in **-ch**, **-sh**, **-s**, **-ss**, **-x**, or **-z** to make them plural.

 one fox  two foxes

Now you try . . .

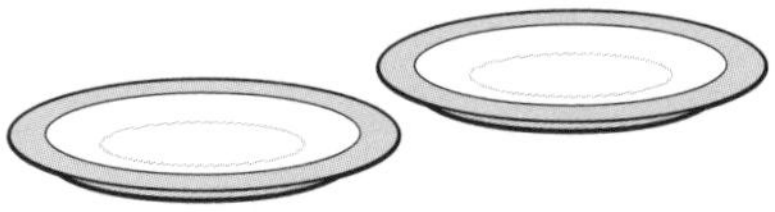

dish ____________ **bus** ____________

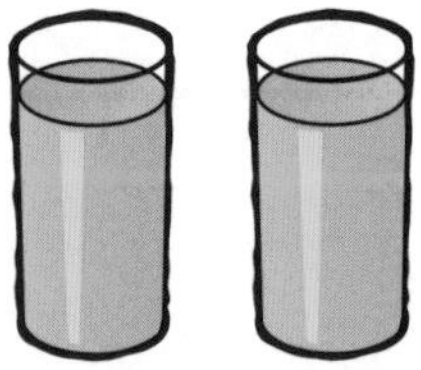

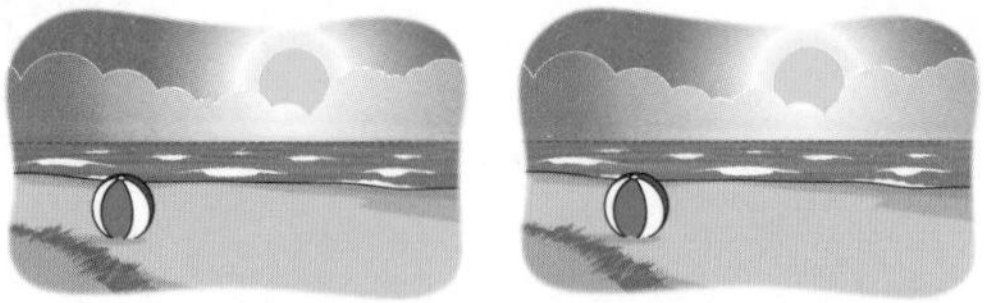

glass ____________ **beach** ____________

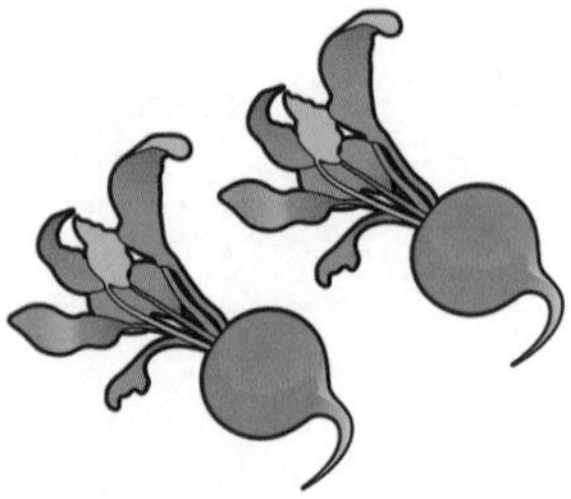

dress ____________ **radish** ____________

Plural Nouns

When a word ends in **-f** or **-fe**, change the **f** or **fe** to a **v** before adding **-es**.

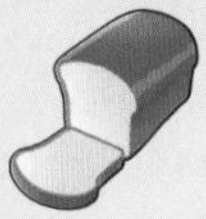 one **loaf** 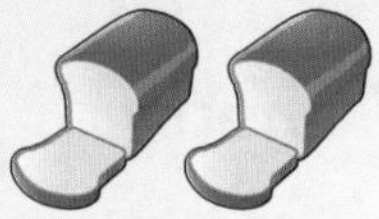 two **loaves**

Draw a line from the **singular word** to its **plural**.

	wolf	leaves
	shelf	wolves
	leaf	knives
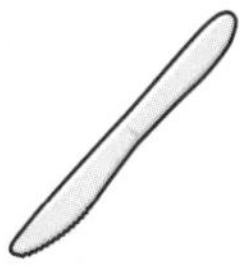	knife	shelves
	scarf	elves
	elf	scarves

Plural Nouns

When the letter before a **y** is a consonant, change the **y** to an **i** before adding **-es**.

cherry

cherries

Now you try . . .

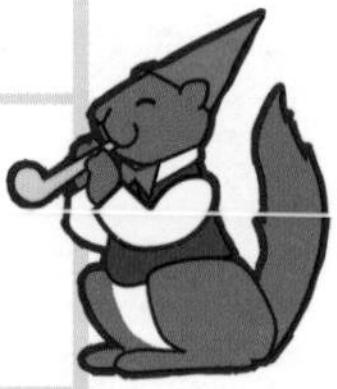

Singular	Plural
baby	
daisy	
story	
party	
sky	
pony	
bunny	

Plural Nouns

When a word ends in **-ay**, **-ey**, **-iy**, **-oy**, or **-uy**, just add an **-s** to make it plural.

 toy  toys

Now you try . . .

day ____________________

boy ____________________

X-ray ____________________

valley ____________________

guy ____________________

key ____________________

Irregular Plural Nouns

Some **nouns** change spelling to name **more than one**.

Examples:

man — men **woman — women**
child — children **foot — feet**
tooth — teeth **mouse — mice**
person — people **goose — geese**

Circle the correct **noun** to complete the sentence.

Many (man, men) played tennis.

One (woman, women) is driving.

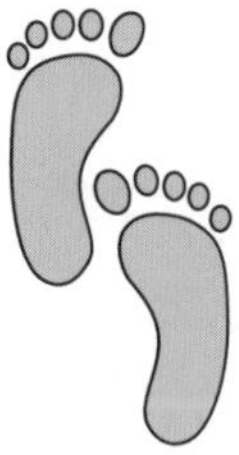

Don't forget to put shoes on your (foot, feet).

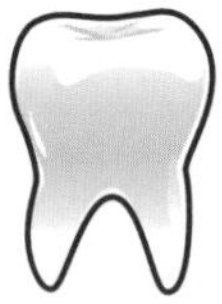

My one (tooth, teeth) is loose.

There are many (mouse, mice) in the barn.

There were many (child, children) at my birthday party.

Many (person, people) have birthdays in the summer.

There is a (goose, geese) in my pond.

Irregular Plural Nouns

WORDS

Make the noun mean more than one.
Write the **plural noun** to complete the sentence.

The ________________ went to the gym.
(man)

The ________________ jogged around the lake.
(woman)

All of the ________________ played in the park.
(child)

My ________________ are cold!
(foot)

I brushed all of my ________________ very well.
(tooth)

________________ love to eat cheese.
(Mouse)

There are so many ________________ on the swings.
(person)

I like to feed the ________________.
(goose)

Irregular Plural Nouns

WORDS

Help the **mouse** find his **mice** friends.

Collective Nouns

A **collective noun** is a word that refers to a group of people or things.

Example:
A **herd** of cows.
Herd is a collective noun.

Complete the sentences using a **collective noun** from the word bank below.

team | class | flock | bunch | fleet

We picked a ______________ of flowers from the garden.

There's a ______________ of ships in the harbor.

We saw a ______________ of sheep on the hill.

The principal visited a ______________ of children.

We passed a ______________ of soccer players on the field.

Collective Nouns

Choose one of these **collective nouns** to complete each sentence.

swarm **pack** **family** **forest** **team**

A collection of playing cards is called a ______________.

A group of baseball players is called a

______________.

A group of people who are related is called a ______________.

A large group of trees is called a

______________.

A bunch of bees is called a

______________.

Collective Nouns

Draw a line from the **collective noun** to the word it matches.

bunch	bees	
flock	whales	
herd	wolves	
batch	birds	
school	elephants	
swarm	cookies	
pack	grapes	

Pronouns

A **pronoun** is a word used in place of a noun or another pronoun. A **personal pronoun** is a word used in place of a noun or another pronoun that refers to specific people, places, things, and ideas.

Karen ate pizza.
She was hungry.

The personal pronoun is **she**.

Underline the appropriate **personal pronoun** in each of these sentences.

(We, Us) love to play in the snow.

Is this ball (your, yours)?

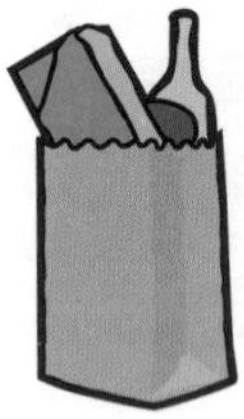

Please help (they, us) bring in the groceries.

Please show (him, his) how to get to class.

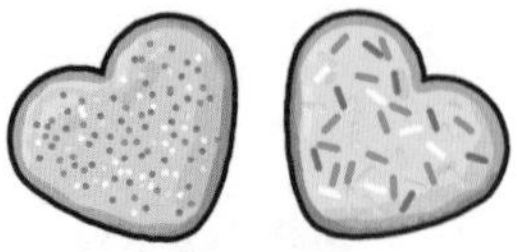

(I, Me) like to bake cookies!

(She, Her) is my best friend.

Personal Pronouns

Fill in the blanks using the correct **personal pronoun** from the word bank.

I	She	He	It	They	We

This ball is small. ________ is small.

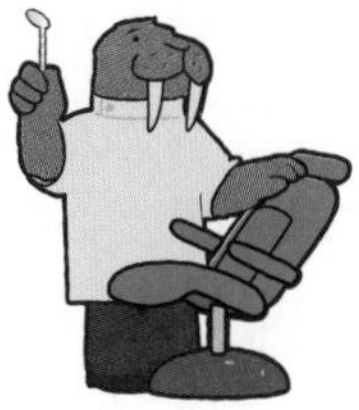

My father is a dentist. ________ is a dentist.

My mother is a teacher. ________ is a teacher.

The girls are soccer players. ________ are soccer players.

My dad and I like to fish. ________ like to fish.

Reflexive Pronouns

A **reflexive pronoun** is formed by adding **-self** or **-selves** to a **personal pronoun**.

Bob finished the homework **himself**.
The reflexive pronoun is **himself**.

Use the **reflexive pronouns** in the word bank to complete the sentences. Then underline the person, people, or noun to which the reflexive pronoun is referring.

itself **themselves** **myself** **yourself**
ourselves **herself**

I went to the store by ____________________.

The dog played by ____________________.

They went on a holiday by ____________________.

Did you do this all by ____________________?

She baked a cake all by ____________________.

We will take out the trash all by ____________________.

Reflexive Pronouns

Draw a line from the correct **personal pronoun** to its **reflexive pronoun**. The first one has been done for you.

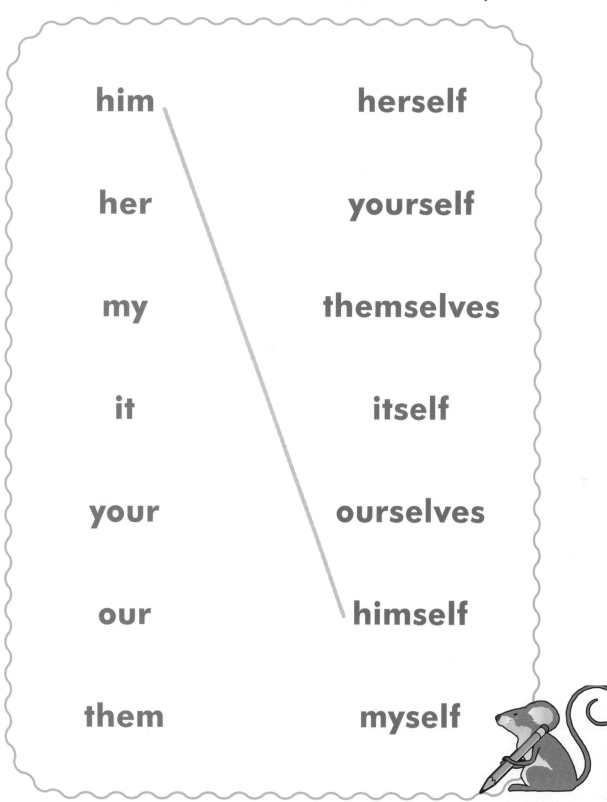

him	herself
her	yourself
my	themselves
it	itself
your	ourselves
our	himself
them	myself

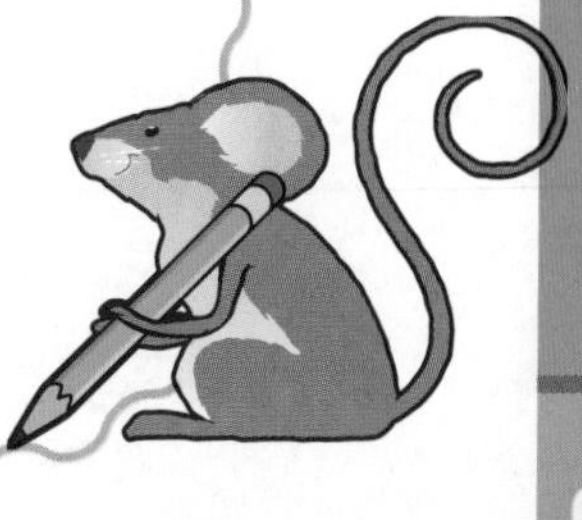

Periods and Question Marks

Put a **period** at the end of a sentence that tells something.

Example: I like to play.

Put a **question mark** at the end of a sentence that asks something.

Example: What is your favorite sport?

Finish each sentence with either a **period** if it tells something or a **question mark** if it asks something.

What time is it ____

I am going to the park ____

I like to jump rope ____

Is it time for dinner ____

What is your name ____

How are you ____

I have a new puppy ____

The Period Is a Little Dot
The period is a little dot,
He says he is my friend.
And when I write to tell a thought,
He must be at the end.
—Author Unknown

Periods

A **period** ends a statement and also appears at the end of people's titles, such as **Mr.**, **Mrs.**, **Ms.**, and **Dr.**

Example: Mrs. Smith is my teacher.

Correct the following paragraph by adding **periods** where they are needed. Color in the park below.

Today, my friends and I are going to the park
Mrs Smith is going to drive us   At the park, we
will go on the swings and down the slides When
we are finished, Mr Jones will drive us home

Question Marks and Exclamation Points

Remember, use a **question mark (?)** at the end of a **question**.

Use an **exclamation point (!)** at the end of an **exclamation**. An exclamation is a sentence that shows excitement or strong feelings.

Example: What a great time!

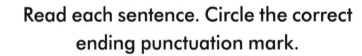

Read each sentence. Circle the correct ending punctuation mark.

What time is it	?	!
Help	?	!
Where are you going	?	!
What day is today	?	!
Hurray, we won	?	!
Are you having fun	?	!
Oh, no, I'm late	?	!
Where do you live	?	!

Apostrophes

An **apostrophe** (') is a punctuation mark that looks like a flying comma.

We can use the apostrophe (') to show who owns something. Add an apostrophe and an **s** to a singular noun, even if it ends in **s**.
For example: the **boy's** house / **Jess's** pencil

Add only an apostrophe to a plural noun ending in **s**. For example: the **boys'** club

Add an apostrophe and an **s** to irregular plural nouns that do not end in **s**. For example: the **women's** hats

Put an **apostrophe** in the correct place in the sentences below.

Jennys mom made cookies.

The coachs team won all of their games.

The childrens car wash raised lots of money!

The childrens toys were all over the room.

The chickens eggs were hatching.

Commas

Where are commas used?

Use a **comma (,)** between a city and a state or a city and a country.
Examples: Warwick, New York   Osaka, Japan

Use a comma in dates between the day and the year.
Example: April 13, 2006

Use a comma in letters, after the greeting and closing of any letter.
Examples: Dear Mom,   Sincerely, Claire

Read the following letter.
Add **commas** where they are needed.

May 13 2021

Dear Gran and Granddad

I am having so much fun at camp. It is beautiful here in Hudson New York. We have done so many things. Sailing is my favorite. Maybe I can show you how to sail next time I see you. I miss you both.

Love

Sylvie

Commas

Commas are also used to separate three or more things.
Use the comma after each item except the last one.

Examples:

My favorite colors are blue, green, and red.

In our garden, we grow carrots, radishes, and tomatoes.

Name your favorite things. You must list three things for each topic and don't forget your **commas**!

My favorite animals are ______________________________
____.

My favorite colors are ______________________________
____.

My favorite sports are ______________________________
____.

My favorite foods are ______________________________
____.

My favorite holidays are ______________________________
____.

Silent Letters

Some words in the English language contain letters that are not pronounced. These are called **silent letters**.

Study the six groups of words below.
In each group there is a **silent letter** that appears in each word.
Figure out the silent letter and write it on the line.

hour what why school rhyme

Silent letter ________

knife knee know knock knowledge

Silent letter ________

yolk half salmon talk should

Silent letter ________

wrap write who wrong whom

Silent letter ________

climb crumb dumb comb doubt

Silent letter ________

castle fasten listen whistle often

Silent letter ________

Silent Letters

Match the words to their picture and then circle the **silent letters**.

knight

knee

scissors

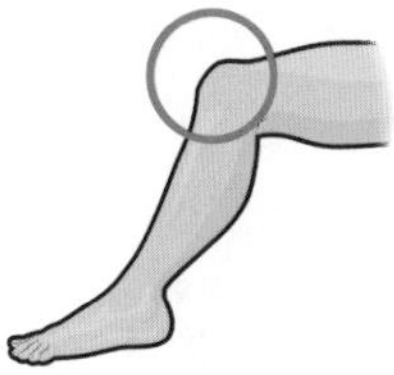

lamb

knife

whale

sign

Silent Letters gh

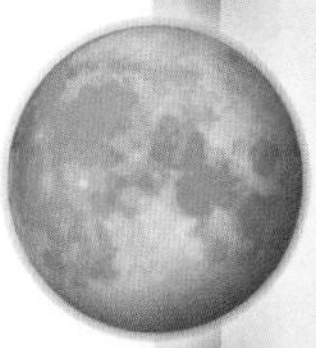

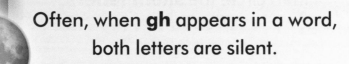

Often, when **gh** appears in a word, both letters are silent.

The moon is out in the ni**gh**t sky.

Read the sentence and choose the correct word from the word bank. Write it on the line and then circle the silent **gh**.

light **bright** **high** **taught** **doughnut**

My favorite treat is a ________________.

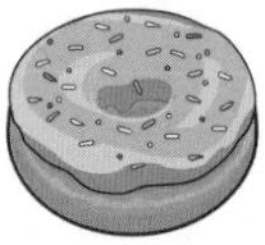

The sun is very ________________ today.

My dad ________________ me how to play checkers.

Please turn off the ________________ when you leave the room.

With my new sneakers on, I can jump very ________________.

Double Vowels oo

In some words, **oo** has the **vowel** sound you hear in the word l**oo**k.

Draw a line to match the word to its picture.

foot 

book 

cookies 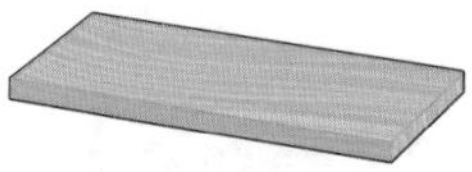

wood 

look 

Double Vowel oo

In some words, **oo** has the vowel sound you hear in the word st**oo**l.
Draw a line to match the word to its picture.

zoo

moon

food

school

balloon

goose

Double Vowel ee

Double vowel **ee** makes the long **e** sound,
as in n**ee**d, gr**ee**d, and f**ee**d.

Look at each picture and say what it is out loud.
Then write it on the line below. Remember the **ee**.

q ____ ____ ____ ____

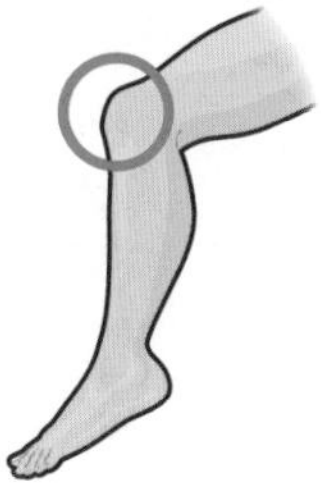

k____ ____ ____

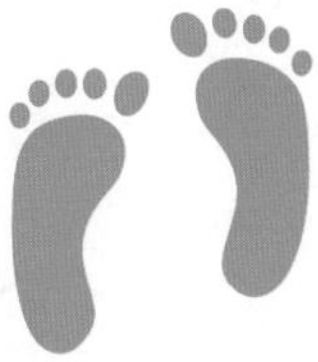

f ____ ____ t

f ____ ____ ____ ____ ____ ____ ____

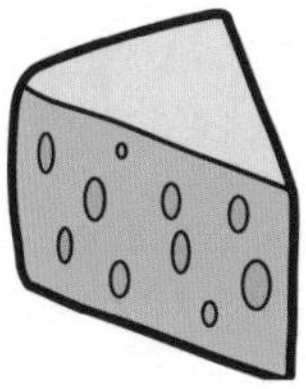

c ____ ____ ____ ____ ____

b____ ____

t ____ ____ ____

s ____ ____ ____ ____

Word Search

Find the **ee** words in the word search below.
The words are listed in the bank at the bottom of the page.
Words can go up, down, across, or diagonally.

T	I	K	C	H	S	P	E	E	L
V	H	A	I	D	T	I	N	F	G
B	I	E	P	H	R	R	I	T	R
E	R	S	E	L	A	B	P	R	L
E	P	I	I	L	I	E	S	I	I
P	H	A	R	T	E	S	C	C	N
I	R	E	I	K	H	N	H	F	G
T	Q	L	M	A	T	D	E	I	T
N	E	E	D	L	E	Z	E	P	H
I	E	N	G	O	M	T	K	S	W

HEEL PEEL CHEEK KEEP
BEEP NEEDLE

Vowel Combination oa

The vowel combination **oa** makes the long vowel sound **o**.
Example: lo**a**d

Trace the **oa** words and then read the sentence out loud.

There is a toad
in the road!

Circle the **oa** words.

toaster	bow	rope
coat	coal	snow
float	snow	roam

Complete the words using the vowel combination **oa**.

s___ ___ ___

c___ ___ ___

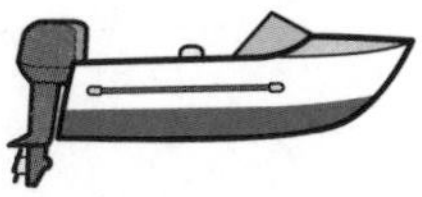
b___ ___ ___

g___ ___ ___

Vowel Combinations ow and ou

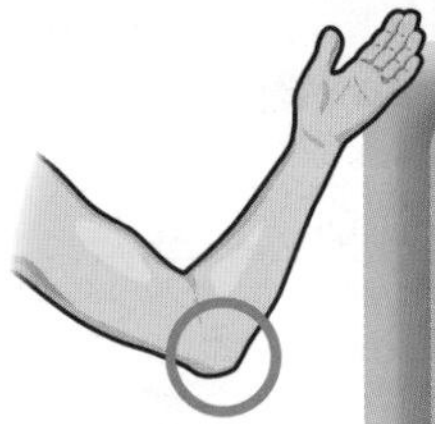

The vowel combination **ow** makes a long **o** vowel sound, as in elb**ow**, or the sound you hear in c**ow**. The vowel combination **ou** makes the sound you hear in m**ou**se.

Draw a line from each picture to the word it matches with either the **ow** or the **ou** sound.

flower

house

owl

clown

snow

cloud

Vowel Combination ay

The vowel combination **ay** makes the sound you hear in cr**ay**on.

Say the word crayon. Listen for the long vowel sound **ay**. Write a rhyming word with the same **ay** combination in the crayons at the right.

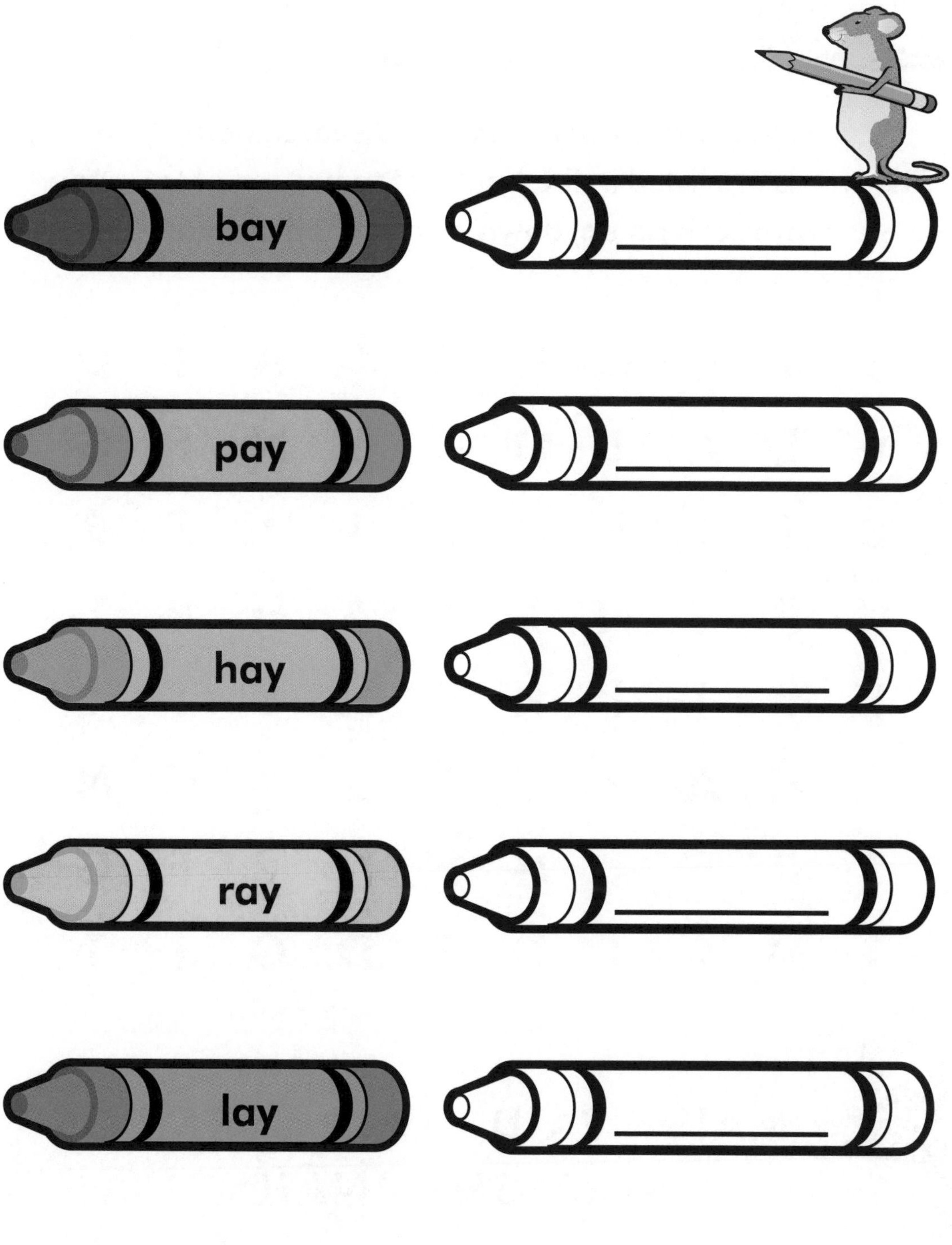

Vowel Combination ai

The vowel combination **ai** makes the long **a** sound, as in the word sn**ai**l or the word m**ai**l.

Find the **ai** words in the word search below.
The words are listed in the bank at the bottom of the page.
Words can go up, down, across, or diagonally.

T	I	K	C	H	S	P	A	I	D
V	L	A	I	D	T	L	N	F	G
B	I	I	P	H	R	I	I	T	R
U	R	S	N	L	A	A	H	R	L
R	P	I	I	K	I	N	S	I	I
N	H	A	R	T	G	S	A	C	N
I	R	E	I	H	H	N	P	F	G
T	M	A	I	D	T	D	G	I	T

MAID PAID LAID TRAIL
STRAIGHT NAIL

Vowel Combination ea

The vowel combination **ea** makes the long **e** sound you hear in the word l**ea**f.

Color in each leaf that has a word with the long vowel combination **ea** in it.

Vowel Combinations oy and oi

The vowel combinations **oy** and **oi** make the sound you hear in the words b**oy** and c**oi**n.

Make words by adding the vowel combinations **oi** and **oy** to the letters in any order. The first one has been done for you.

spl — spoil

pnt — ______

l — ______

nse — ______

enj — ______

t — ______

b — ______

j — ______

Common and Proper Nouns

A **common noun** names **any** person, place, or thing.
A **proper noun** names a **special** person, place, or thing.
Proper nouns must be capitalized.

Examples:
A **waterfall** is a common noun.
Niagara Falls is a proper noun and should be capitalized.

Determine whether each noun is a **common noun** or a **proper noun**. If it is common, write common on the line. If it is proper, rewrite the word on the line using the correct capitalization.

holiday ______________	november ______________
chicago ______________	city ______________
jones street ______________	state ______________
avenue ______________	america ______________

WORDS

Common and Proper Nouns

Put all of these **common** and **proper nouns** in alphabetical order.

flag 1 ____________________

Boston 2 ____________________

America 3 ____________________

president 4 ____________________

democracy 5 ____________________

Washington 6 ____________________

coin 7 ____________________

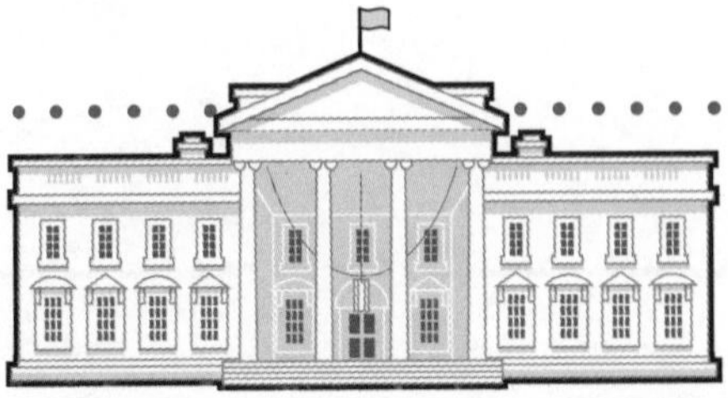

Days of the Week

Days of the week are **proper nouns**. Each day must be capitalized.
Write the days of the week in order.
Don't forget to start with a capital letter!

Thursday Sunday Tuesday

Saturday Wednesday Monday Friday

1 ______________________

2 ______________________

3 ______________________

4 ______________________

5 ______________________

6 ______________________

7 ______________________

How many days are in a week? ☐

What days do you go to school?

____

____

Which days fall on the weekend?

____

____

Days of the Week

Days of the Week Crossword Puzzle

Fill in the days of the week in the crossword puzzle below, based on the clues for Across and Down.

There are seven days in the week. The week starts with Sunday and ends with Saturday.

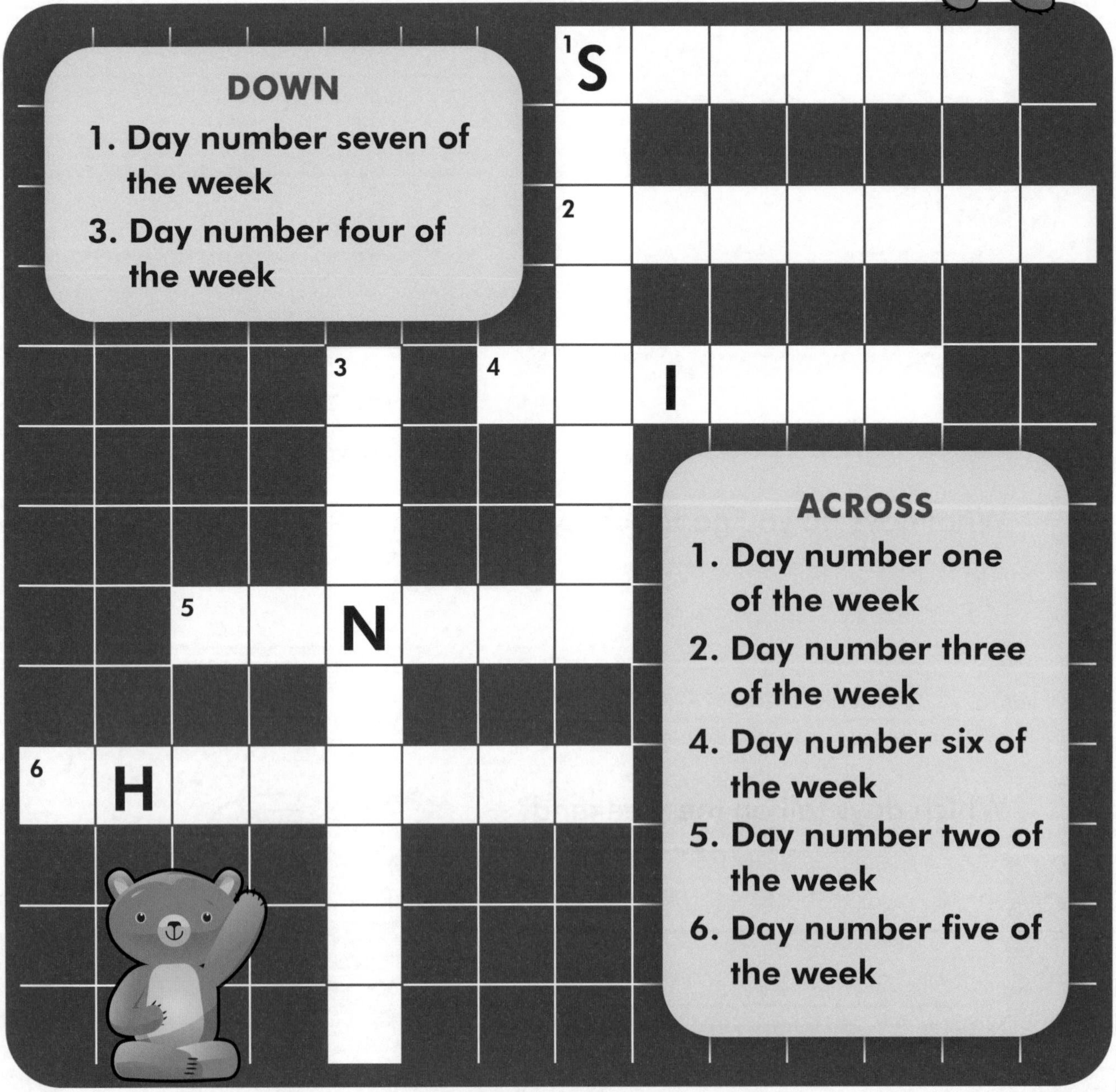

DOWN

1. Day number seven of the week
3. Day number four of the week

ACROSS

1. Day number one of the week
2. Day number three of the week
4. Day number six of the week
5. Day number two of the week
6. Day number five of the week

Proper Nouns: Months

Months of the year are **proper nouns**.
Each month must be capitalized. Read each clue.
Write the answer using the word bank below.

January February March April
May June July August
September October November December

Third month of the year	First month of the year
Month after May	Month before October
Month before December	Month after April
Last month of the year	Seventh month of the year
Second month of the year	Month after July
Month between March and May	Month between September and November

Proper Nouns: Continents

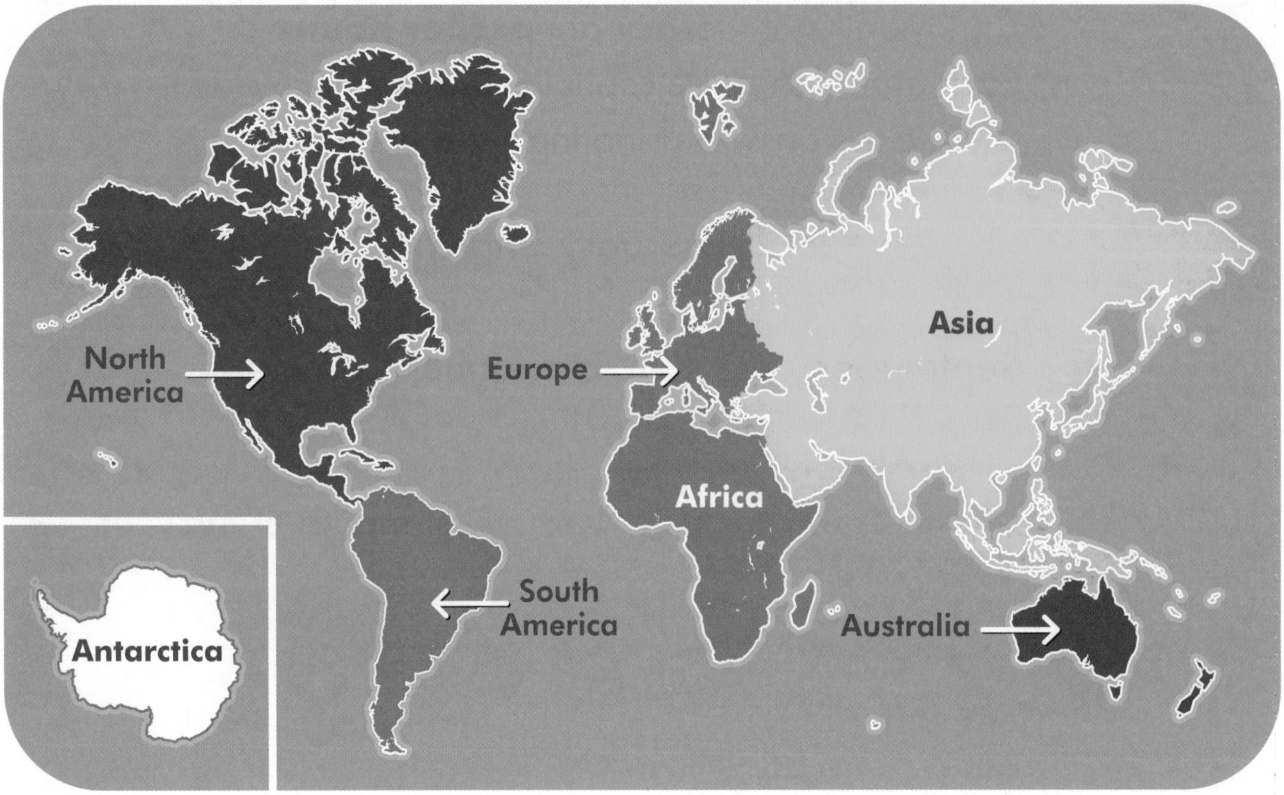

Which continent is the biggest?

____

Which continent do you live on?

____

Which continent is the smallest?

____

What continent is directly south of North America?

____

Parts of Speech

A **noun** is a word that names a person, place, or thing.

Example: An **elephant** walked into the room. **Elephant** is a noun.

Circle the **noun**.

dog skip beautiful sad

A **verb** is an action word. Verbs tell what a person, place, or thing does.

Example: The baby **cries** a lot. **Cries** is a verb.

Circle the **verb**.

cat run large small

An **adjective** is a describing word. It describes a noun.

Example: That is a **juicy** peach. **Juicy** is an adjective.

Circle the **adjective.**

tree jog rock small

Parts of Speech

Circle the **nouns**.
Put an X through the **verbs**.
Underline the **adjectives**.

beautiful
quiet
fish
skip
drives
dirty
run
bird
walk
sunny
jumps
sad
mom
sleepy
dog
room
crawl
turtle

Proofreading

Look at the pictures below. There are three spellings next to each picture. Circle the correct spelling.

bare **bear** **bair**

nect **neste** **nest**

shoos **shoese** **shoes**

spin **span** **spine**

son **sun** **sune**

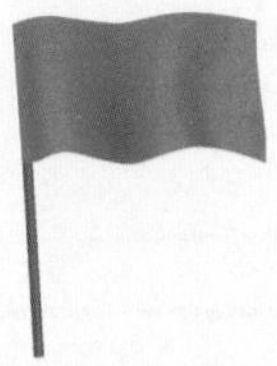

flad **flaag** **flag**

Proofreading

Read each sentence below.
Rewrite each sentence using correct
punctuation and capitalization on the line below.

my cat's name is fluffy

____

would you like to come over

____

mrs bucci is my teacher

____

i live in boston?

____

my birthday is in january.

____

how are you today.

____

Proofreading

Read the paragraph below. Add any missing punctuation and correct any words that need to be capitalized.

today is my birthday I will be nine years old. I am having a party and I invited all of my friends We will have cake and play games. after that I will open my presents Will i get the football I asked for today is going to be a great day!

SENTENCES

Writing a Sentence

Read each sentence. Circle the **naming part**.
Underline the **action part**.

The kids play in the park.

The boy goes down the slide.

The sun is shining.

The kids run around the park.

Some kids wait in line for the slide.

Writing Sentences

Write each of these words in a sentence. The sentences can be about yourself, your friends, your family, or your pets. Remember, a sentence tells a complete thought. It begins with a capital letter and ends with a period, a question mark, or an exclamation point.

excited **brave**
cute **hot** **quick**

Turn the Questions Around

When asked a question, you can usually take off the beginning of the question to help write a **response sentence**.

Examples: What is your favorite thing to do?
My favorite thing to do is . . .

Why do you like to read?
I like to read because . . .

Now try answering the questions below in **response sentences**.

Who is the most important person in your life?

____

What is your favorite color?

____

What is your favorite book?

____

What is your favorite season?

____

Vivid Verbs

A good writer uses verbs to create a picture for the reader. Some verbs are overused, such as **went**, **said**, and **liked**.

The children **went** to school.

A more exciting way to say this would be:
The children **skipped** to school, or
The children **hurried off** to school.

Write different ways to say the **verbs** below. The first one has been started for you.

said	liked	looked
exclaimed answered added expressed responded		
ran	**cried**	**jumped**

Sequencing

Transition words help move a story forward
and show the **sequence** or **order** of events.

first	next	then	last
One time	Later	Also	Finally
To begin with	Soon	Thirdly	In conclusion
To start	After that	In addition	As you can see
In the beginning	Secondly	Another	In the end

Write a sentence for each picture.
Don't forget to use your **transition words**!

Sequencing

Look at each picture and label them 1–4 in order of how a plant grows. When you are finished, write four sentences describing the process using your **transition words**.

first	next	then	last
One time To begin with To start In the beginning	Later Soon After that Secondly	Also Thirdly In addition Another	Finally In conclusion As you can see In the end

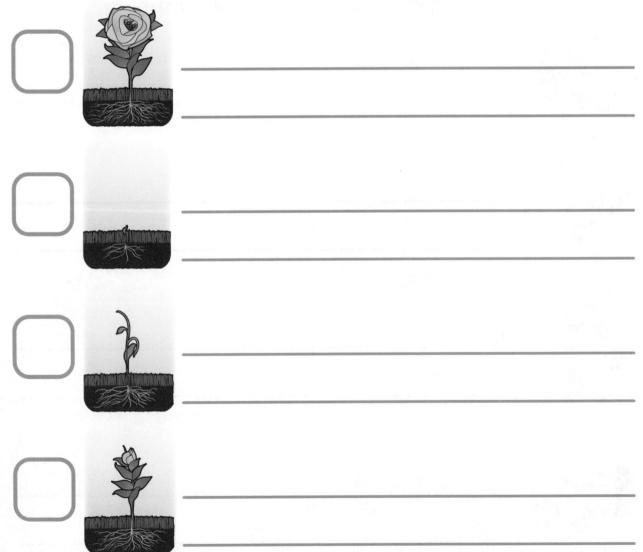

☐  ________________________________

____

☐  ________________________________

____

☐  ________________________________

____

☐  ________________________________

____

The 5 Ws

Answer the following questions.

Who → person   When → time   Why → reason
What → thing   Where → place

Who ate dinner with you last night?

___

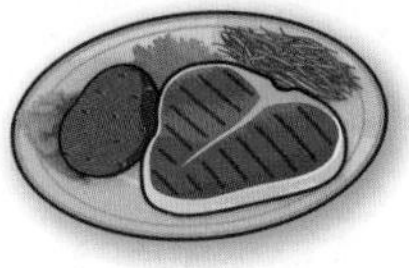

What did you have for dinner?

___

When, or what time, did you have dinner?

___

Where did you have dinner?

___

Why is it important to eat your vegetables at dinner?

___

The 5 Ws

Fill in the missing words from the word bank.

Who What When
Where Why

_____________ do you live?
I live in New York.

_____________ is your best friend?
Mike is my best friend.

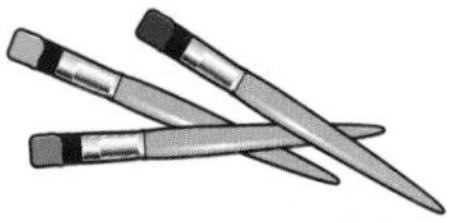

_____________ is your favorite color?
Green is my favorite color.

_____________ is your bedtime?
My bedtime is 7:30.

_____________ are you sad?
I am sad because it is the last day of summer.

The 5 Ws

Finish the title with your own answer. Draw a picture in the box below and then answer the questions.

My Favorite Trip Was to

____

Where did you go? ______________________________

What did you do when you got there? ______________________________

____

Who went with you? ______________________________

Why was it your favorite trip? ______________________________

____

When did you go? ______________________________

Descriptive Writing

Look at the picture. On the lines next to each picture, write a sentence that **describes** the picture.

Descriptive Writing

Write two sentences about your favorite things.
Try to use as many **descriptive** words as you can.

My favorite game:

My favorite thing to do in the winter:

My favorite person:

Writing a Paragraph

Write a paragraph about your favorite animal. Make sure you hook your reader with an interesting **topic sentence**, give them **three details** about your animal, and end your paragraph with a concluding sentence.

Paragraph Planner

Topic: My Favorite Animal

Topic Sentence/Main Idea:

Detail:

Detail:

Detail:

Concluding Sentence:

What Do You See?

Butterflies are very beautiful.
Color in the butterfly and the flower below and write three sentences describing what you see.

READING

Parts of a Story

Every story has a . . .

Beginning Should catch your attention and make you want to read more.

Middle Should contain details about the topic and hold your attention. The middle is usually the longest part of the story.

End Should bring the story to a close. The ending should keep you thinking about the topic.

Draw a scene from your favorite book.

Beginning, Middle, and End

READING

Think about three things you do before you go to bed.
Draw three pictures to show what you do **first**, **next**, and **last**.
Then write a sentence telling about each picture.

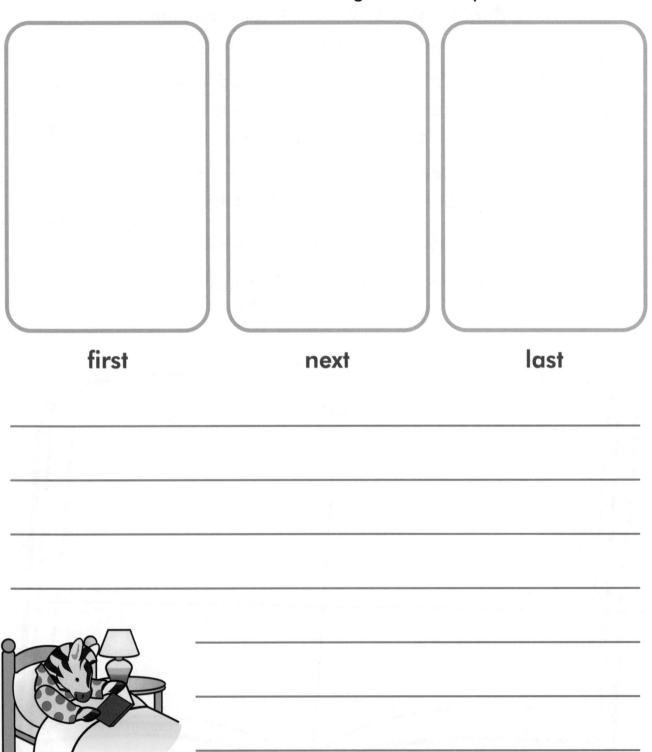

first

next

last

Putting It Together

Now put sentences together to tell the story of what you do in the morning before you go to school.

Write Your Own Story

Write your own story using the three pictures below. Be sure there is a beginning, a middle, and an end. Watch your punctuation!

Poems

An **acrostic** is a **poem** built on a special word. The word is written vertically. Then, each letter of that word serves as the first letter of a line of the poem.

Example: **Fall**

Falling leaves
Apples
Light the fireplace
Leaf piles

Now you try using the word **apple**.

A ______________________________

P ______________________________

P ______________________________

L ______________________________

E ______________________________

Poems

Poems are often stories that rhyme. Here are a bunch of words that rhyme with **cat**. Think of some lines about a cat, using these **rhyming words** in the word bank. Don't forget to come up with a title for your poem.

that hat bat rat mat sat fat pat

Title ____________________

____

____

____

____

____

____

____

____

____

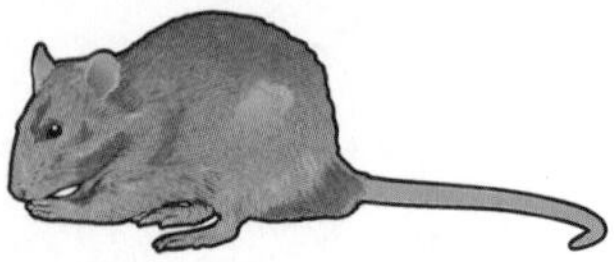

Poems

Not all **poems** have to rhyme.
Fill in the blanks below to create your own poem about **Today**.

Today Poem

Today is ______________________.

It is ______________________.
(morning, afternoon, or evening)

I feel ______________________.

I see ______________________.

I smell ______________________.

I wonder ______________________.

Tomorrow will be ______________________.

MATH

Number Words

Number words from eleven to twenty are very different from other number words. These are also important to learn.

Trace the numbers from eleven to twenty.

11 eleven

12 twelve

13 thirteen

14 fourteen

15 fifteen

16 sixteen

17 seventeen

18 eighteen

19 nineteen

20 twenty

Write the **number word**.

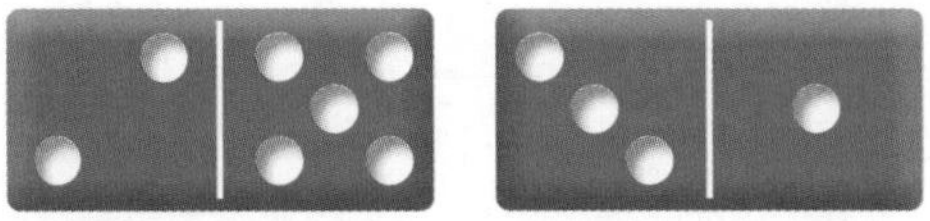

________________ dots

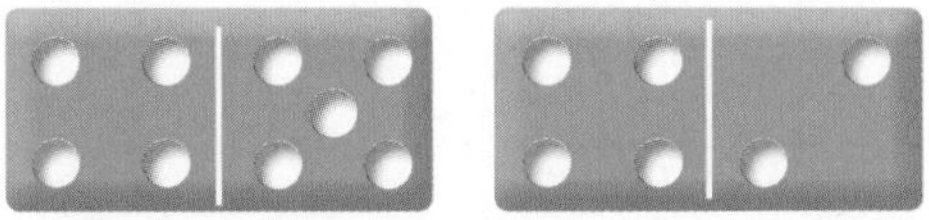

________________ dots

________________ dots

Number Words

After learning the **number words** up to twenty, it is important to learn the number words such as thirty, forty, fifty, sixty, up to one hundred.

Trace the numbers from thirty to one hundred.

30 thirty

40 forty

50 fifty

60 sixty

70 seventy

80 eighty

90 ninety

100 one hundred

Find and circle the **number words** (horizontal, vertical, or diagonal).

s	i	x	t	y	o	y	r	y	z	e	t	w	y	e
a	h	o	c	d	t	s	t	s	f	f	h	c	n	i
d	a	y	i	n	m	f	u	p	y	a	i	p	h	g
g	t	j	e	p	i	u	b	x	f	o	r	t	y	h
b	n	v	q	f	n	i	n	e	t	y	t	i	f	t
f	e	k	n	v	z	b	t	y	b	x	y	d	s	y
s	t	e	y	h	o	n	e	h	u	n	d	r	e	d

Number Words

MATH

Once you know these **number words**, it is easy to make number words for higher-value numbers by putting them together.

63 = sixty-three 24 = twenty-four 36 = thirty-six

When you put two number words together, you separate them with a **hyphen**, which looks like –.

Now you try! Use your **Number Word Charts**, from the previous pages, to help you.

Number	Number Word
53	fifty-three
84	
47	
79	
22	
71	

MATH

Place Value

Each column in a number holds a different **place value**.

For example: In the number **245** the 2's place value is in the **hundreds** column, the 4's place value is in the **tens** column, and the 5's place value is in the **ones** column.

245		
Hundreds	Tens	Ones
2	4	5

Practice writing three-digit numbers. Fill in the boxes.

548		
Hundreds	Tens	Ones

284		
Hundreds	Tens	Ones

984		
Hundreds	Tens	Ones

574		
Hundreds	Tens	Ones

274		
Hundreds	Tens	Ones

965		
Hundreds	Tens	Ones

123		
Hundreds	Tens	Ones

759		
Hundreds	Tens	Ones

Place Value

Write how many hundreds, tens, and ones there are.

three-digit numbers

hundred	ten	one
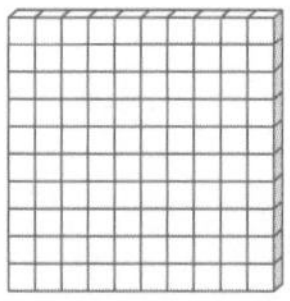		
100	10	1

	hundreds	tens	ones
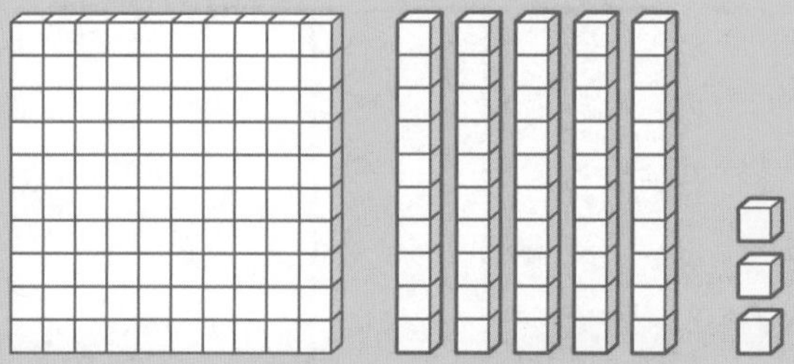			
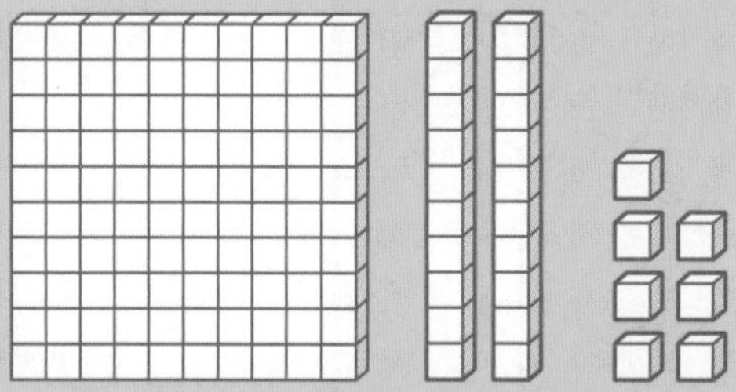			
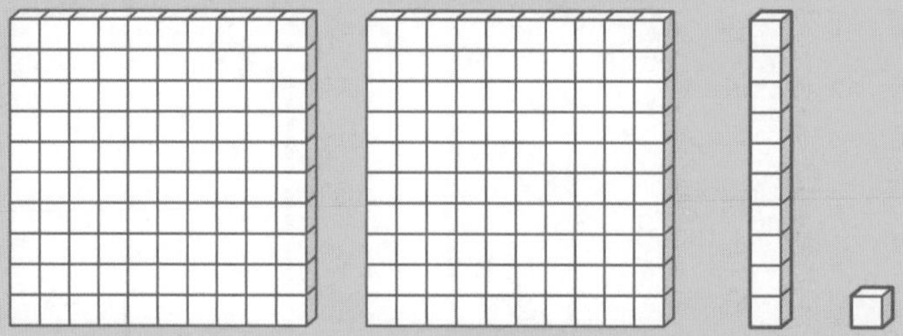			
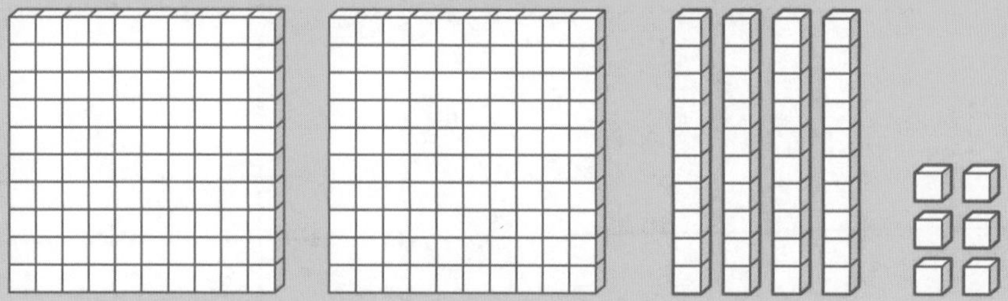			

Place Value

Write how many hundreds, tens, and ones there are.

three-digit numbers

hundred	ten	one
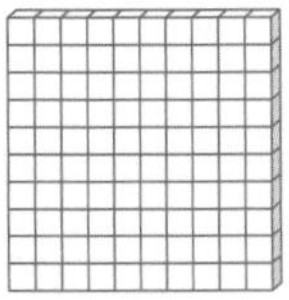		
100	10	1

	hundreds	tens	ones
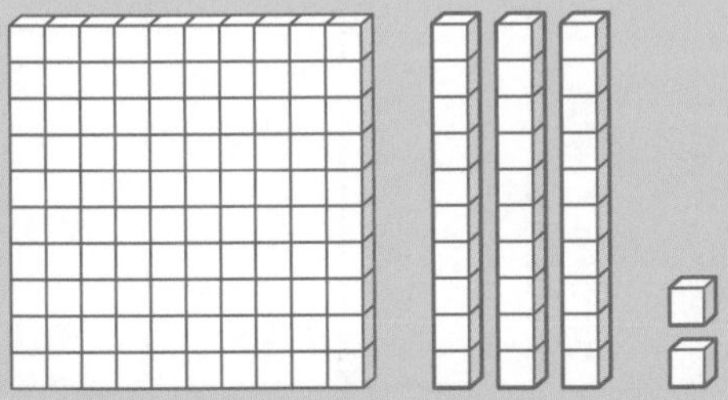			
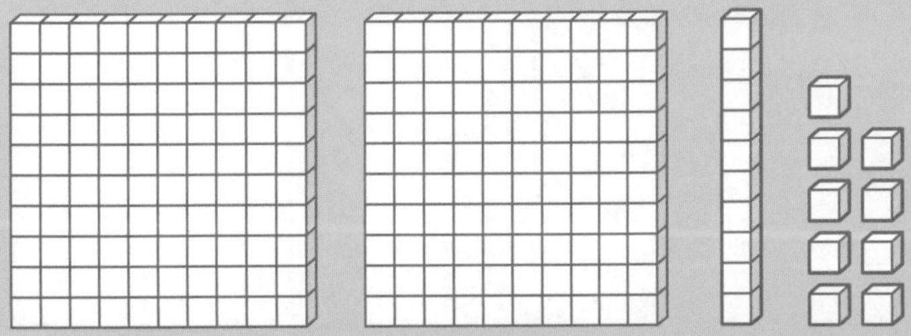			
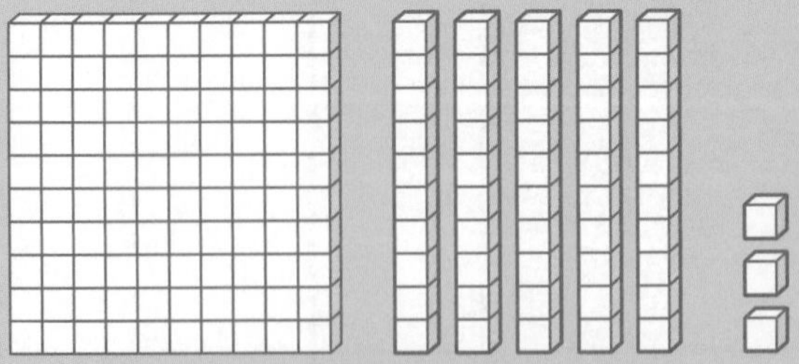			
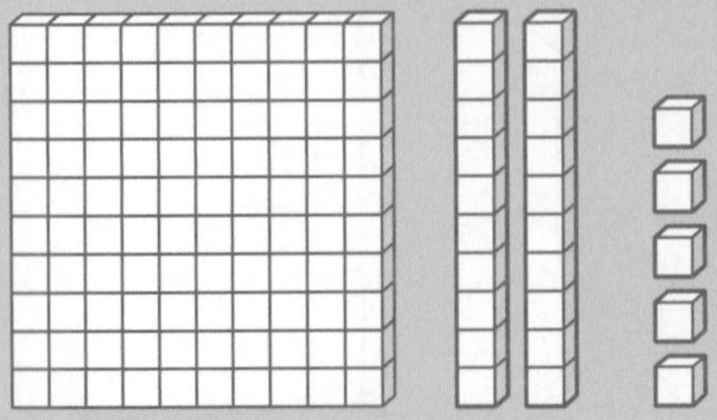			

Place Value: Tens and Ones

Write how many tens and ones are pictured
and then write an addition sentence.
The first one has been done for you.

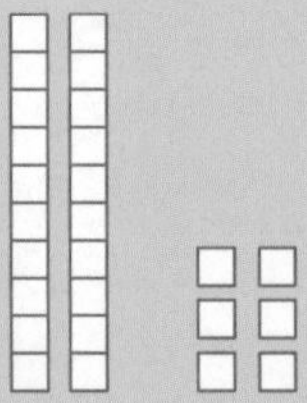

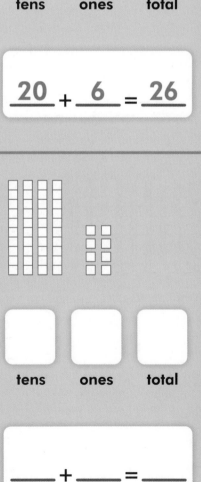

2	6	26
tens	ones	total

20 + 6 = 26

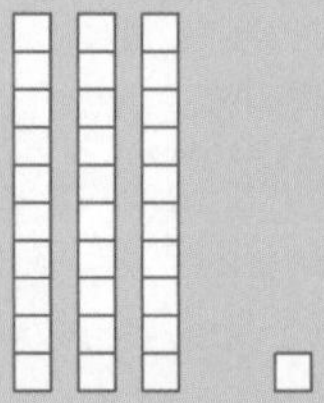

tens	ones	total

____ + ____ = ____

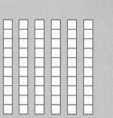

tens	ones	total

____ + ____ = ____

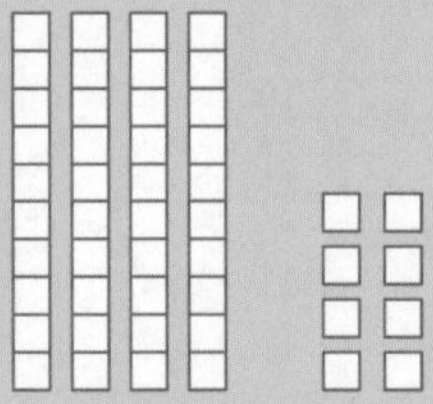

tens	ones	total

____ + ____ = ____

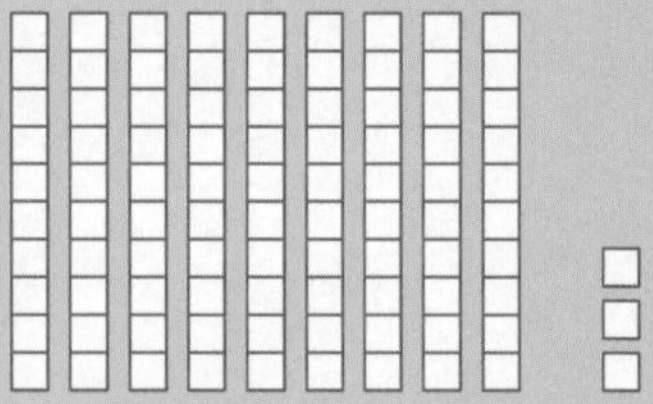

tens	ones	total

____ + ____ = ____

tens	ones	total

____ + ____ = ____

Place Value: Tens and Ones

Write how many tens and ones are pictured and then write an addition sentence. The first one has been done for you.

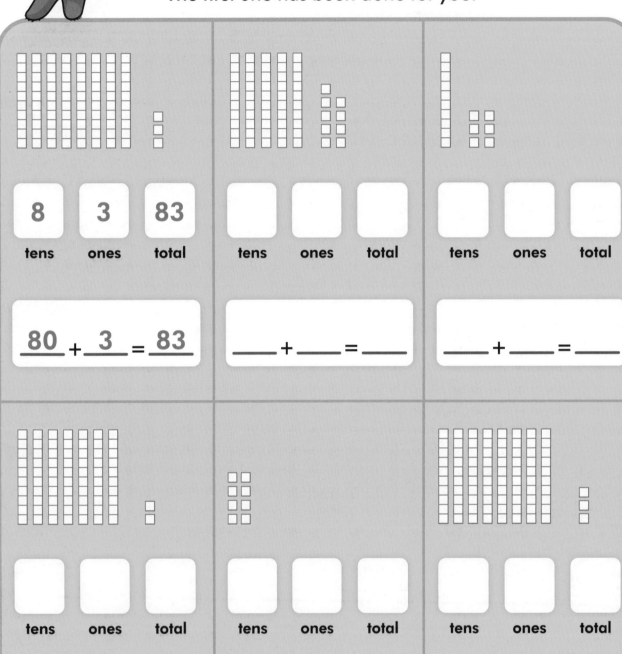

8	3	83
tens	ones	total

80 + 3 = 83

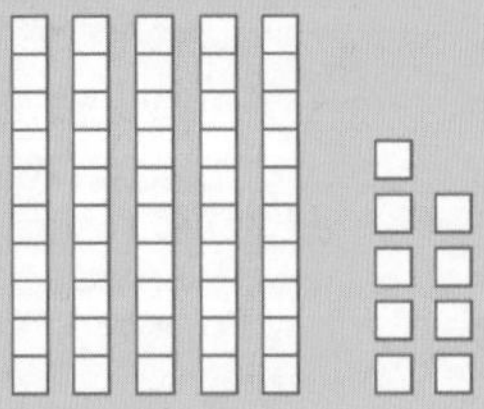

tens	ones	total

____ + ____ = ____

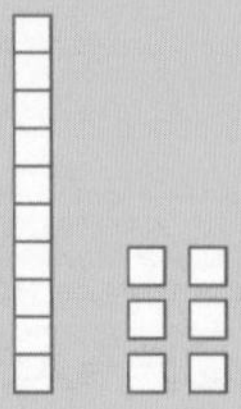

tens	ones	total

____ + ____ = ____

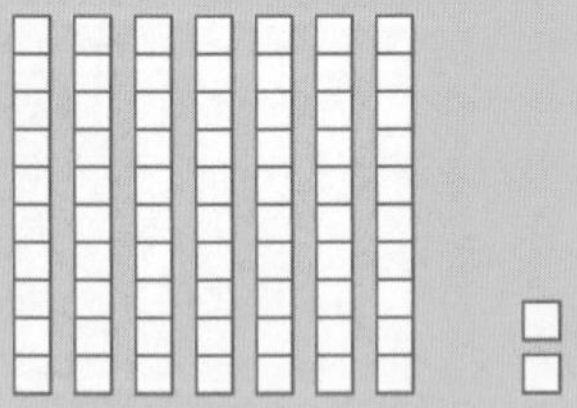

tens	ones	total

____ + ____ = ____

tens	ones	total

____ + ____ = ____

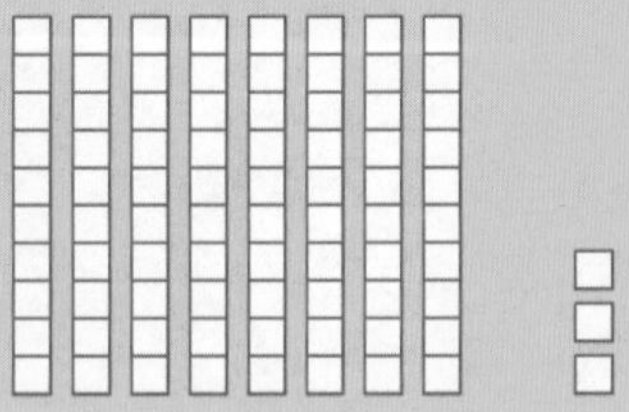

tens	ones	total

____ + ____ = ____

Place Value: Hundreds, Tens, and Ones

Write how many hundreds, tens, and ones are pictured and then write an addition sentence. The first one has been done for you.

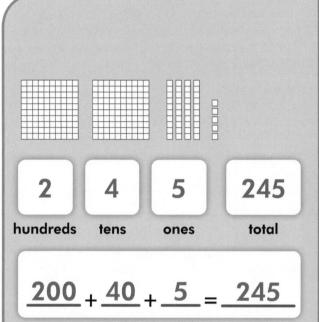

2	4	5	245
hundreds	tens	ones	total

200 + 40 + 5 = 245

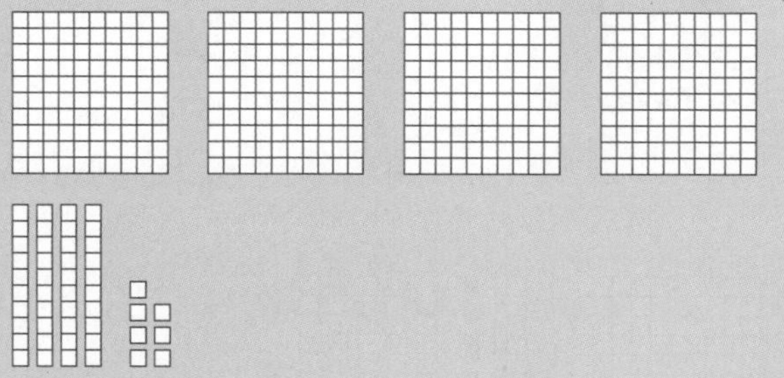

hundreds	tens	ones	total

____ + ____ + ____ = ______

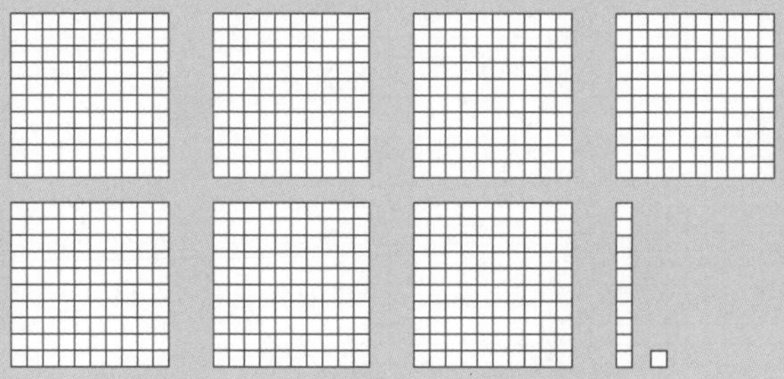

hundreds	tens	ones	total

____ + ____ + ____ = ______

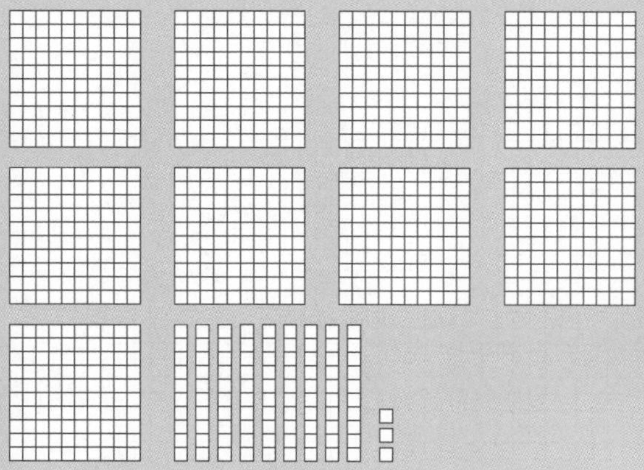

hundreds	tens	ones	total

____ + ____ + ____ = ______

Place Value: Hundreds, Tens, and Ones

MATH

Write how many hundreds, tens, and ones are pictured and then write an addition sentence. The first one has been done for you.

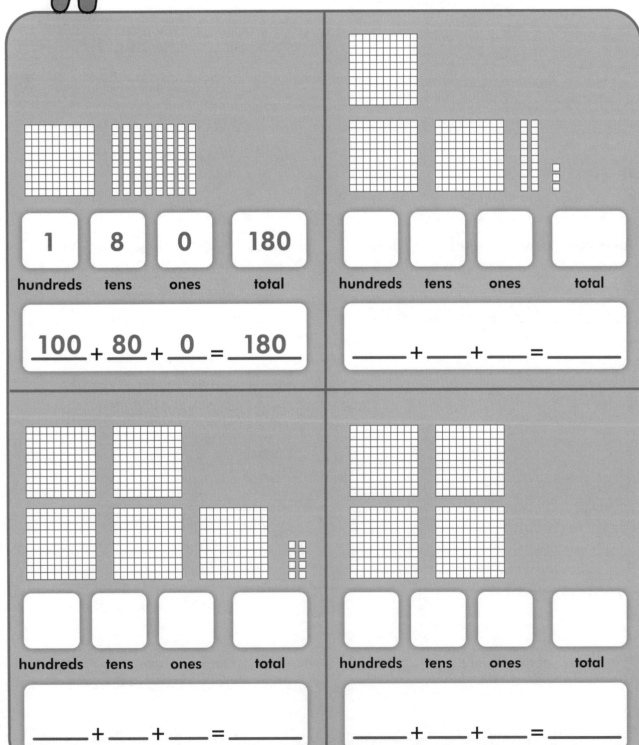

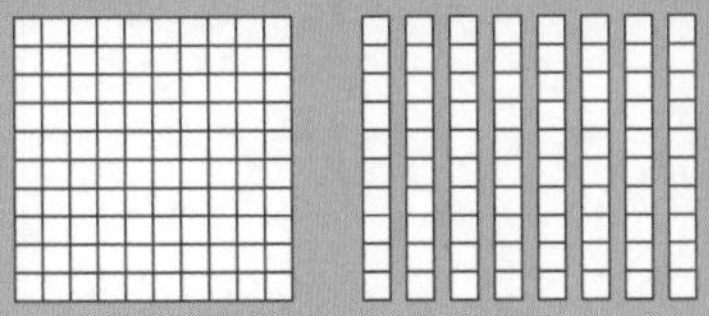

1	8	0	180
hundreds	tens	ones	total

100 + 80 + 0 = 180

hundreds	tens	ones	total

____ + ____ + ____ = ______

hundreds	tens	ones	total

____ + ____ + ____ = ______

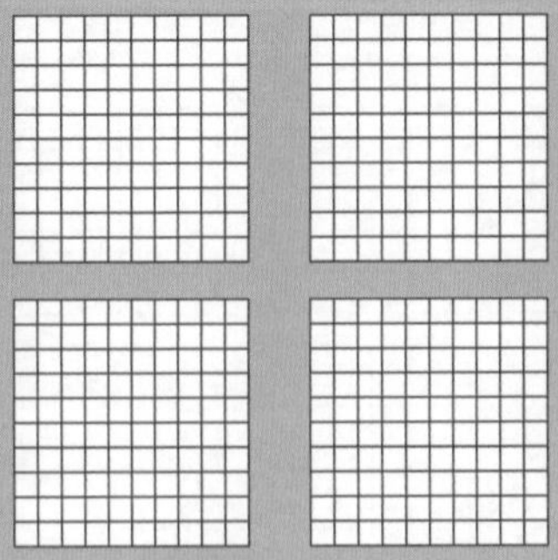

hundreds	tens	ones	total

____ + ____ + ____ = ______

Greater Than • Less Than

MATH

Alligators are hungry animals. They always want to eat the bigger number. Think of the open end of the symbol < as the open mouth of an alligator trying to eat the bigger number.

Now you try. Have the alligator eat the bigger number. Draw a < (the **less than** symbol) if the number on the right is bigger or a > (the **greater than** symbol) if the number on the left is bigger.

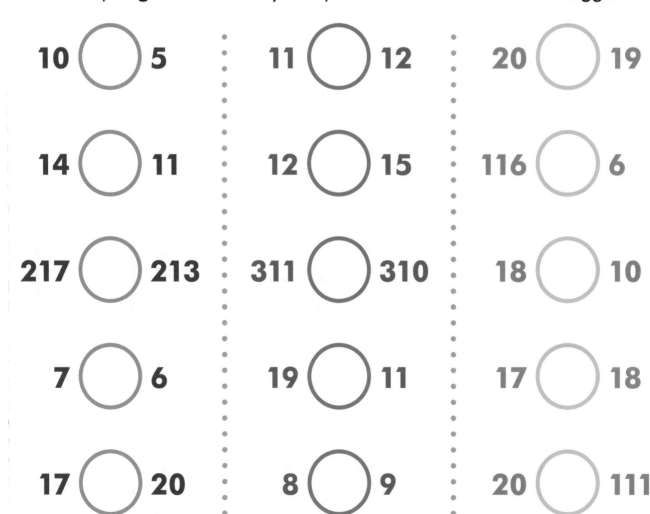

10	◯	**5**	**11**	◯	**12**	**20**	◯	**19**
14	◯	**11**	**12**	◯	**15**	**116**	◯	**6**
217	◯	**213**	**311**	◯	**310**	**18**	◯	**10**
7	◯	**6**	**19**	◯	**11**	**17**	◯	**18**
17	◯	**20**	**8**	◯	**9**	**20**	◯	**111**

MATH

Comparing Numbers

Draw number blocks to represent the circled numbers. Then write whether the first number is **greater** or **less** than the second number. The first one has been done for you.

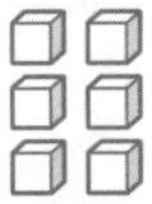

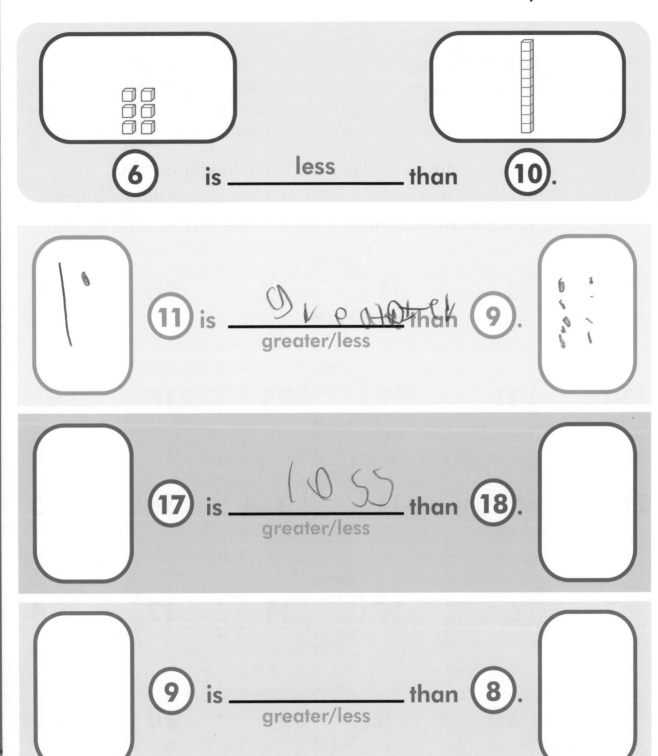

(6) is less than (10).

(11) is ______________ than (9).
greater/less

(17) is ______________ than (18).
greater/less

(9) is ______________ than (8).
greater/less

Ordinal Numbers

Ordinal numbers tell you the position of things.
Look at the shapes below from left to right.
Follow the directions for each shape.

Color the 2nd and 5th circles yellow.

Color the 1st and 9th triangles green.

Color the 4th and 6th hearts red.

Color the 3rd and 7th squares purple.

Ordinal Numbers

Read the question. Look at the rabbits for your answer and circle the correct answer below each question.

1 2 3 4 5 6 7 8 9 10

11 12 13 14 15 16 17 18 19 20

Which rabbit comes before the 10th rabbit in line?

4th **9th** **12th**

Which rabbit is just after the 14th rabbit?

15th **19th** **2nd**

Which rabbit comes between the 5th rabbit and 7th rabbit?

7th **12th** **6th**

Which rabbit is the very last?

3rd **19th** **20th**

Which rabbit is at the very beginning?

1st **10th** **19th**

Odd and Even Numbers

Even numbers are when you count by **2**s starting at **2**
Example: **4**, **6**, **8**, **10**, **12**

Odd numbers are when you count by **2**s starting at **1**
Example: **3**, **5**, **7**, **9**, **11**, **13**

You must always look at the digit in the one's place to see if it is an odd or even number.

346 **6** is an **even** number, so 346 is even.

263 **3** is an **odd** number, so 263 is odd.

Circle all the **even** numbers.
Put an **X** through all the **odd** numbers.

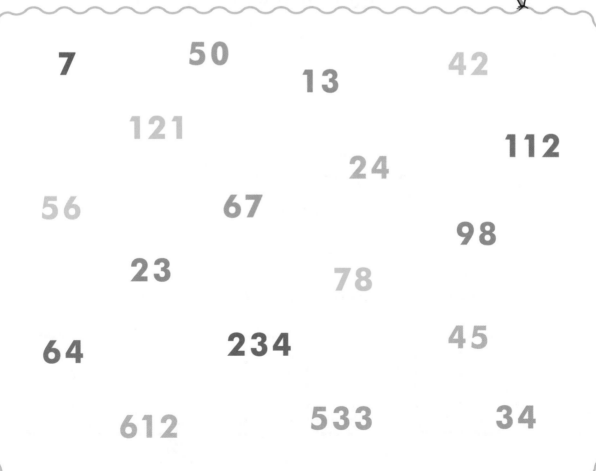

7 50 13 42

121 112

24

56 67

98

23 78

64 234 45

612 533 34

Odd and Even Numbers

Look at these three numbers:

2 7 8

Sort them to make the **largest even number** you can.

Sort them to make the **largest odd number** you can.

Sort them to make the **smallest even number** you can.

Now look at these four numbers:

2 5 9 4

Use them to make six different two-digit even numbers:

Odd and Even Numbers

Below are a lot of numbers that are multiples of 5.
Write them under the proper column.

Even numbers:
2, **4**, **6**, **8**, **10**, **12**, and so on

Odd numbers:
1, **3**, **5**, **7**, **9**, **11**, and so on

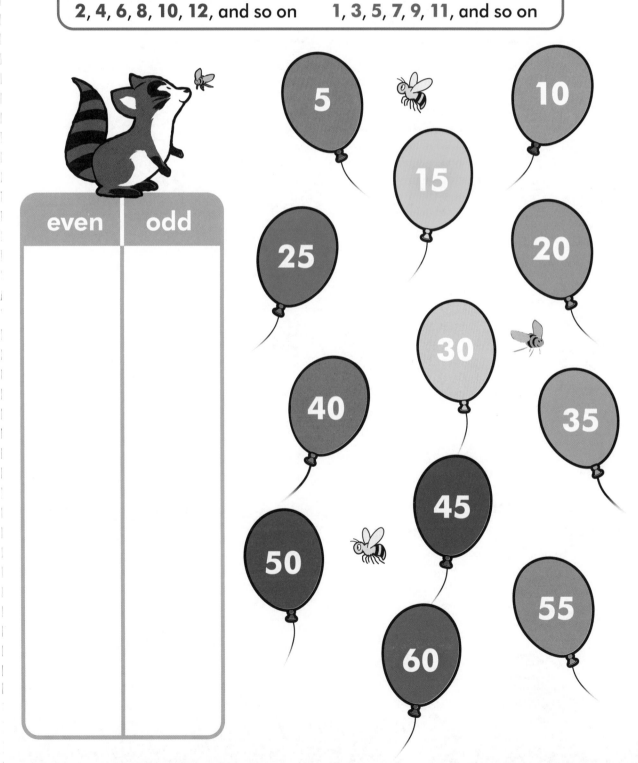

even	odd

Skip-Counting by 2s

Fill in the missing numbers by **skip-counting** by 2s.

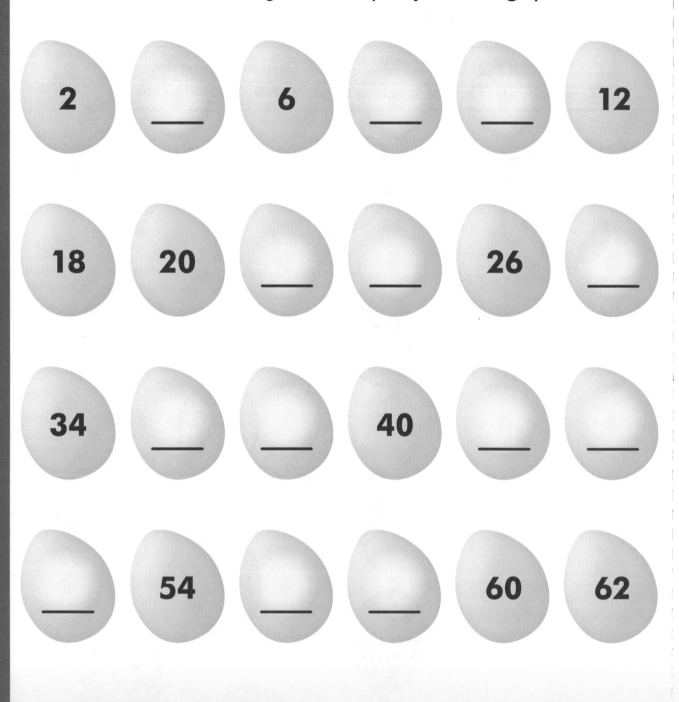

2	___	6	___	___	12
18	20	___	___	26	___
34	___	___	40	___	___
___	54	___	___	60	62

Skip-Counting by 5s

Fill in the missing numbers by **skip-counting** by 5s.

5	____	15	____	____	30
15	20	____	____	35	____
40	____	____	55	____	____
____	75	____	____	90	____

MATH

Skip-Counting by 10s

Fill in the missing numbers by **skip-counting** by 10s.

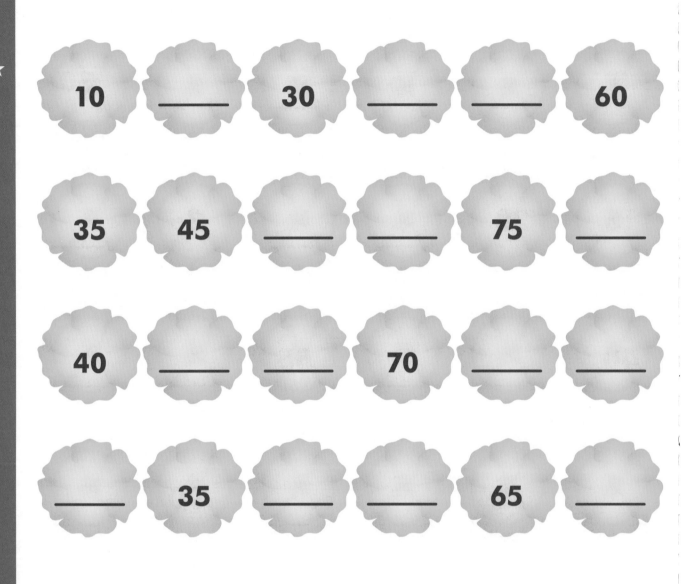

10	____	30	____	____	60
35	45	____	____	75	____
40	____	____	70	____	____
____	35	____	____	65	____

Pictograph

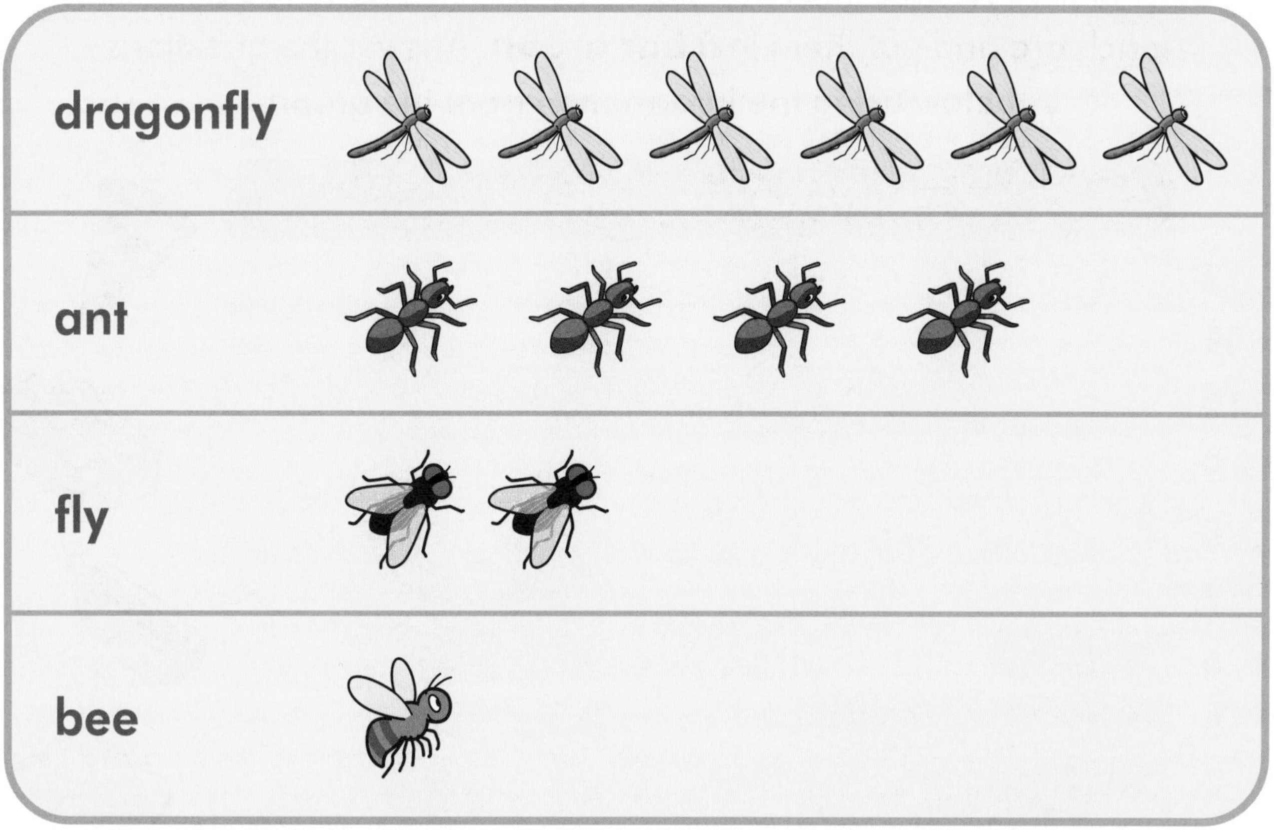

Use the **pictograph** above to solve the following problems:

How many flies are there? ________

Which group of bugs is the smallest? ________

Which group of bugs is the largest? ________

 = ________ +  = ________ = ________

 = ________ +  = ________ = ________

Bar Graph

Mrs. Bucci asked her students what their favorite foods for lunch are and put them in a **bar graph**. Answer the questions below using the information from the graph.

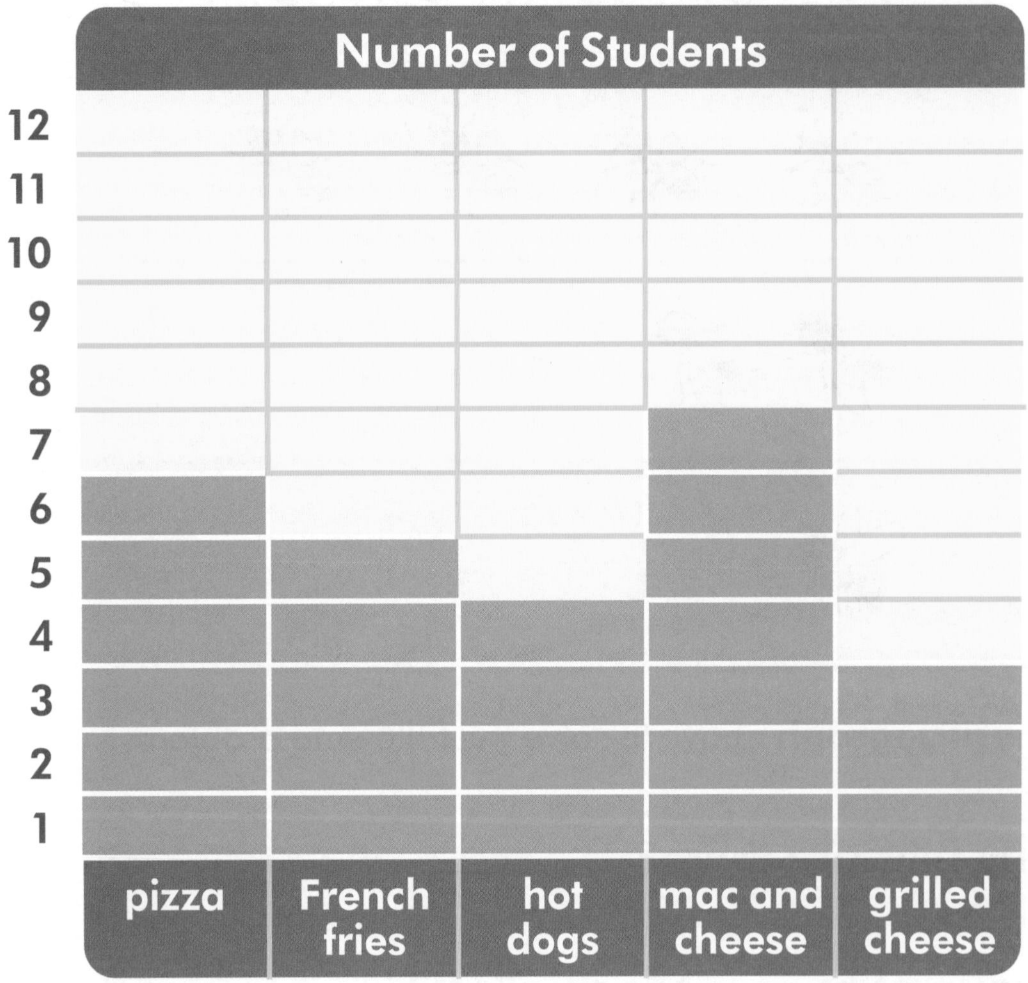

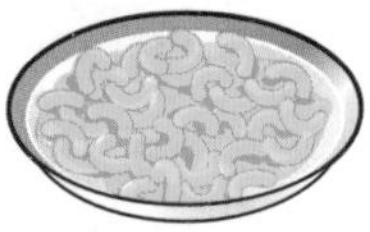

How many students love pizza? ________

How many more people like mac and cheese than hot dogs? ________

How many people like both French fries and pizza? ________

What is the students' favorite food? ________________________

Same Sums

Draw a line from the left column to the right column where the **sums** match.

TOTAL = 5

TOTAL = 5

7 + 3	9 + 7
8 + 8	8 + 3
6 + 6	5 + 8
5 + 6	9 + 3
9 + 4	9 + 5
7 + 7	6 + 4

Two-Digit Addition

Count the blocks and then add them up.
The first problem has been solved for you.

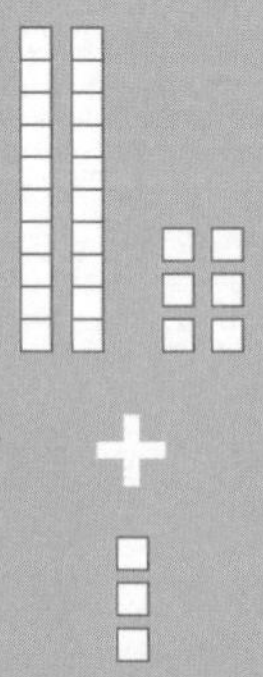

start ↓

	tens	ones
	2	6
+	0	3
total	2	9

start ↓

	tens	ones
+		
total		

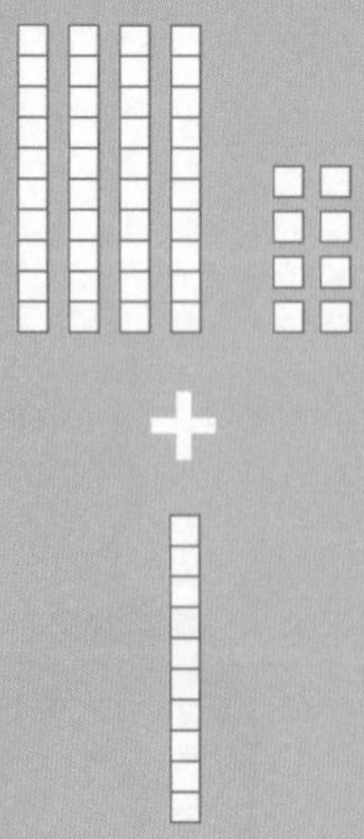

start ↓

	tens	ones
+		
total		

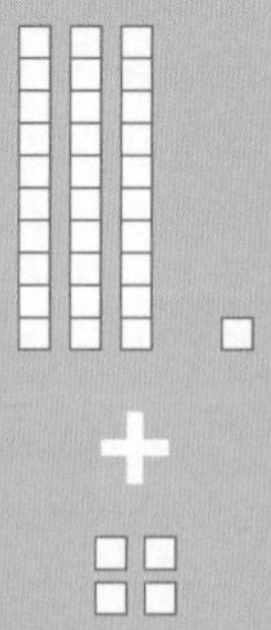

start ↓

	tens	ones
+		
total		

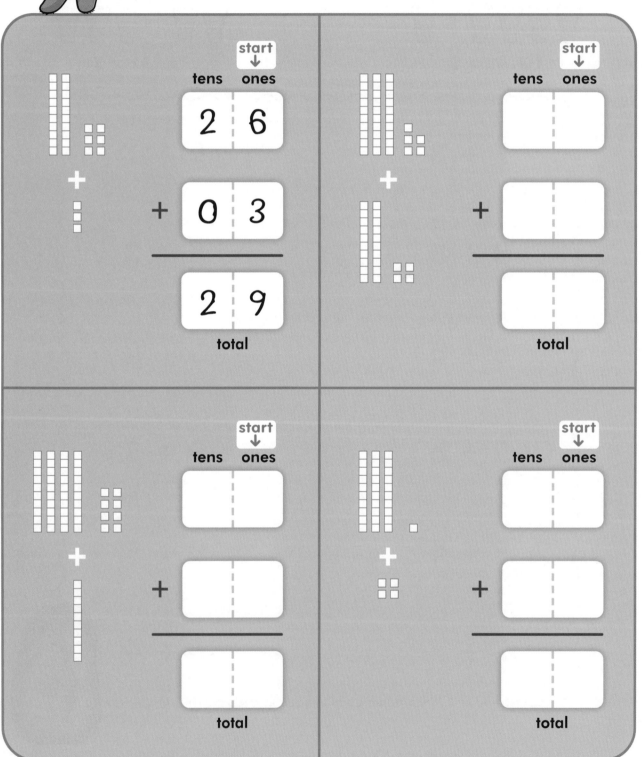

Two-Digit Addition

Write how many tens you have in each box, and then how many ones you have. When adding two-digit numbers, you always want to start in the ones place to add, then go to the tens place to add.

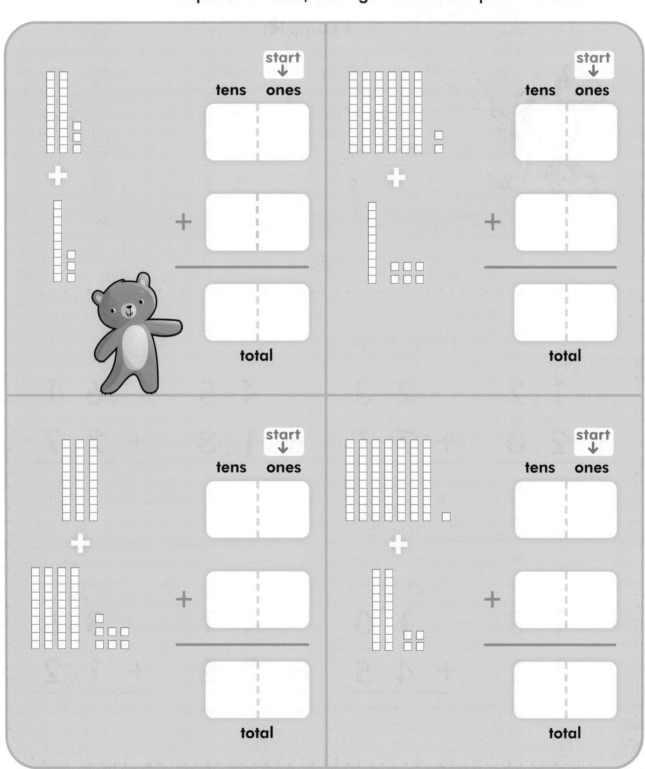

start ↓

tens | ones

\+

total

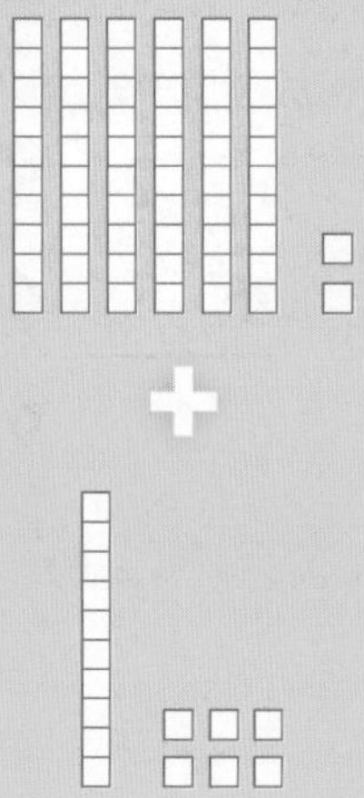

start ↓

tens | ones

\+

total

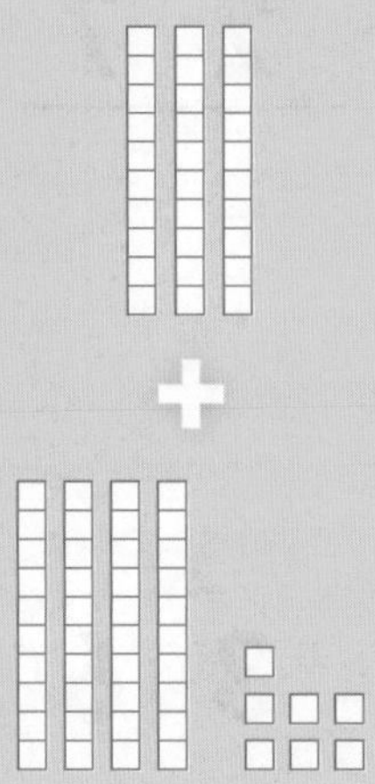

start ↓

tens | ones

\+

total

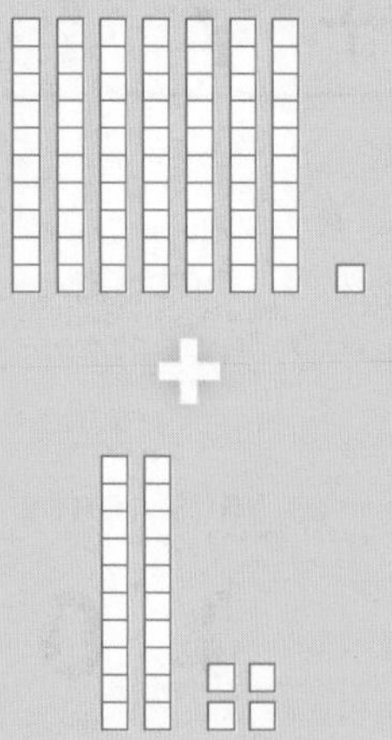

start ↓

tens | ones

\+

total

MATH

Two-Digit Addition

When adding two-digit numbers, first add the ones, then add the tens.

Example:

	tens	ones (start)
	2	5
+	1	4
		9

	tens	ones (start)
	2	5
+	1	4
	3	9

Add.

	tens	ones (start)
	1	2
+	2	0

	tens	ones (start)
	2	3
+	7	1

	tens	ones (start)
	4	5
+	1	3

	tens	ones (start)
	6	1
+	2	7

	tens	ones (start)
	1	3
+	6	1

	tens	ones (start)
	1	0
+	4	5

	tens	ones (start)
	4	1
+	2	8

	tens	ones (start)
	3	6
+	1	2

Adding Two-Digit Numbers

Add.

	tens	ones
	2	2
+	4	5

	tens	ones
	3	5
+	1	4

	tens	ones
	1	0
+	3	9

	tens	ones
	1	8
+	5	0

	tens	ones
	1	6
+	3	0

	tens	ones
	2	2
+	4	2

	tens	ones
	4	0
+	1	0

	tens	ones
	1	1
+	2	5

	tens	ones
	1	2
+	5	0

	tens	ones
	2	2
+	6	1

	tens	ones
	1	5
+	4	0

	tens	ones
	3	6
+	1	2

(Each problem: "start ↓" above the ones column.)

Adding Two-Digit Numbers: Regrouping

When we add numbers in columns, we can think of each column as a set. We add up the numbers in each set. First we add all the numbers in the ones place and then the tens place.

If we have more than 9 in one set, we have to regroup, which means that we have to move the digits that are higher than 9 to the next column.

Example:

```
  [1]
   1 6
+  1 5
------
   3 1
```

Add.

	tens	ones (start)
	6	8
+	1	5

	tens	ones (start)
	3	7
+	4	7

	tens	ones (start)
	3	4
+	4	8

	tens	ones (start)
	1	8
+	1	5

	tens	ones (start)
	2	6
+	4	6

	tens	ones (start)
	3	8
+	4	2

Adding Two-Digit Numbers: Regrouping

Add the numbers in the columns, using each box to regroup.

$\square$ start
tens ones

$$\begin{array}{cc} 5 & 6 \\ + \ 2 & 7 \\ \hline \end{array}$$

$\square$ start
tens ones

$$\begin{array}{cc} 4 & 8 \\ + \ 1 & 3 \\ \hline \end{array}$$

$\square$ start
tens ones

$$\begin{array}{cc} 6 & 9 \\ + \ 2 & 2 \\ \hline \end{array}$$

$\square$ start
tens ones

$$\begin{array}{cc} 7 & 9 \\ + \ 1 & 1 \\ \hline \end{array}$$

$\square$ start
tens ones

$$\begin{array}{cc} 2 & 8 \\ + \ 5 & 3 \\ \hline \end{array}$$

$\square$ start
tens ones

$$\begin{array}{cc} 1 & 7 \\ + \ 5 & 4 \\ \hline \end{array}$$

$\square$ start
tens ones

$$\begin{array}{cc} 3 & 4 \\ + \ 4 & 7 \\ \hline \end{array}$$

$\square$ start
tens ones

$$\begin{array}{cc} 2 & 1 \\ + \ 1 & 9 \\ \hline \end{array}$$

$\square$ start
tens ones

$$\begin{array}{cc} 3 & 4 \\ + \ 3 & 8 \\ \hline \end{array}$$

$\square$ start
tens ones

$$\begin{array}{cc} 4 & 5 \\ + \ 2 & 6 \\ \hline \end{array}$$

$\square$ start
tens ones

$$\begin{array}{cc} 8 & 0 \\ + \ 1 & 8 \\ \hline \end{array}$$

MATH

Adding Two-Digit Numbers: Regrouping

Add the numbers in the columns, using each box to regroup.

start → tens ones

23 + 19	39 + 32	13 + 27	54 + 18
39 + 32	47 + 25	48 + 37	44 + 29
	54 + 8	44 + 17	44 + 16

Subtraction with Base Ten

Draw the base ten blocks for each number. Then cross out the ones to subtract. Write the answer under the line.

Example:

$$\begin{array}{r} 67 \\ -\ \ 7 \\ \hline 60 \end{array}$$

67 ←1
7 ←2
60 ←3

1 Draw the larger number with base ten blocks.

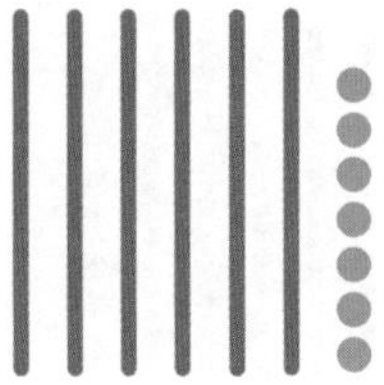

67

2 Take away the smaller number by crossing it out.

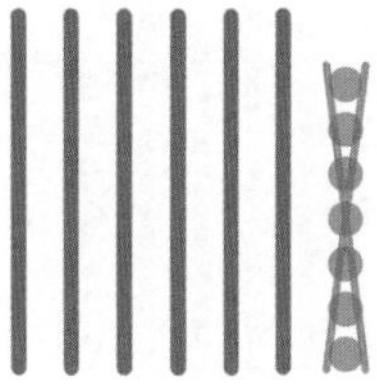

~~7~~

3 Count what you have left.

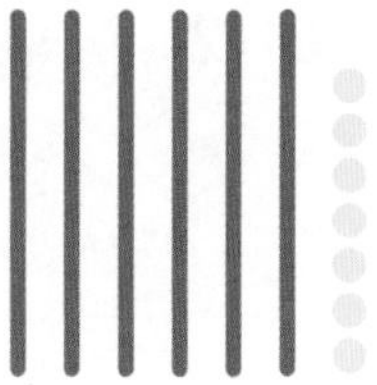

60

$$\begin{array}{r} 35 \\ -\ \ 4 \\ \hline \end{array}$$

$$\begin{array}{r} 18 \\ -\ \ 5 \\ \hline \end{array}$$

$$\begin{array}{r} 56 \\ -\ \ 6 \\ \hline \end{array}$$

$$\begin{array}{r} 47 \\ -\ \ 3 \\ \hline \end{array}$$

$$\begin{array}{r} 83 \\ -\ \ 1 \\ \hline \end{array}$$

$$\begin{array}{r} 77 \\ -\ \ 4 \\ \hline \end{array}$$

Subtraction with Base Ten

Draw the base ten blocks for each number. Then cross out the tens and ones to subtract. Write the answer under the line.

Example:

```
  6 7  ← 1
– 3 2  ← 2
  3 5  ← 3
```

1. Draw the larger number with base ten blocks.
2. Take away the smaller number by crossing it out.
3. Count what you have left.

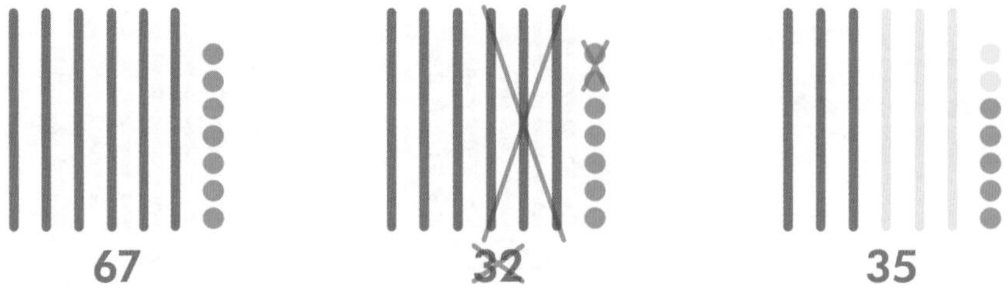

$$\begin{array}{r} 25 \\ -\ 10 \\ \hline \end{array}$$

$$\begin{array}{r} 46 \\ -\ 20 \\ \hline \end{array}$$

$$\begin{array}{r} 61 \\ -\ 30 \\ \hline \end{array}$$

$$\begin{array}{r} 75 \\ -\ 22 \\ \hline \end{array}$$

$$\begin{array}{r} 37 \\ -\ 21 \\ \hline \end{array}$$

$$\begin{array}{r} 54 \\ -\ 12 \\ \hline \end{array}$$

Subtraction

Subtract.

start ↓ tens ones 38 − 21	start ↓ tens ones 87 − 22	start ↓ tens ones 51 − 50	start ↓ tens ones 87 − 6
start ↓ tens ones 15 − 14	start ↓ tens ones 79 − 9	start ↓ tens ones 17 − 3	start ↓ tens ones 59 − 10
start ↓ tens ones 95 − 22	start ↓ tens ones 73 − 73	start ↓ tens ones 85 − 53	start ↓ tens ones 45 − 15

Two-Digit Subtraction with Regrouping

tens	ones
9	1
− 3	5

The first thing to do is subtract the ones. But since we can't subtract 5 from 1, we must borrow from the tens. This is called **regrouping**.

tens	ones
8	11
~~9~~	~~1~~
− 3	5

So we are going to take 1 from the 9 and make it 8. Then we add the 10, since one from the ten spot is 10, to the 1, making it 11.

Once we've finished regrouping, we can subtract. Look at the first example below to see the answer to this problem. Then work out the answers to the other problems on your own.

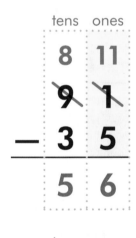

tens	ones
8	11
~~9~~	~~1~~
− 3	5
5	6

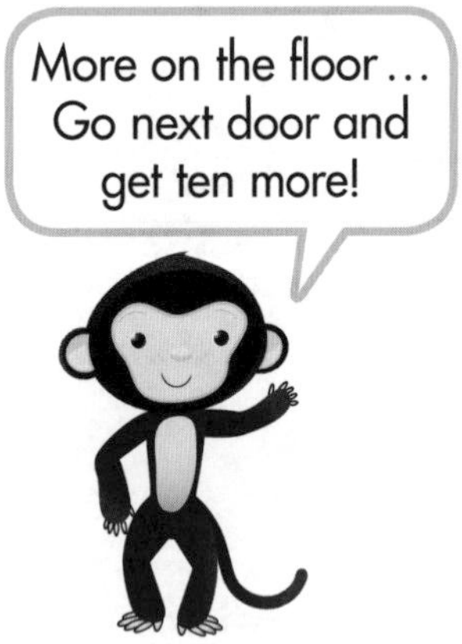
More on the floor… Go next door and get ten more!

tens	ones
☐	☐
3	8
− 2	9

tens	ones
☐	☐
4	2
− 3	7

tens	ones
☐	☐
5	6
− 2	8

tens	ones
☐	☐
6	6
− 3	7

tens	ones
☐	☐
8	4
− 5	5

tens	ones
☐	☐
7	3
− 3	7

Two-Digit Subtraction with Regrouping

Subtract.

	tens	ones
	8	11
	~~9~~	~~1~~
−	3	5
	5	6

More on the floor...
Go next door and
get ten more!

	tens	ones
	5	1
−	1	3

	tens	ones
	3	2
−	1	9

	tens	ones
	9	2
−	5	5

	tens	ones
	6	1
−	5	8

	tens	ones
	7	4
−	4	8

	tens	ones
	8	1
−	4	5

	tens	ones
	2	1
−	1	7

	tens	ones
	9	3
−	2	8

	tens	ones
	4	0
−	2	3

	tens	ones
	8	4
−	6	7

Two-Digit Subtraction with Regrouping

More on the floor…
Go next door and
get ten more!

Subtract. Draw a line connecting the problem to its answer.

tens	ones
5	2
− 1	3

tens	ones
7	3
− 4	8

tens	ones
9	2
− 3	5

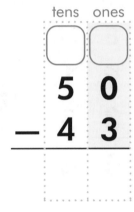

26

13

57

39

25

7

tens	ones
5	0
− 4	3

tens	ones
3	1
− 1	8

tens	ones
8	1
− 5	5

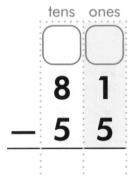

How to Solve a Word Problem

1. Read the problem and circle the important numbers. — A monkey was given 13 bananas. He ate 7. How many were left?

2. Underline the question: What is being asked of you? — A monkey was given 13 bananas. He ate 7. How many were left?

3. Then write an answer sentence. — The monkey had ___ bananas left.

4. Box any key words such as more, less, in all, all together. — The monkey had ___ bananas left.

5. Write a number sentence and solve. — $13 - 7 = 6$

6. Write your answer in the sentence. — The monkey had 6 bananas left.

Word Problems

1 Read the problem and circle the important numbers.
2 Underline the question: What is being asked of you?
3 Then write an answer sentence.
4 Box any key words such as more, less, in all, all together.
5 Write a number sentence and solve.
6 Write your answer in the sentence.

Jenny went to the grocery store to buy fruit for pies.
She bought 12 apples and 16 peaches.
How many pieces of fruit did Jenny buy in all?

Number sentence: ______________________

Answer sentence: ______________________

Amy had 56 jelly beans. She gave 12 to Dylan.
How many jelly beans does Amy have left?

Number sentence: ______________________

Answer sentence: ______________________

Brian had 80 cookies. He gave some to his friend.
Now he only has 42 cookies left.
How many did he give to his friend?

Number sentence: ______________________

Answer sentence: ______________________

Word Problems

1 Read the problem and circle the important numbers.
2 Underline the question: What is being asked of you?
3 Then write an answer sentence.
4 Box any key words such as more, less, in all, all together.
5 Write a number sentence and solve.
6 Write your answer in the sentence.

In my classroom, there are 14 boys and 12 girls. How many kids all together are there in my classroom?

Number sentence: ____________________

Answer sentence: ____________________

Dave had some fish in a fish tank. Paul gave him 10 more fish. Now he has 35 fish. How many fish did Dave begin with?

Number sentence: ____________________

Answer sentence: ____________________

There are 13 birds on a fence. Another 12 birds land on the fence. How many birds in all are on the fence?

Number sentence: ____________________

Answer sentence: ____________________

TIME AND MONEY

Counting Money

When counting coins, always count from the highest-value coin to the lowest-value coin.

Quarter = 25 cents = 25¢	Dime = 10 cents = 10¢	Nickel = 5 cents = 5¢	Penny = 1 cent = 1¢

25¢ 25¢ 10¢ 10¢ 5¢ 1¢ 1¢

.25 + .50 + .60 + .70 + .75 + .76 + .77 = 77¢

Write the sum of each coin as you count.

25¢ 5¢ 5¢ 1¢

___ + ___ + ___ + ___ = ___¢

25¢ 10¢ 5¢ 1¢

___ + ___ + ___ + ___ = ___¢

25¢ 5¢ 1¢ 1¢

___ + ___ + ___ + ___ = ___¢

10¢ 5¢ 1¢ 1¢

___ + ___ + ___ + ___ = ___¢

Counting Money

When counting coins, always count from the highest-value coin to the lowest-value coin.

Quarter = 25 cents = 25¢	Dime = 10 cents = 10¢	Nickel = 5 cents = 5¢	Penny = 1 cent = 1¢

25¢ 25¢ 10¢ 10¢ 5¢ 1¢ 1¢

.25 + .50 + .60 + .70 + .75 + .76 + .77 = 77¢

Write the sum of each coin as you count.

25¢ 10¢ 10¢ 1¢

____ + ____ + ____ + ____ = ____¢

25¢ 5¢ 5¢ 5¢

____ + ____ + ____ + ____ = ____¢

10¢ 10¢ 5¢ 5¢

____ + ____ + ____ + ____ = ____¢

10¢ 5¢ 5¢ 1¢

____ + ____ + ____ + ____ = ____¢

Counting Money

When counting coins, always count from the highest-value coin to the lowest-value coin.

Quarter =	Dime =	Nickel =	Penny =
25 cents = 25¢	10 cents = 10¢	5 cents = 5¢	1 cent = 1¢

25¢ 25¢ 10¢ 10¢ 5¢ 1¢ 1¢

.25 + .50 + .60 + .70 + .75 + .76 + .77 = 77¢

Write the sum of each coin as you count.

25¢ 10¢ 1¢ 1¢

___ + ___ + ___ + ___ = ___¢

25¢ 5¢ 5¢ 1¢

___ + ___ + ___ + ___ = ___¢

25¢ 25¢ 5¢ 5¢

___ + ___ + ___ + ___ = ___¢

25¢ 25¢ 25¢ 5¢

___ + ___ + ___ + ___ = ___¢

Counting Money

When counting coins, always count from the highest-value coin to the lowest-value coin.

Quarter =	Dime =	Nickel =	Penny =
25 cents = 25¢	10 cents = 10¢	5 cents = 5¢	1 cent = 1¢

25¢ 25¢ 10¢ 10¢ 5¢ 1¢ 1¢

.25 + .50 + .60 + .70 + .75 + .76 + .77 = 77¢

Write the sum of each coin as you count.

25¢ 25¢ 5¢ 5¢ 1¢

___ + ___ + ___ + ___ + ___ = ___¢

25¢ 10¢ 5¢ 1¢ 1¢

___ + ___ + ___ + ___ + ___ = ___¢

10¢ 10¢ 10¢ 5¢ 5¢

___ + ___ + ___ + ___ + ___ = ___¢

10¢ 5¢ 5¢ 1¢ 1¢

___ + ___ + ___ + ___ + ___ = ___¢

Counting Money

When counting coins, always count from the highest-value coin to the lowest-value coin.

Quarter = 25 cents = 25¢	Dime = 10 cents = 10¢	Nickel = 5 cents = 5¢	Penny = 1 cent = 1¢

25¢ 25¢ 10¢ 10¢ 5¢ 1¢ 1¢

.25 + .50 + .60 + .70 + .75 + .76 + .77 = 77¢

Write the sum of each coin as you count.

25¢ 10¢ 5¢ 5¢ 1¢

____ + ____ + ____ + ____ + ____ = ____¢

25¢ 25¢ 5¢ 1¢ 1¢

____ + ____ + ____ + ____ + ____ = ____¢

10¢ 10¢ 5¢ 5¢ 5¢

____ + ____ + ____ + ____ + ____ = ____¢

10¢ 10¢ 5¢ 1¢ 1¢

____ + ____ + ____ + ____ + ____ = ____¢

Counting Money

When counting coins, always count from the highest-value coin to the lowest-value coin.

Quarter = 25 cents = 25¢ | **Dime =** 10 cents = 10¢ | **Nickel =** 5 cents = 5¢ | **Penny =** 1 cent = 1¢

25¢ 25¢ 10¢ 10¢ 5¢ 1¢ 1¢

.25 + .50 + .60 + .70 + .75 + .76 + .77 = 77¢

Write the sum of each coin as you count.

25¢ 25¢ 25¢ 10¢

___ + ___ + ___ + ___ = ___¢

25¢ 25¢ 10¢ 5¢ 1¢ 1¢

___ + ___ + ___ + ___ + ___ + ___ = ___¢

10¢ 10¢ 5¢ 5¢ 5¢ 1¢

___ + ___ + ___ + ___ + ___ + ___ = ___¢

10¢ 10¢ 5¢ 1¢

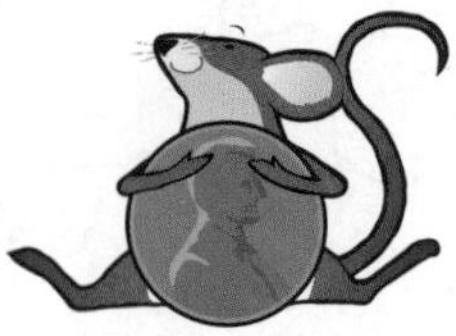

___ + ___ + ___ + ___ = ___¢

Two Different Ways

Quarter = 25 cents = 25¢	Dime = 10 cents = 10¢	Nickel = 5 cents = 5¢	Penny = 1 cent = 1¢

Show two different coin combinations to make the value shown for each toy. The first one has been done for you.

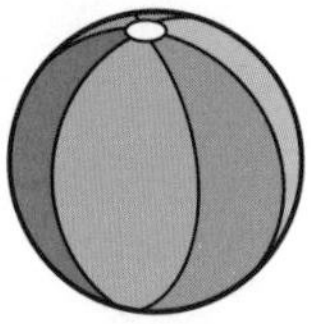

65¢ Q Q D N

Q D D D N N

79¢

28¢

99¢

53¢

Comparing Money

Quarter = 25 cents = 25¢	Dime = 10 cents = 10¢	Nickel = 5 cents = 5¢	Penny = 1 cent = 1¢

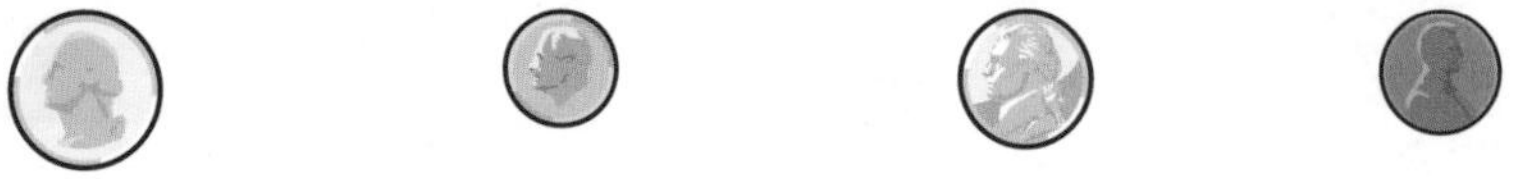

Add up the coins on the left and right of each row. Then fill in the **greater than** or **less than** symbol in the circle. The first one has been done for you.

25¢ 10¢ 10¢ 5¢ 1¢

.25 + .35 + .45 + .50 + .51

= 51 ¢

(>)

25¢ 10¢ 5¢ 5¢ 5¢

.25 + .35 + .40 + .45 + .50

= 50 ¢

10¢ 10¢ 10¢ 5¢ 1¢

___ + ___ + ___ + ___ + ___

= ___¢

( )

25¢ 5¢ 5¢ 5¢ 1¢

___ + ___ + ___ + ___ + ___

= ___¢

25¢ 25¢ 5¢ 1¢ 1¢

___ + ___ + ___ + ___ + ___

= ___¢

( )

25¢ 10¢ 5¢ 5¢ 1¢

___ + ___ + ___ + ___ + ___

= ___¢

Comparing Money

Quarter =	Dime =	Nickel =	Penny =
25 cents = 25¢	10 cents = 10¢	5 cents = 5¢	1 cent = 1¢

Add up the coins on the left and right of each row. Then fill in the **greater than** or **less than** symbol in the circle. The first one has been done for you.

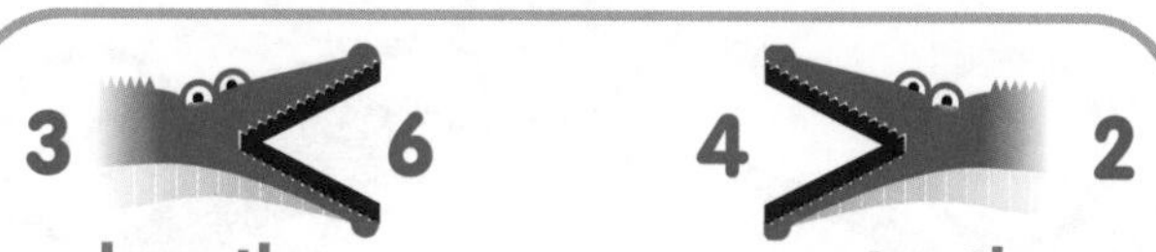

25¢ 5¢ 5¢ 5¢ 1¢ | 10¢ 10¢ 5¢ 5¢ 5¢

.25 + .30 + .35 + .40 + .41 = 41 ¢ (>) .10 + .20 + .25 + .30 + .35 = 35 ¢

10¢ 10¢ 5¢ 5¢ 1¢ | 25¢ 10¢ 5¢ 5¢ 1¢

___ + ___ + ___ + ___ + ___ = ___¢ ( ) ___ + ___ + ___ + ___ + ___ = ___¢

25¢ 10¢ 5¢ 5¢ 1¢ | 25¢ 10¢ 10¢ 10¢ 5¢

___ + ___ + ___ + ___ + ___ = ___¢ ( ) ___ + ___ + ___ + ___ + ___ = ___¢

Telling Time

A clock shows 12 hours, which is half a day.
There are 24 hours in a day. So the clock goes around two times in one full day.

Fill in the missing hours.

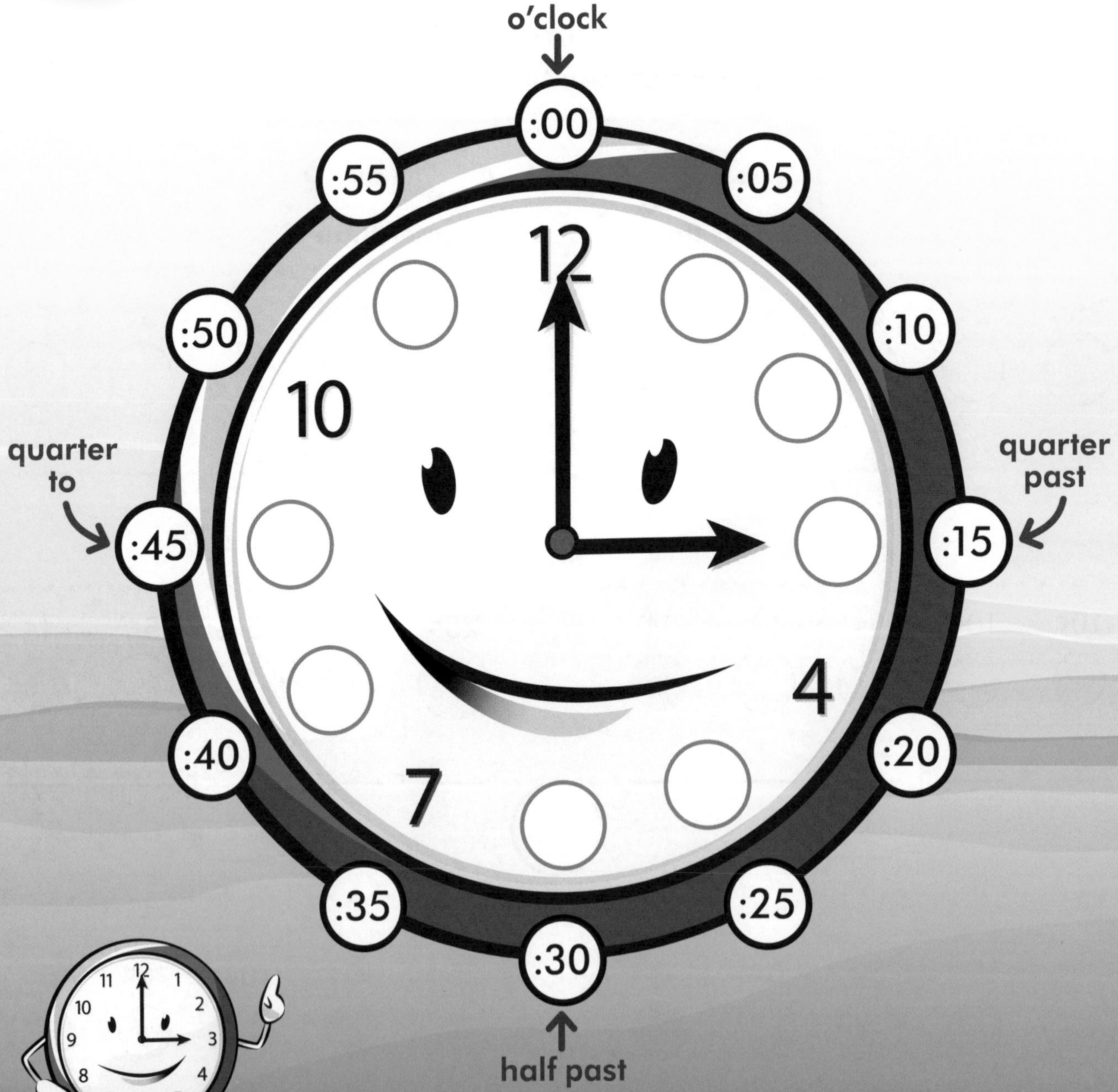

Telling Time

There are 24 hours in each day.
There are 60 minutes in each hour.

A.M. is time before noon.
P.M. is time after noon.

There are twelve numbers on a clock, each representing one hour. To read the hours on a clock, you begin at 12, then go clockwise to 1, 2, 3, and so on.

A clock face has two hands.
The smaller hand points to the hour.
The longer hand points to the minute.

The time on this clock is two o'clock, or 2:00.

Write out the times.

four o'clock ____ : ____ five o'clock ____ : ____

twelve o'clock ____ : ____ one o'clock ____ : ____

Telling Time by the Half Hour

Every thirty-minute period is equal to one half of an hour.

4:30
four thirty
half past four

2:00
two o'clock

Write the time.

____ : ____

____ : ____

____ : ____

____ : ____

____ : ____

____ : ____

____ : ____

____ : ____

____ : ____

What does the clock say? Write the time in word form.

____

Telling Time by the Quarter Hour

Every fifteen-minute period is equal to one fourth of an hour or one quarter hour. Two quarters of an hour is the same as one half of an hour.

2:45
two forty-five
quarter to three

4:15
four fifteen
quarter past four

Write the time.

____ : ____

____ : ____

____ : ____

____ : ____

____ : ____

____ : ____

____ : ____

____ : ____

____ : ____

What does the clock say? Write the time in word form.

____

Telling Time by the Quarter Hour

Draw the clock hands to show the correct time.

1:15

11:30

4:00

2:45

11:15

1:30

7:00

8:45

10:15

Telling Time

Match the clocks that tell the same time.

Can You Find the Pattern?

Draw the next clock in each pattern.

Your Schedule

Read the question. Write your answer by drawing the hands on the clock.

What time do you wake up?

What time do you eat lunch?

What time do you get out of school?

What time do you go to bed?

MEASUREMENTS

Measuring Inches

Look at each item next to the ruler.
Write down how many inches each item is to the 1/2 inch.

inches→

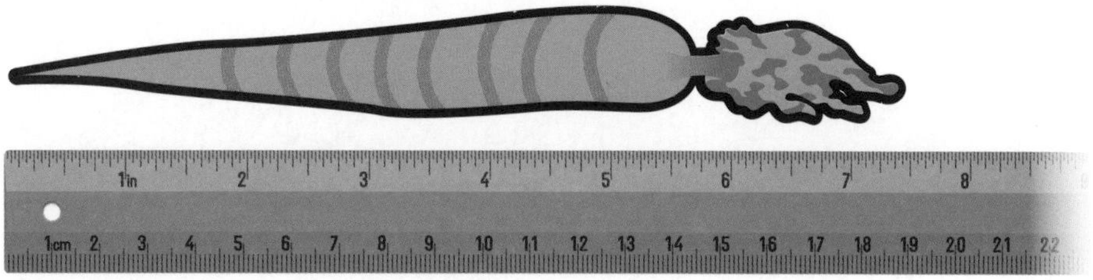

About _______ inches

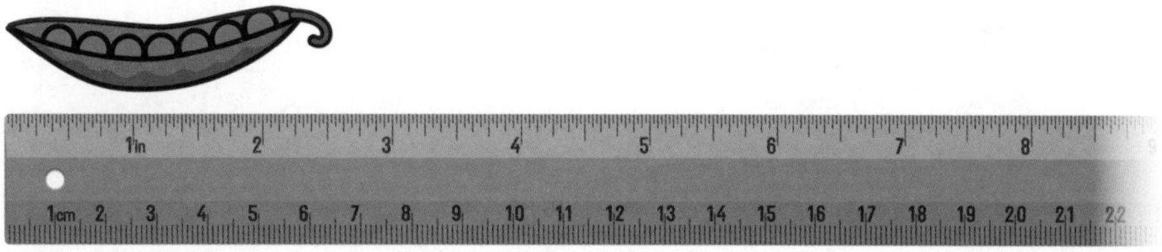

About _______ inches

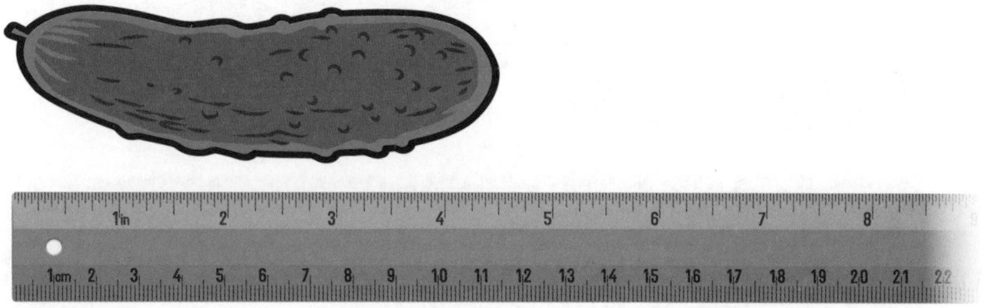

About _______ inches

Measuring Centimeters

Look at each item next to the ruler.
Write down how many centimeters each item is.

centimeters →
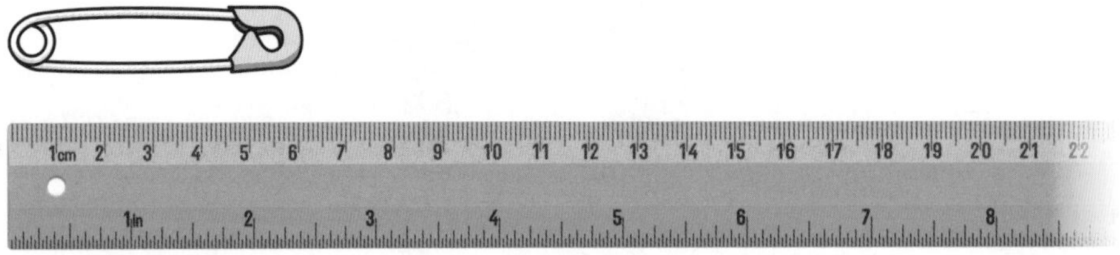

About ________ centimeters

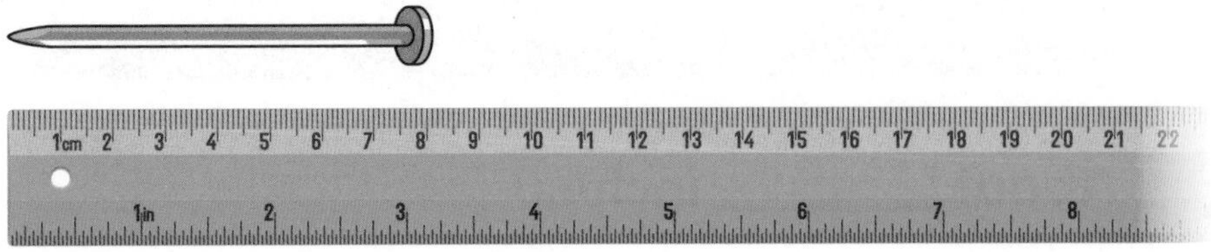

About ________ centimeters

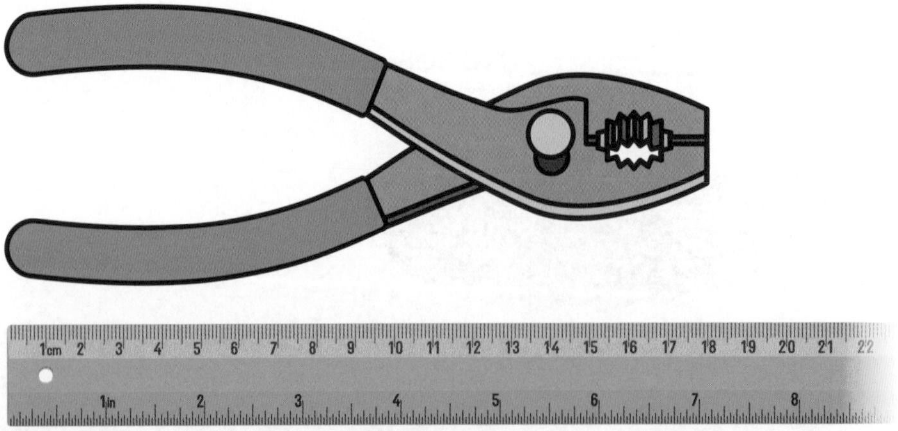

About ________ centimeters

Feet and Yards

There are 12 inches in a foot.

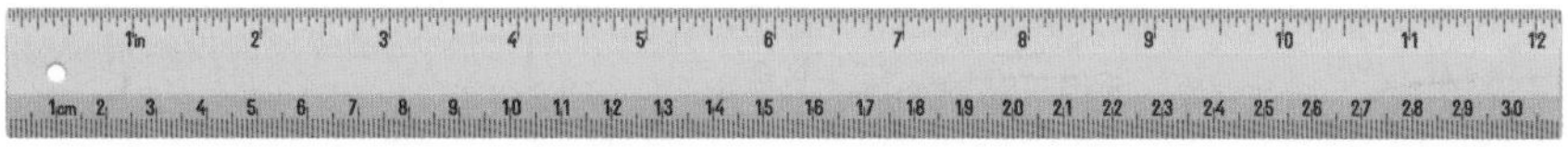

← inches

There are 3 feet in a yard.

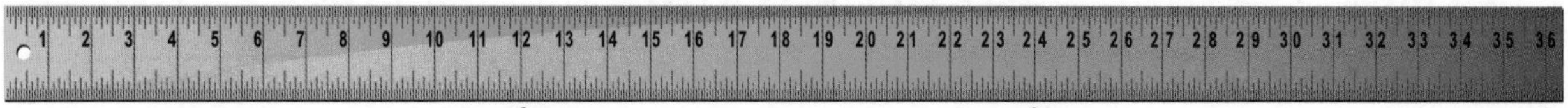

↑ 1 foot ↑ 2 feet ↑ 3 feet

Read the number of inches below. Write how much that would be in feet and yards. The first one is done for you.

30 inches = __2 1/2__ feet

36 inches = ________ feet = ________ yard(s)

24 inches = ________ feet

48 inches = ________ feet

18 inches = ________ feet

72 inches = ________ feet = ________ yard(s)

Cups, Pints, and Quarts

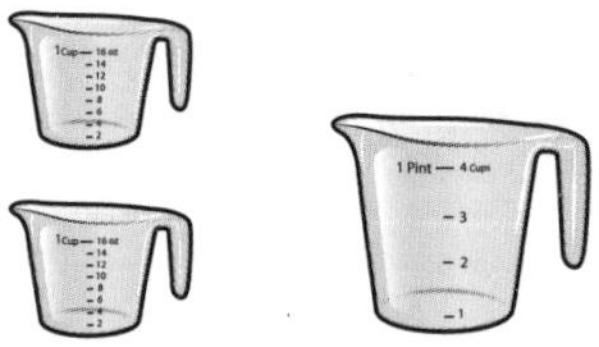

2 cups = 1 pint

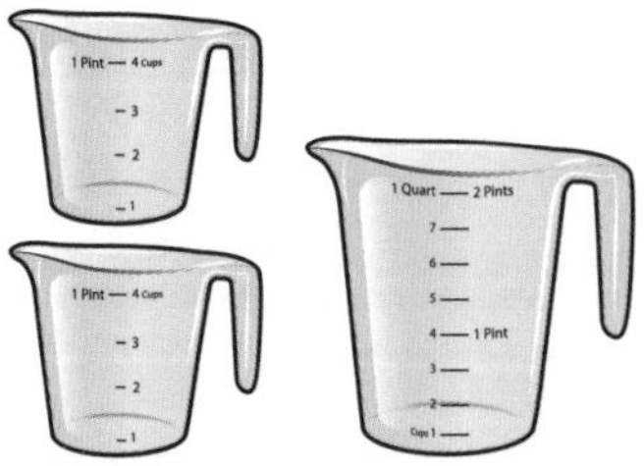

2 pints = 1 quart

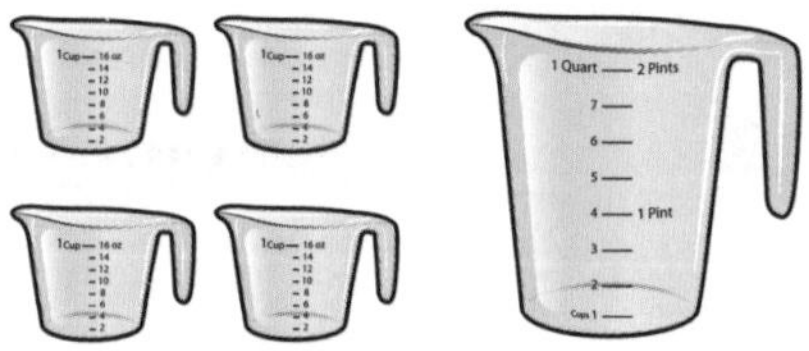

4 cups = 1 quart

Look at each measuring cup on the left. Circle how many of the measuring cups on the right are needed to fill it.

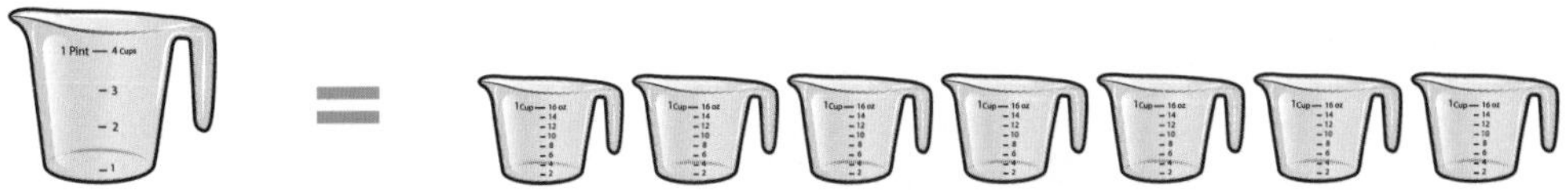

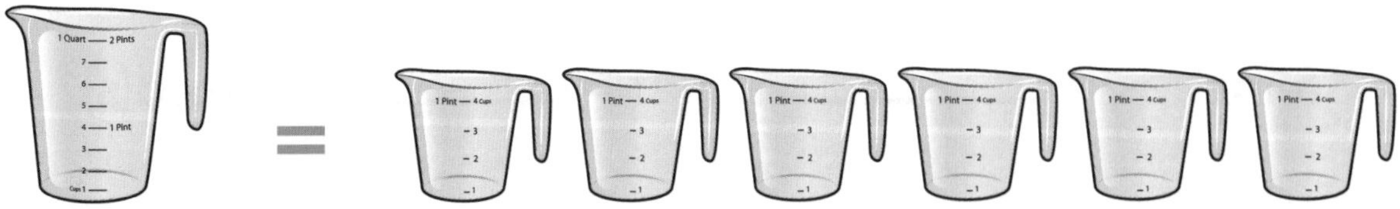

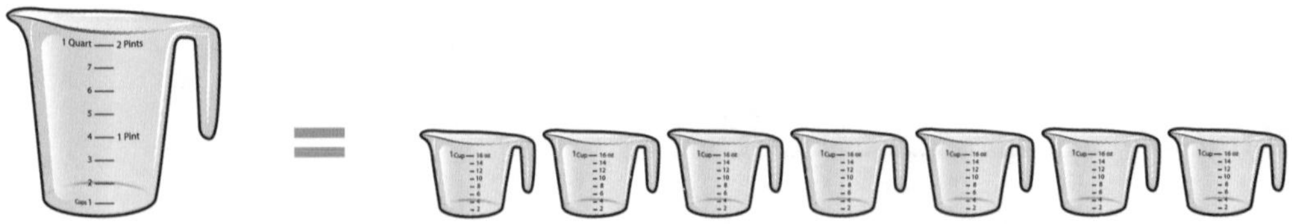

Cups, Pints, and Quarts

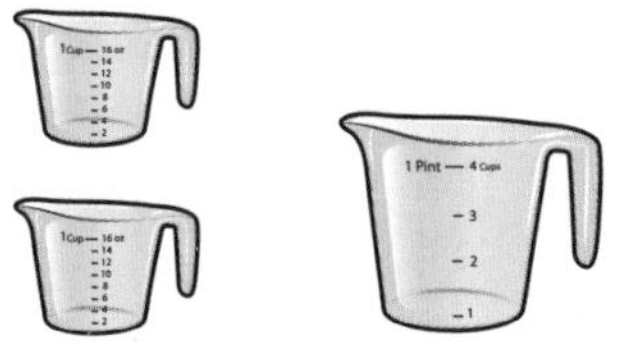

2 cups = 1 pint

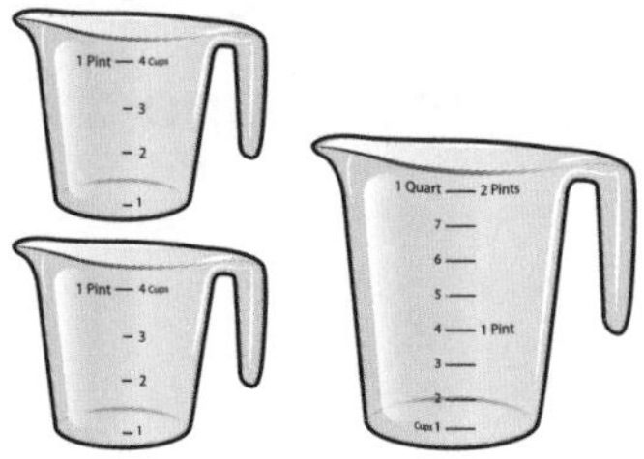

2 pints = 1 quart

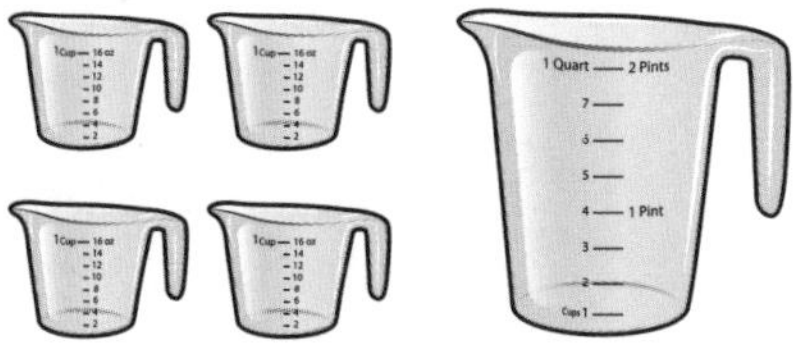

4 cups = 1 quart

You need to make fruit punch for a party. The recipe is below. The problem is you only have a one-cup measuring cup. How many cups of each item will you need to make the punch?

Fruit Punch

2 quarts water ______ cups water

1 quart grape juice ______ cups grape juice

1 pint orange juice ______ cups orange juice

Geometric 2-D Shapes

Draw a line from the shape to its name. Trace the shape word. Then try drawing the shape on your own.

You draw the shape.

circle

square

rectangle

oval

triangle

Geometric 3-D Shapes

Draw a line from the 3-D shape to its name.

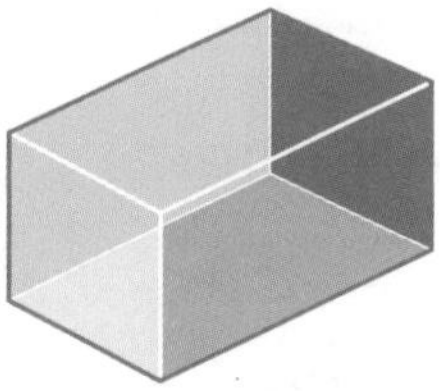

cone

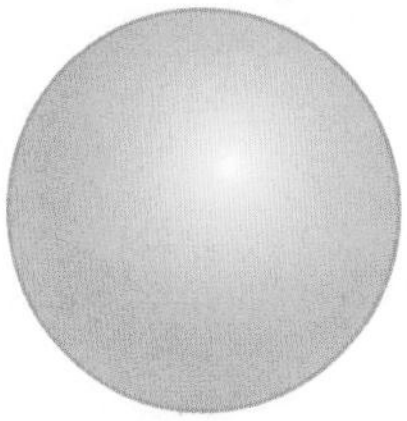

cube

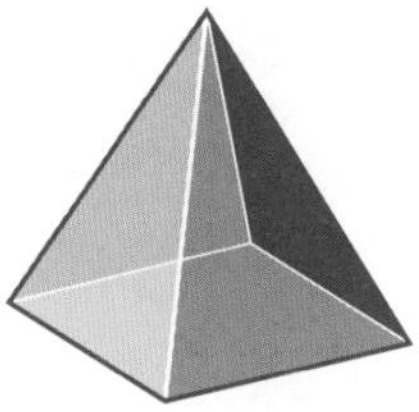

pyramid

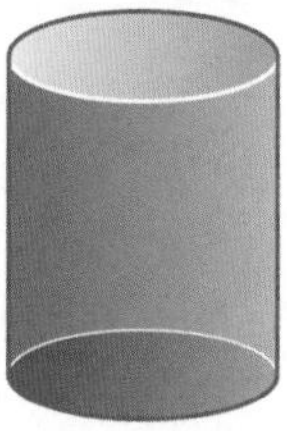

sphere

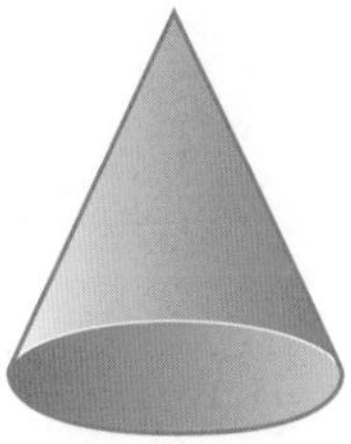

cylinder

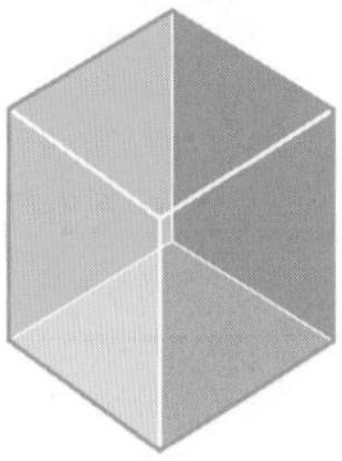

rectangular prism

Geometric 3-D Shapes

The **face** of an object is any surface that is flat.
A **cube** has **6 faces**.
An **edge** is the line that connects **2 faces** together.
A **cube** has **12 edges**.
The **vertex** is the point, or corner, on a shape.
This is where the faces and edges meet.
A **cube** has **8 vertices**.

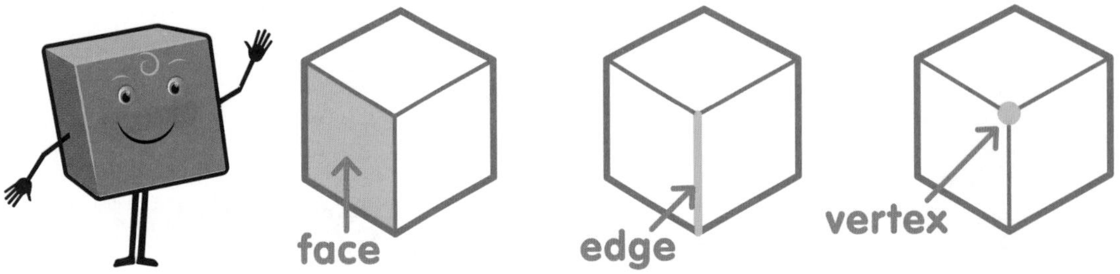

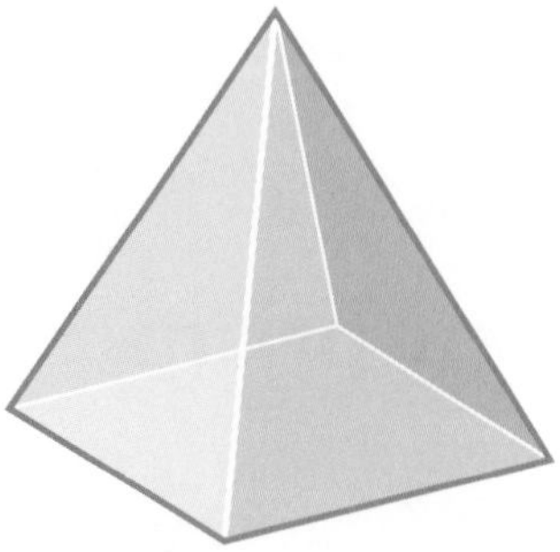

A pyramid has ________ faces.

A pyramid has ________ edges.

A pyramid has ________ vertices.

Geometric Shapes

Look at this shape.

Describe the shape.

How many faces do you see? ________

How many edges do you see? ________

How many vertices do you see? ________

What is its name? ____________________

Name the Shape

Shapes with different numbers of sides have different names.

A triangle has 3 sides.

A pentagon has 5 sides.

An octagon has 8 sides.

A quadrilateral has 4 sides.

A hexagon has 6 sides.

Name the shapes below.

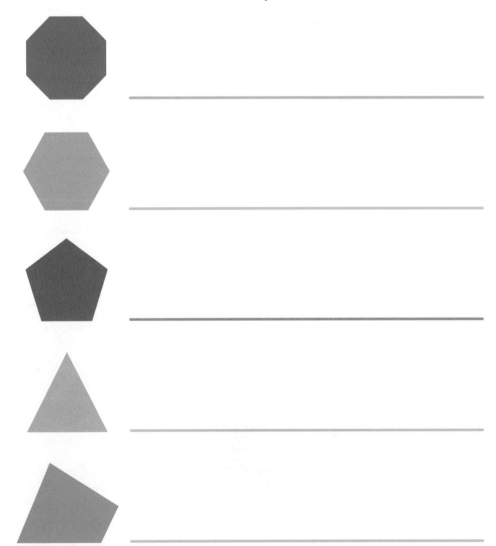

____

____

____

____

____

What Geometric Shape Am I?

Read the clue below and circle the correct answer.

I have three sides.

square triangle

I am round with no sides.

circle rectangle

I have four sides and all my sides are of equal length.

rectangle square

My opposite sides are equal.

circle rectangle

I am the shape of a stop sign.

square octagon

Symmetry

Symmetry means that something is the same on both sides.

If you were to draw a line dividing something into two parts, both parts would be identical to each other.

Example: 

Both sides of this heart are exactly the same. They are **symmetrical**.

Draw a line through each of these **symmetrical** shapes.

Now, can you draw a second line of **symmetry** through each shape?

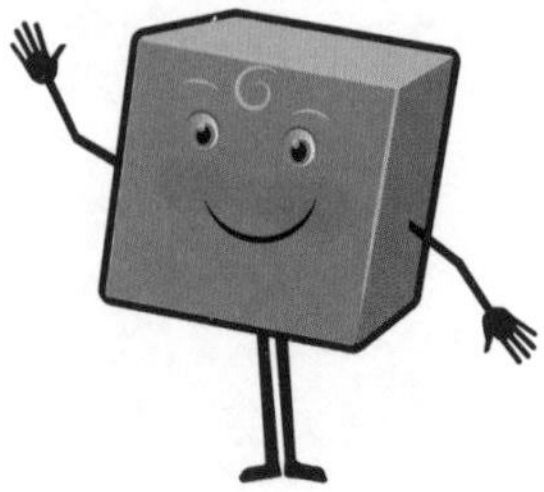

Symmetry

Tell whether or not the line on each picture is a line of **symmetry**. Circle yes or no.

yes no

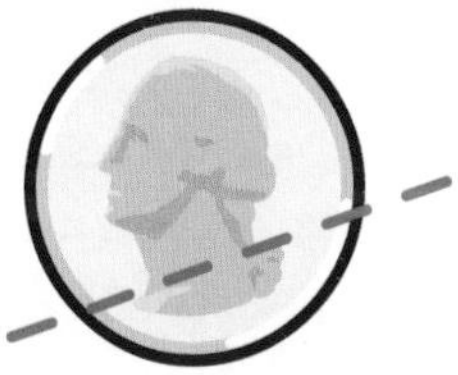

yes no

yes no

yes no

yes no

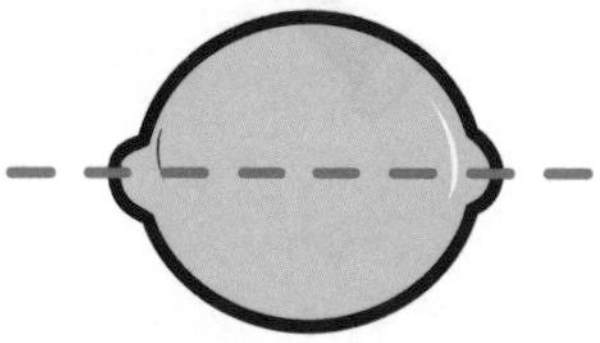

yes no

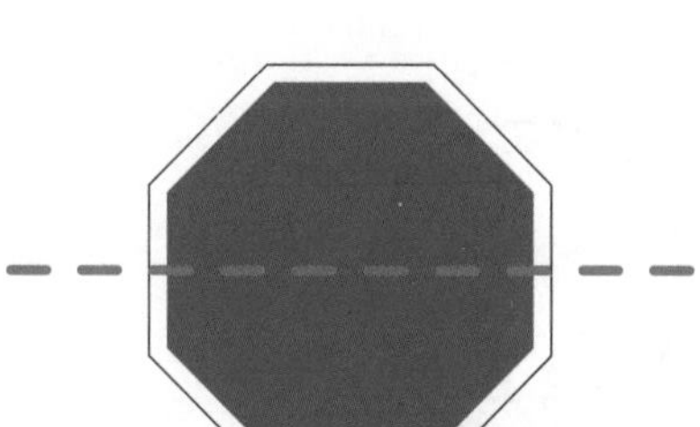

yes no

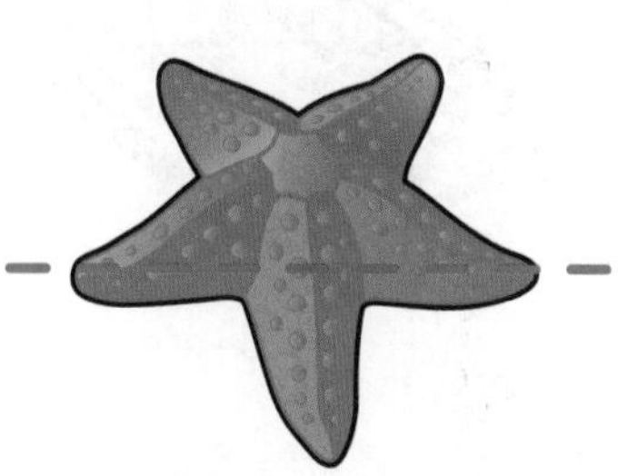

yes no

Am I Symmetrical?

If you fold a shape and the two halves match up exactly, the shape has **symmetry**. Look at the shapes and figures below and circle the ones that have symmetry.

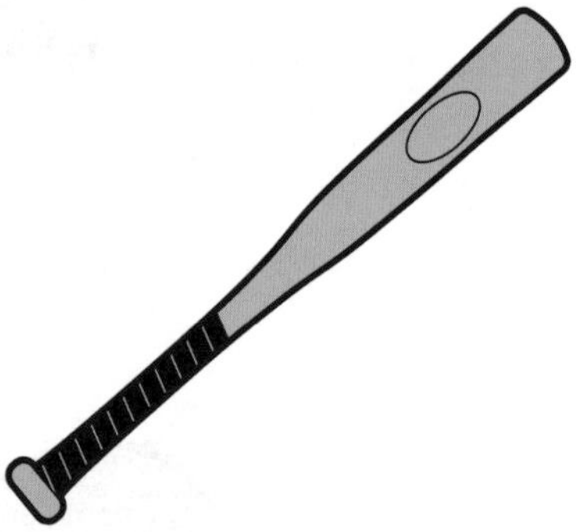

Symmetry

Draw the second half of each **symmetrical** shape.

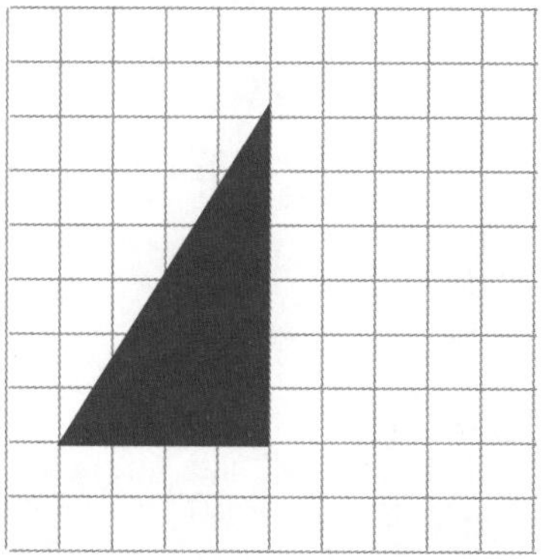

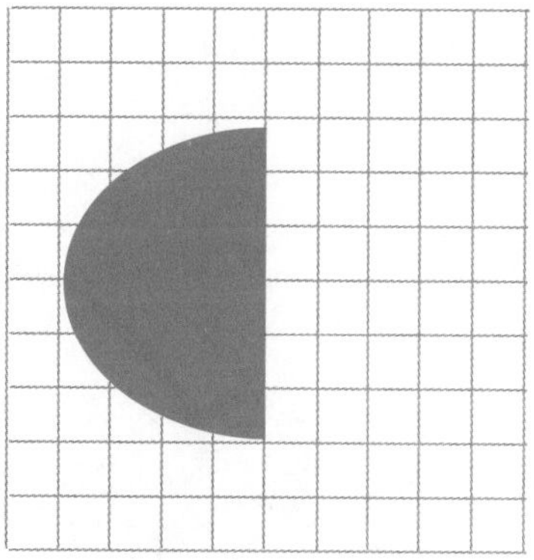

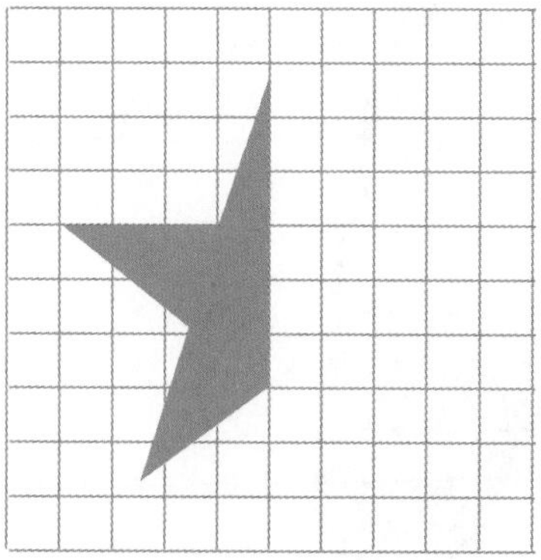

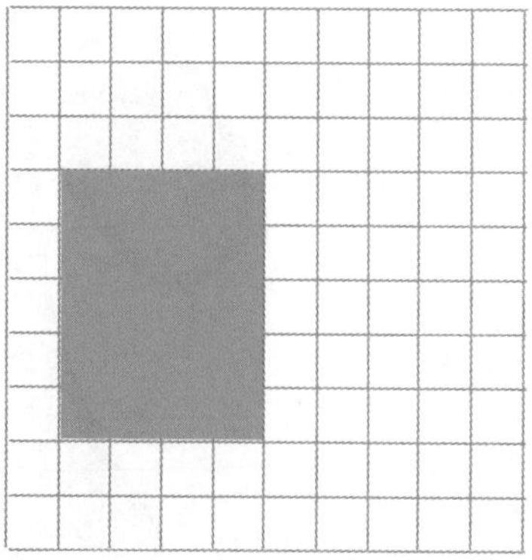

SCIENCE AND NATURE

Animal Classification

Circle the correct **classification** for each animal.

mammal reptile

bird

bird fish

mammal

bird fish

mammal

reptile bird

fish

bird mammal

reptile

mammal fish

reptile

mammal reptile

bird

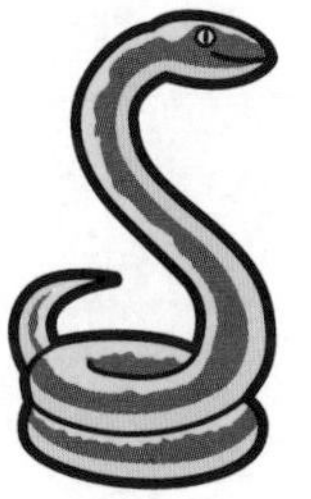

reptile mammal

fish

bird mammal

reptile

Animal Classification: Warm-Blooded Animals

Mammals and birds are **warm-blooded**, which means that they can make their own body heat even when it is cold outside. It does not matter whether it is hot or cold outside, warm-blooded animals have body temperatures that usually stay the same.

The animals in the word bank below are all **warm-blooded**. Find and circle them in the word search. They can be horizontal, vertical, or diagonal.

H	L	M	A	S	A	O	M	C
U	I	G	I	R	A	F	F	E
M	O	N	K	E	Y	Z	R	H
A	N	H	J	G	H	P	D	F
N	E	L	E	P	H	A	N	T
S	O	H	S	H	E	E	P	T

LION SHEEP ELEPHANT
HUMANS MONKEY

Animal Classification: Cold-Blooded Animals

Cold-blooded animals become hotter and colder depending on the weather outside. Cold-blooded animals include reptiles, amphibians, and fish.

Circle all the **cold-blooded** animals below.

Life Cycles: Butterfly

The life cycle of a butterfly starts out with the **egg** that a butterfly lays on a leaf.

Next, the egg hatches and out comes a **caterpillar**, or larva.

The third stage is when the caterpillar creates a **chrysalis** around its body.

After some time, a **butterfly** comes out of the chrysalis.

Color the **butterfly** below.

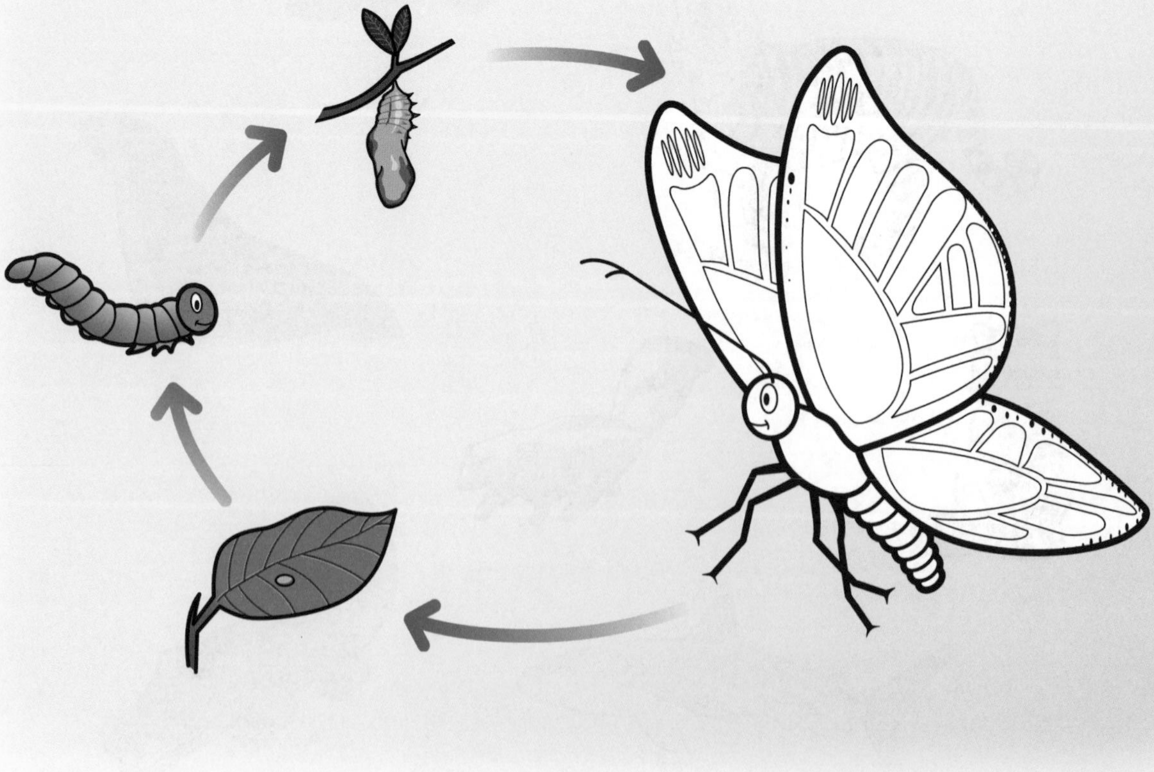

Life Cycles: Butterfly Facts

Answer the questions below.

A butterfly has ____________ stages in its life cycle.

The first stage is when a female butterfly lays an

____________________ on a leaf.

When the egg hatches, out comes a

____________________.

The caterpillar eventually creates a

____________________ around its body.

What comes out of the chrysalis?

____

Life Cycles: Frog

The Life Cycle of a Frog

Stage 1: **Eggs** take about 6 to 21 days to hatch. Frogs can lay up to 4,000 eggs at one time!

Stage 2: **Tadpoles** hatch from eggs and live in the pond.

Stage 3: A tadpole begins to grow legs.

Stage 4: A tadpole turns into a **froglet**, sprouting arms and legs but still has its tail!

Stage 5: By about 16 weeks, the tadpole has grown into a **frog**.

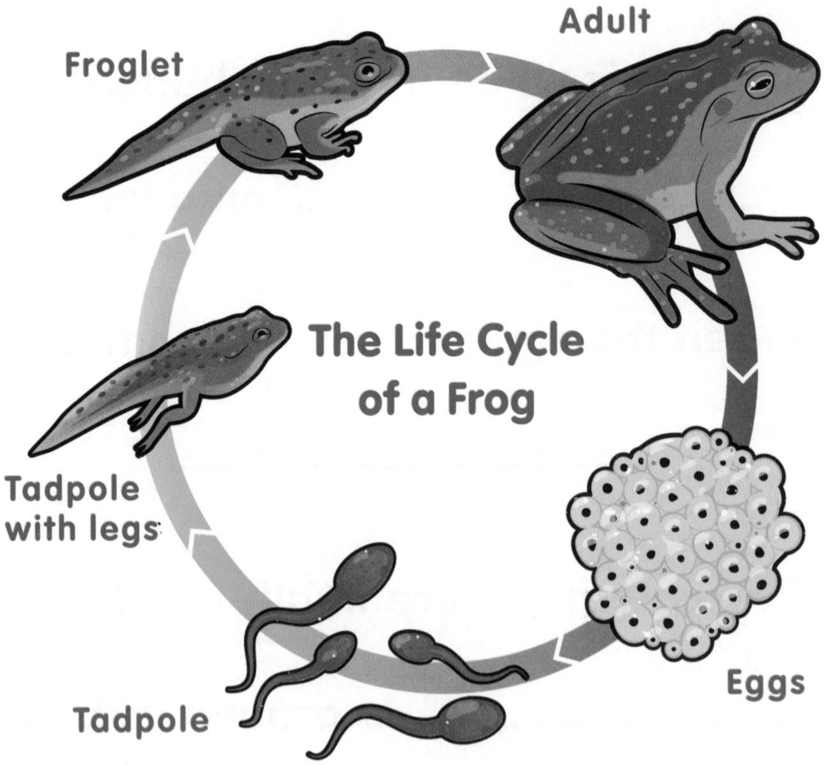

Based on what you just read, put the following stages in order.

_____ adult frog _____ tadpole _____ tadpole with legs

_____ egg _____ froglet

Life Cycles: Flowering Plant

1

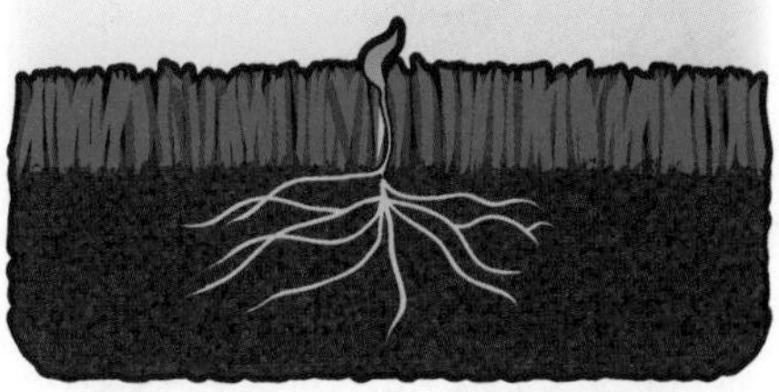

Flowering plants begin their lives as **seeds**. When a seed begins to grow, this is called **germination**.

2

When the first sign of life appears above the soil, this is called a **sprout**, or **seedling**.

3

The seedling will continue to grow into a full mature plant with leaves, roots, and stems.

4

The mature plant will grow flowers. Through **pollination**, the flowers will produce seeds. When the seeds end up on the ground, the cycle will begin again.

Life Cycles: Tomato Plant

Look at each picture. Then write a one-word description for each step on the lines provided.

Life Cycles: People

Even **people** have a **life cycle**.
Can you draw your life cycle?

1

When you were a baby

2

Who you are now

3

When you grow up

Life Cycles: Stages

What will these babies look like when they grow up?
Draw a line to match the baby animal to its adult version.

Healthy Living

The five food groups are:

Grains: Examples are cereal, rice, and whole-grain bread. They provide energy and fiber in your diet.

Fruits: Examples are bananas, apples, and pears. They provide your body with vitamins, minerals, and fiber you need to stay healthy.

Vegetables: Examples are broccoli, carrots, and Brussels sprouts. They provide vitamins, minerals, and fiber to help your body stay healthy.

Dairy: Examples are milk, cheese, and yogurt. They are often a great source of calcium, which is important for strong bones.

Protein: Examples are lean meats, fish, poultry, eggs, beans, and tofu. Protein is an important building block for bones and muscles.

The plate below shows how much of each **food group** you should eat in a meal.

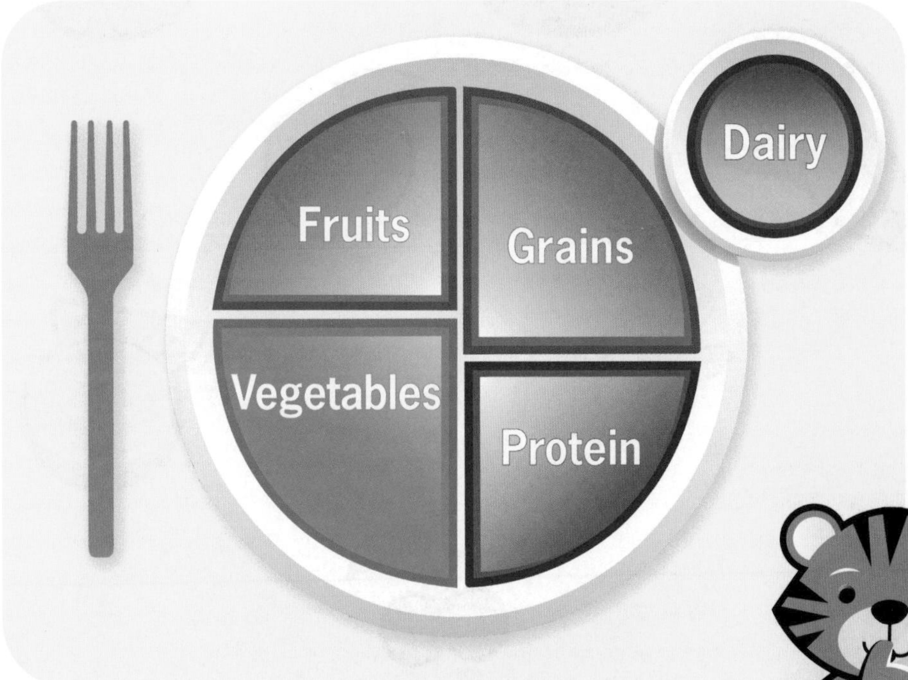

Are half of your meals made up of fruits and vegetables?

Healthy Living: Fruit or Vegetable

The difference between a **fruit** and a **vegetable** is whether or not it has seeds. Fruits have seeds and vegetables do not. For example, a watermelon has seeds, so it is a fruit. So while you may think cucumbers or tomatoes are vegetables, they have seeds, so they are actually fruits.

Circle all the **fruits** and put a box around all the **vegetables**.

Healthy Living: Fruit or Vegetable

Match the foods on the left with
their correct **food group** on the right.

Dairy Group

Protein Group

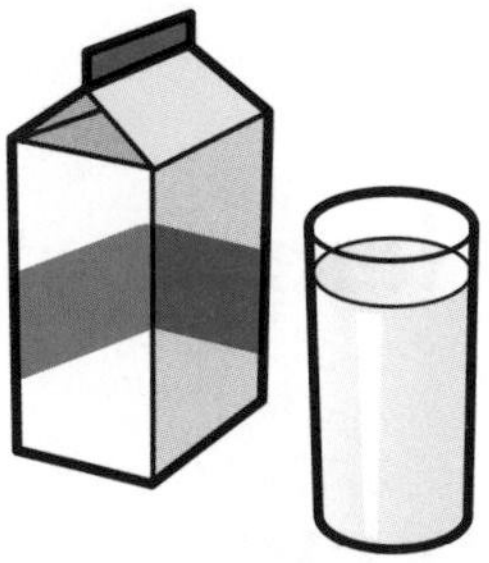

Fruit Group

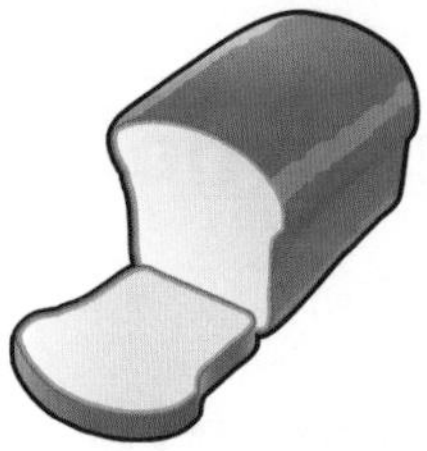

Vegetable Group

Grain Group

Healthy Living: What Am I?

Everything on this page is a member of the **fruit food group**. Fruits come in all different sizes, shapes, and colors. Eating fruit keeps you healthy and feeling great!

Draw a line from the **fruit** to its name.

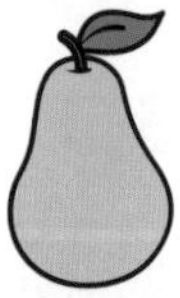

grapes

strawberry

apple

lemon

banana

watermelon

orange

pear

cherries

Healthy Living: Food Groups

Some of the foods below do not belong in a
healthy diet and others are in the wrong group.
Put an **X** through the foods that don't belong in each row.

Dairy Group

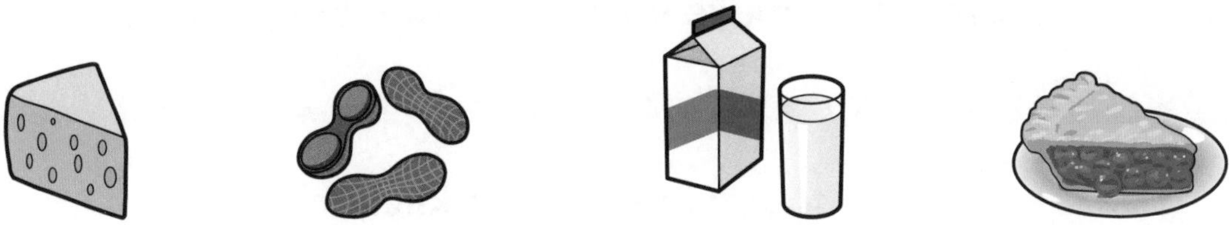

Fruit Group

Grain Group

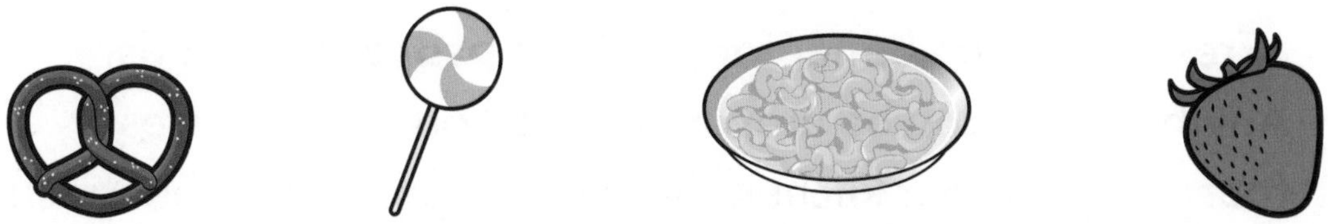

Protein Group

Healthy Eating: Food Processing

Most foods that are in a packet, tub, or box are **processed**, or made in a factory. These foods are not always good for you because the manufacturers add lots of salt, sugar, and fat to make them taste really good. They also add a lot of chemicals to make the foods last a long time.

List four things in your kitchen cabinets that are **processed**.

____

____

____

____

Fresh foods are better for you than **processed** foods. Anything that can be grown or raised on a farm is fresh. List four things in your kitchen that are not processed, but fresh.

____

____

____

____

Healthy Eating: Farm or Factory

Many things come from a **farm**, such as fruits, vegetables, and many dairy products. Other foods are produced in a **factory**. The more foods you eat that come right from the farm, the healthier you will be.

Label the pictures below as **farm** or **factory**, based on where they are grown or produced.

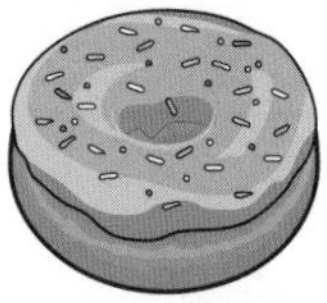

Healthy Living: Exercise Is Important, Too!

Exercise is the activity of exerting your muscles in various ways to stay fit.

Exercise is just as important as a healthy diet.

Exercise gives us more energy and strength.

Exercise also helps us to live longer and happier lives.

Everyone should get at least **60 minutes** of exercise every day!

List five ways that you can get **exercise** every day.

1. ______________________________

2. ______________________________

3. ______________________________

4. ______________________________

5. ______________________________

Seasonal Cycles: What Is Weather?

Weather is the state of the atmosphere, or the mass of air surrounding the Earth at any time. Weather can refer to many things, such as temperature, precipitation, air pressure, or cloud cover. Weather changes daily. Weather changes from season to season because of the Earth's rotation around the Sun.

Draw a line connecting the adjective on the left to its **opposite** on the right.

sunny	cool
cloudy	clear
hot	dry
wet	cold
warm	rainy

Seasonal Cycles

As the Earth spins on its axis, producing night and day, it also orbits around the Sun, taking 365 days to complete one orbit. This tilt of the Earth's axis is why we have **seasons**. When the Earth's axis is pointing toward the Sun, it is **summer** for that hemisphere, or side of Earth. When it points away from the Sun, it is **winter**.

Look at the diagram of the Earth rotating around the Sun. Write on each line whether that side is experiencing **winter** or **summer**.

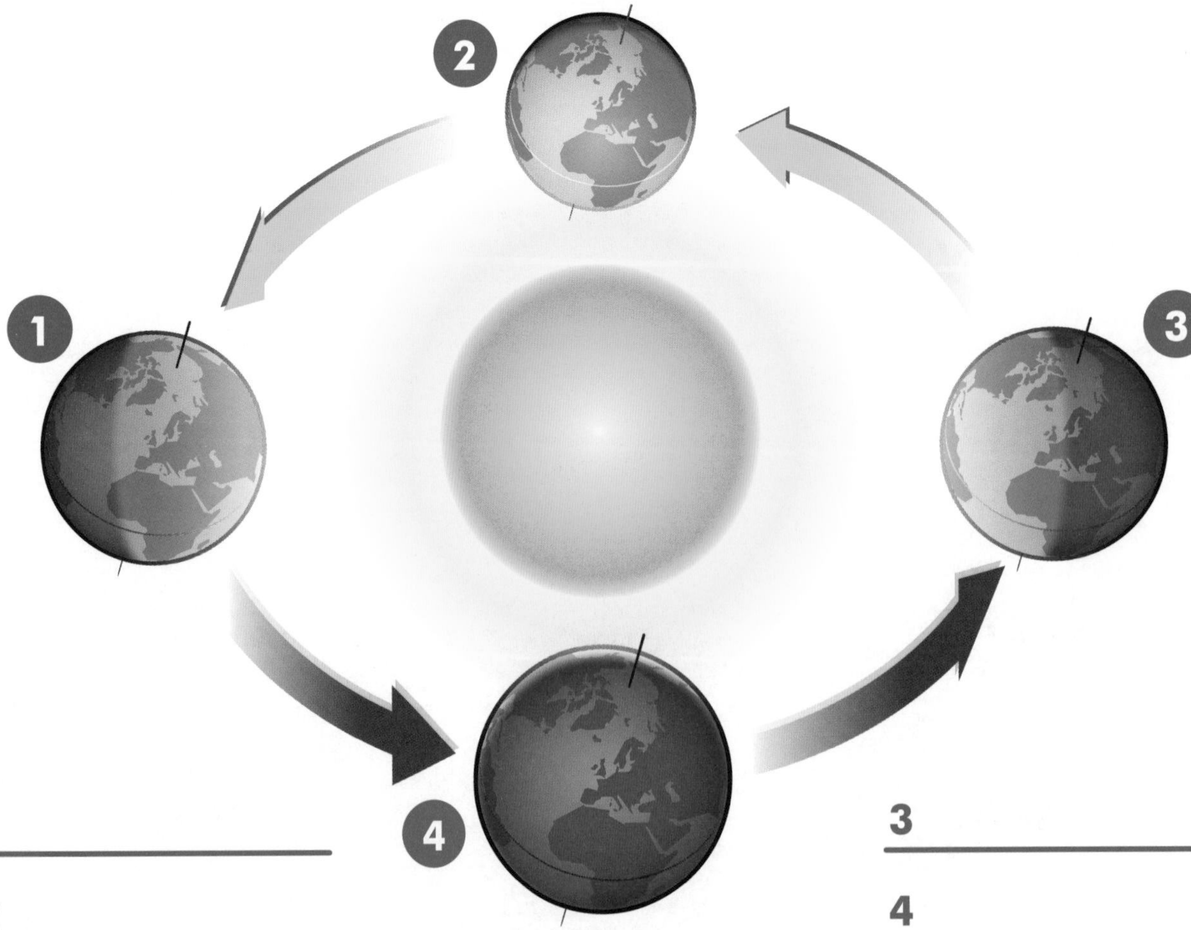

1 ____________

2 ____________

3 ____________

4 ____________

Seasonal Cycles

Read the sentences below and complete the last sentence in each group of sentences.

Some days are really sunny. It is the Sun that heats the Earth. When it is sunny, I like to

____

____

The weather changes every day. Some days are windy, which means the air is moving. When it is windy out, I like to

____

____

Some days are rainy. The rain falling from the clouds is called precipitation. On rainy days, I like to

____

____

Some days are snowy. Snow is made up of ice crystals. On snowy days I like to

____

____

Joke Time

To figure out the riddle below, fill in the correct letter for each number.

1=e 2=l 3=d 4=a 5=p 6=u

What do you call a snowman in the summer?

___ ___ ___ ___ ___ ___ ___
4 5 6 3 3 2 1

The Water Cycle: How Clouds Form

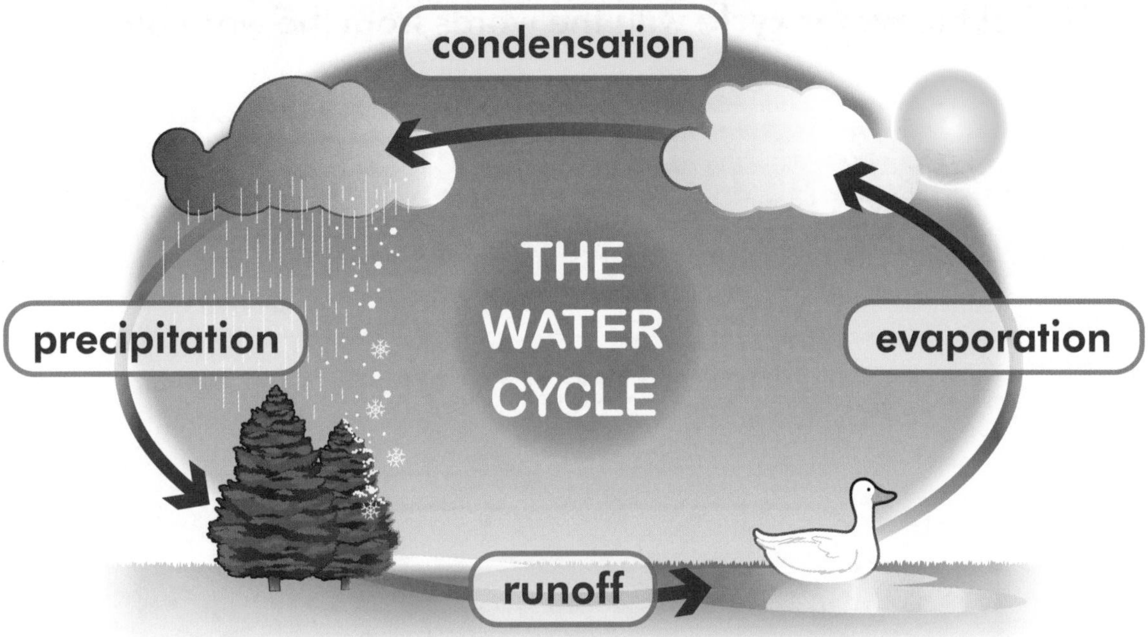

All **clouds** are made up of water. The path water takes from the ground to the sky and back again, by **evaporation**, **condensation**, **precipitation**, and **runoff** is called the **water cycle**.

Evaporation occurs when the Sun shines on the Earth, providing light and heat. This heat warms up the water on the ground, turning it from a liquid to a gas, or vapor. The vapor rises from the ground and returns to the Earth's atmosphere. This can happen over all bodies of water, including ponds, lakes, oceans, and even puddles.

Condensation is when this water vapor collects around dust particles and forms larger droplets. As more and more droplets come together, clouds form.

Precipitation happens when clouds become too heavy and must shed some of their weight. The water droplets fall to the ground as rain. If the weather is really cold, the water droplets could turn to snow, sleet, or hail.

Runoff is precipitation that does not evaporate or get absorbed into the soil. It collects on the ground.

The Water Cycle

Label the **water cycle** with the words from the word bank.

condensation evaporation runoff precipitation

The Water Cycle

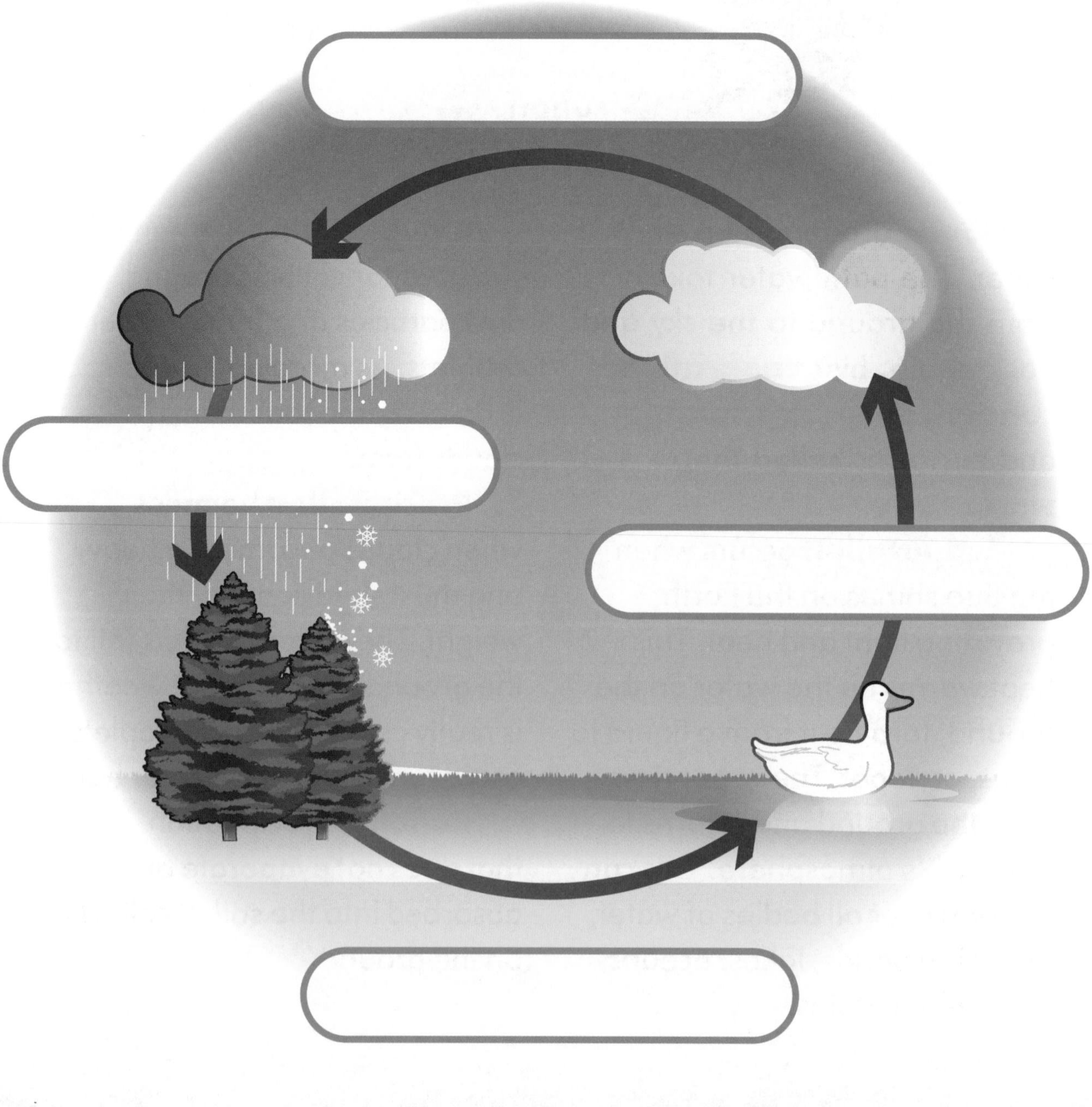

The Water Cycle

SCIENCE AND NATURE

Fill in the blanks below using words from the word bank.

Condensation	water vapor
cloud	Precipitation

1. A ________________ is a large collection of very tiny droplets of water.

2. Water that has evaporated from the surface of the earth is called ________________.

3. ________________ occurs when water droplets form in the atmosphere around dust particles.

4. ________________ happens when clouds become too heavy.

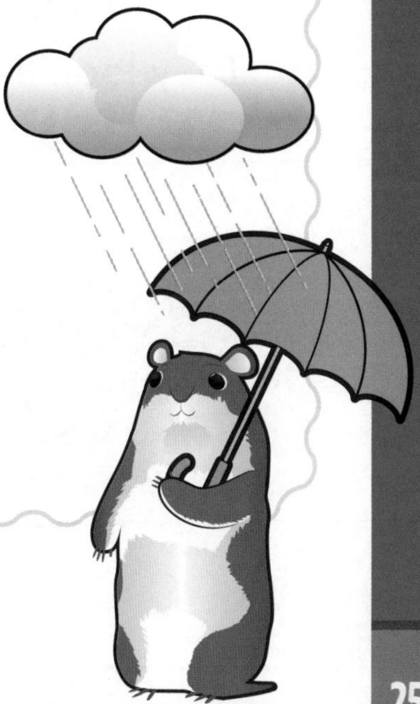

The Water Cycle

Meet the Clouds
by Christine Locke

Cirrus Clouds
These icy clouds are way up high.
They're just like feathers in the sky
or silky strands of cotton curls.
The sun shines through these painted whirls.

Cumulus Clouds
Some clouds look like an ocean whale,
a flock of sheep, a dragon's tail.
Although these clouds are lots of fun,
sometimes tornadoes hide in one!

Stratus Clouds
The clouds that hang low to the ground
often foretell that snow is bound
to fall, or rain, or icy sleet.
They look like soft gray woolly sheets.

Label the **clouds** below.

______________ ______________ ______________

Temperature

Temperature is a degree of coldness or hotness that can be measured using a **thermometer**. We measure temperature using the **Fahrenheit** or the **Celsius** scale.

This thermometer reads 80 degrees Fahrenheit or 80°F.

FREEZING MARK

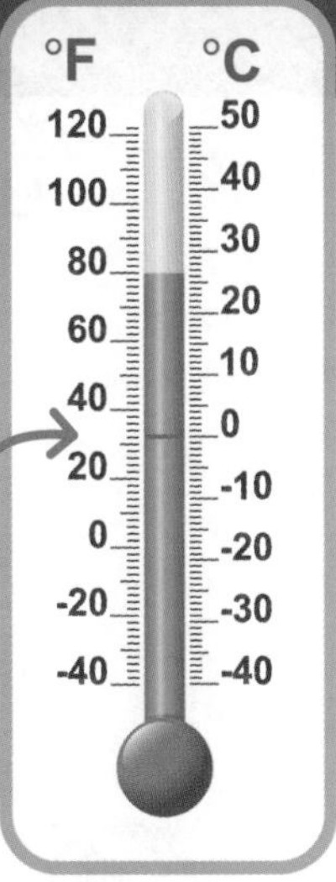

Fill in the **Fahrenheit temperatures** below.

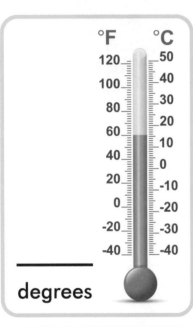

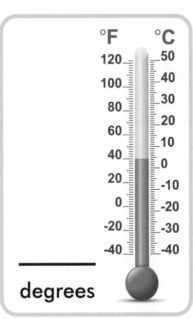

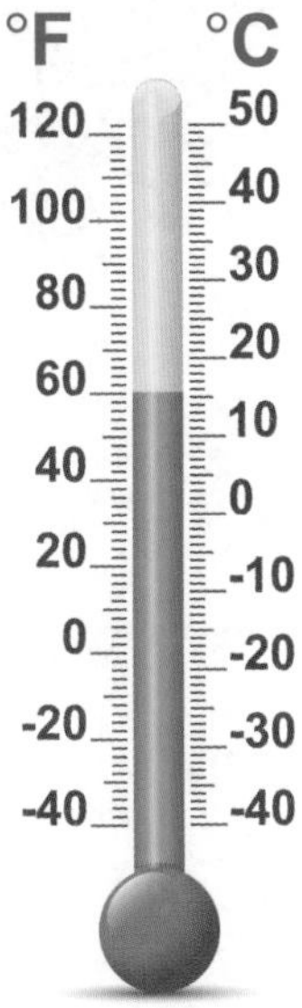

______ degrees

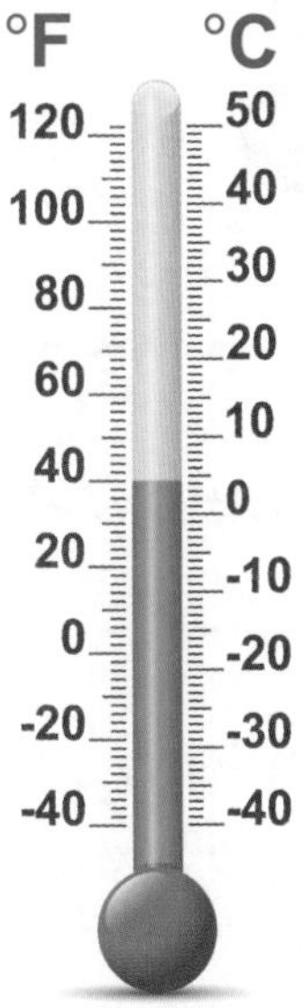

______ degrees

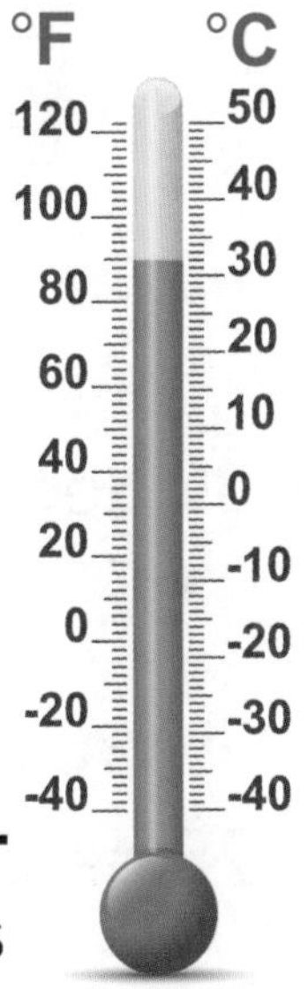

______ degrees

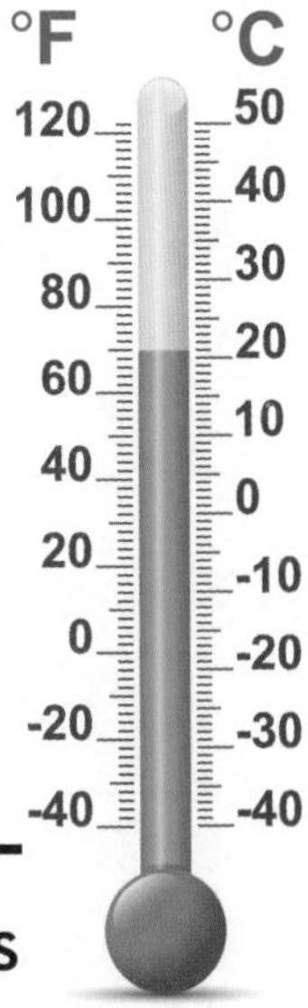

______ degrees

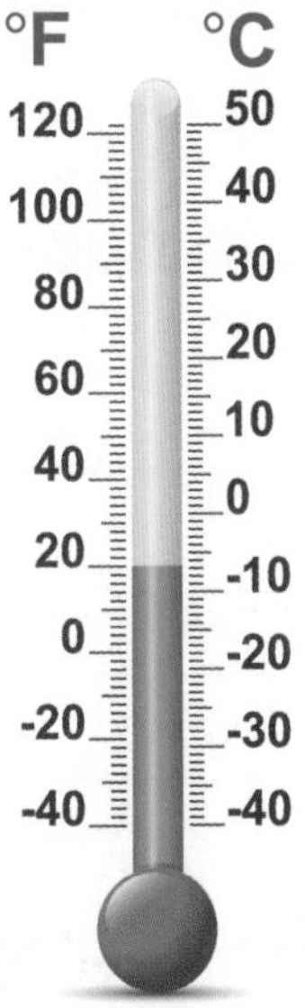

______ degrees

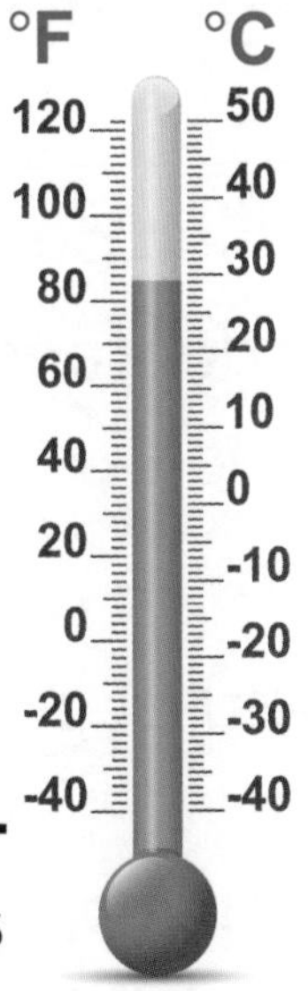

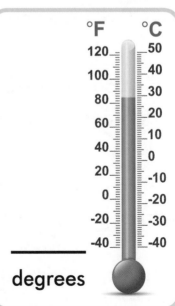

______ degrees

Temperature

Use the thermometers to answer the questions below.
Remember, water freezes at 32°F.

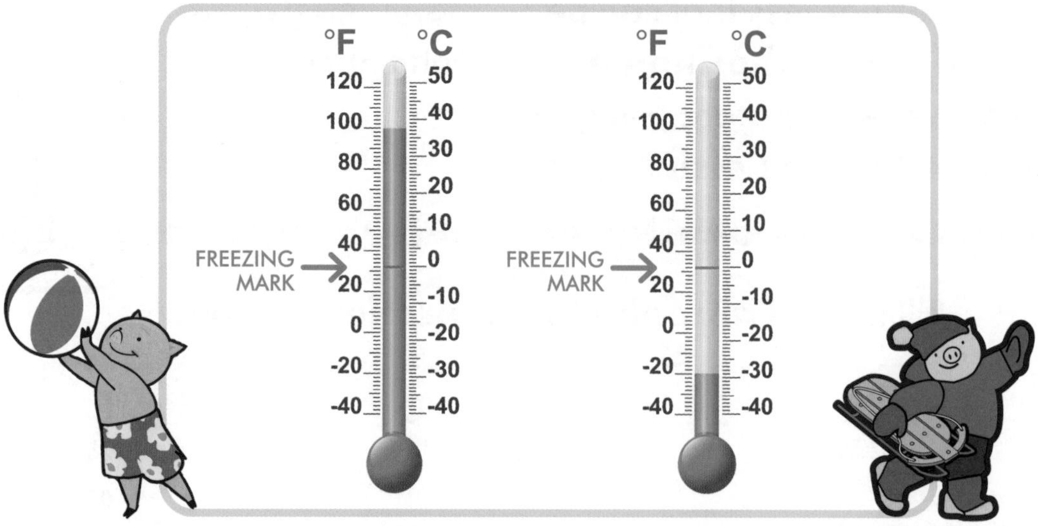

Circle the correct answer.

Is 30 degrees above or below 40 degrees?	above below
Will it rain or snow if the temperature is 28 degrees Fahrenheit?	rain snow
Is –20 degrees above or below 0 degrees?	above below
Will a pond freeze if the temperature is 0 degrees Fahrenheit?	yes no
Which temperature is hotter: –20 degrees or 20 degrees?	–20 20
Will a Popsicle melt in 90-degree weather?	yes no

Types of Matter

Matter can be **solid**, like wood. Solids hold their shape and are visible.

Matter can be a **gas**, like air. Gas changes its shape easily and is usually invisible.

Matter can be a **liquid**, like water. Liquids take the shape of the container they are in and are visible.

Circle the **matter** each object is made of:

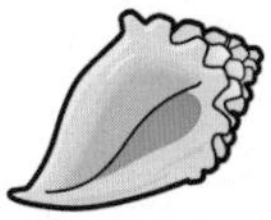

shell solid liquid gas

ocean solid liquid gas

steam solid liquid gas

chair solid liquid gas

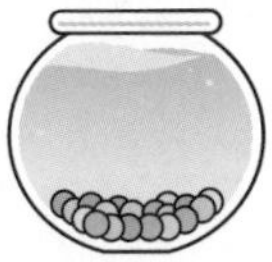

water in a fishbowl solid liquid gas

air in a hot-air balloon solid liquid gas

SCIENCE AND NATURE

Types of Matter: What Am I?

Answer each question.
Write the word from the word bank on the line.

solid   gas   matter   liquid

I have a shape and am visible to the eye. I can be hard or soft and big or small.

What am I? ________________________

I am wet and can take the shape of the container I am in. I can be poured.

What am I? ________________________

You cannot see me. My shape changes easily.

What am I? ________________________

I am what things are made up of.
I can take three different forms: solid, liquid, or gas.

What am I? ________________________

Rainbows: How They Form

After it has rained outside, you might see a **rainbow** in the sky. For this to happen, you need sunshine and rain. Sunshine appears as white light, but it is really made up of many colors: red, orange, yellow, green, blue, indigo, and violet. When the sunlight passes through the raindrops, the white light splits apart into all the colors, forming a rainbow!

Color in the **rainbow** below.

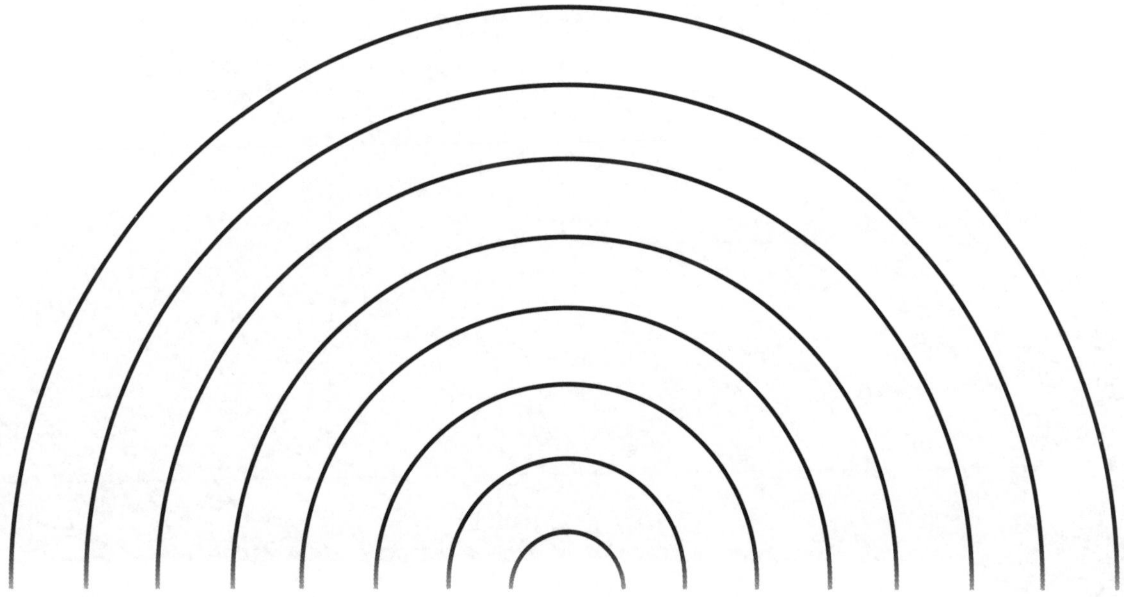

Rainbows

Rainbows are made up of seven colors that we can see.
Fill in all the colors of a rainbow using
the first letter on each line below.

R________________

O________________

Y________________

G________________

B________________

I________________

V________________

Landforms and Bodies of Water

Earth is made up of many different **landforms** and **bodies of water**. Landforms are the way land is shaped, such as a mountain, a hill, or a plain. Bodies of water can be many different sizes, as in oceans, streams, and ponds.

Use the word bank to label the **landforms** and **bodies of water**.

__________ __________ __________

__________ __________ __________

island **river** **mountain** **plains** **beach** **lake**

Landforms

Landforms and **bodies of water** come in many different shapes, colors, and sizes. Find the different landforms in the word search below. The words can be horizontal, vertical, or diagonal.

R	L	S	T	R	E	A	M	A	K
C	O	N	T	I	N	E	N	T	G
R	M	O	U	N	T	A	I	N	H
L	A	K	E	X	Y	F	W	Z	W
P	L	A	I	N	R	V	M	Z	A
W	D	I	S	L	A	N	D	V	D
H	I	L	L	T	Y	S	A	O	F
J	O	V	V	A	L	L	E	Y	Y
G	R	H	J	O	Y	P	D	J	U

PLAIN VALLEY LAKE MOUNTAIN
CONTINENT ISLAND HILL STREAM

Landforms

Draw a line from the **landform** or **body of water** word to its definition.

Desert	body of freshwater with land all around it
Hill	dry place that gets very little water
Island	opening in the Earth's surface where ashes and lava are forced out
Lake	small piece of land surrounded by water
Volcano	raised area of the Earth's surface, shorter than a mountain

Maps

A **map** is a small drawing of a place or location. There are various types of maps, including street maps, landform maps, and navigational maps. People can use maps for many things, such as to help them plan trips or even locate a country.

Answer the questions below.

What is a map? ______________________

____

Name one type of map. ______________________

____

Why do people use maps? ______________________

____

Map Key

A **map key** is a box with symbols representing objects on the map. A **symbol** is a picture on the map that represents something in the real world. Maps use a key to explain the meaning of each of the symbols used in the map.

What do you think the following **symbols** stand for? Write your answer on the line below each one.

______________ ______________ ______________

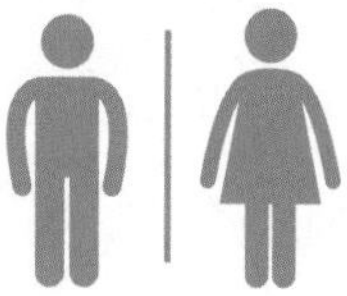

______________ ______________

______________ ______________ ______________

World Map

Maps offer additional information not found in a typical map key. For instance, **green** shading usually stands for land; **blue** shading usually stands for a body of water, such as a pond, a lake, or an ocean; thin blue lines stand for rivers, streams, or creeks; and **brown** or **yellow** shading sometimes stands for land that is a desert or a plain.

Color the **world map** according to the key.

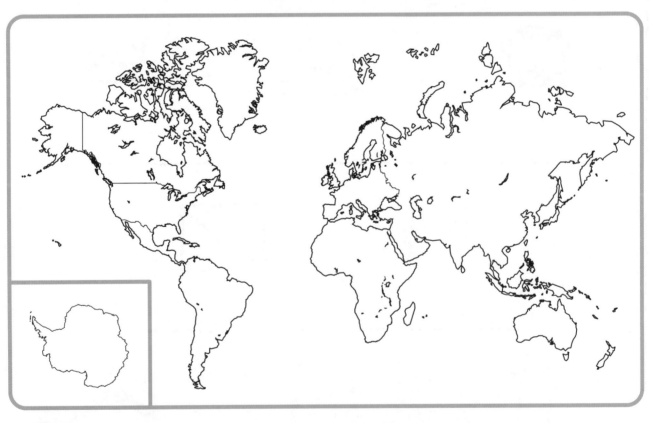

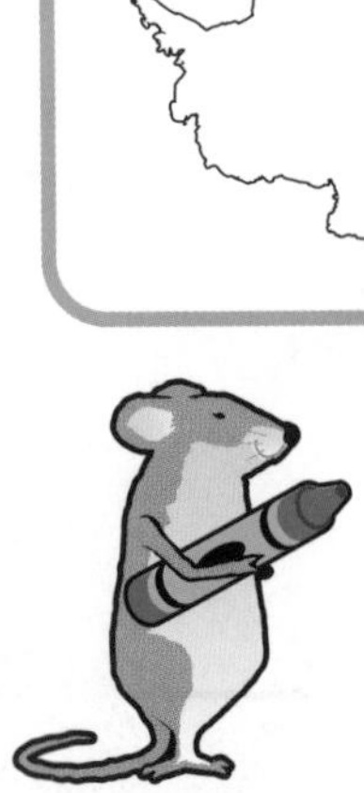

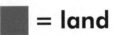

= oceans and seas **= land**

Maps: Drawing a Scale

Remember that a map is a drawing of a much bigger area of land. Maps have to be small to fit everything on them. Imagine drawing a map of the United States with everything its true size! Maps are scaled down to fit on paper and online. To calculate the actual distance between places, we use a **scale**.

Example: |———| 1 inch = 1 mile

If the map **scale** is **1 inch = 1 mile**, fill in the distance between the following:

The church is 3 inches from the bank.

This would be ________ miles.

The park is 5 inches from the school.

This would be ________ miles.

The library is 4 inches from the firehouse.

This would be ________ miles.

The Solar System

Our **solar system** is made up of eight planets that revolve around the **Sun**, which is a star. **Earth** is one of those eight planets. The path the Earth takes around the Sun is called an **orbit**. Our solar system is part of a cluster of millions of stars and planets known as a **galaxy**. Our galaxy is called the **Milky Way**. Our galaxy, with about 6 billion different galaxies, makes up the **universe**!

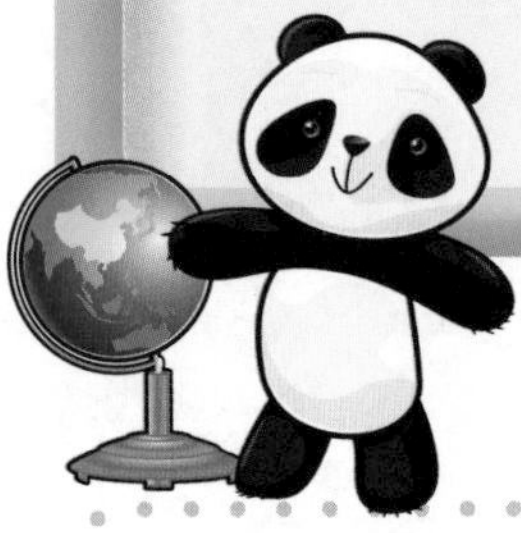

Answer the questions.

What do all the objects in our solar system orbit?

____

How many planets are in our solar system?

____

What planet do we live on?

____

What is our galaxy called?

____

All of the galaxies make up the

______________________________.

The Solar System

Unscramble the letters to find the names of all the planets in our **solar system**.

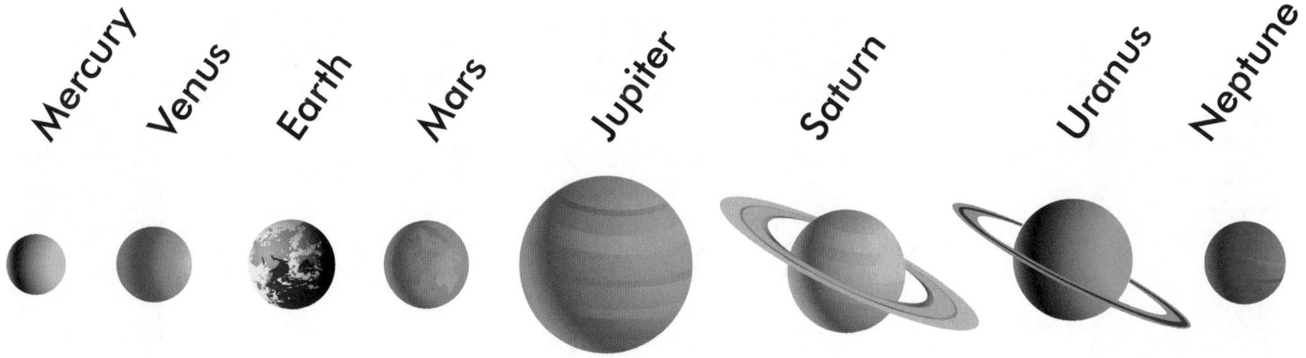

ejurtpi ______________________

rmas ______________________

emcryur ______________________

herat ______________________

arsunt ______________________

npnueet ______________________

vnseu ______________________

asuurn ______________________

The Solar System: Word Search

Find the **solar system** words written below in the word search. They can be horizontal, vertical, or diagonal.

P	L	A	N	E	T	S	J
M	Y	R	O	A	M	O	U
H	A	E	R	T	I	L	N
J	M	A	B	M	L	A	I
G	Y	R	I	O	K	R	V
A	B	T	T	S	Y	S	E
L	I	H	Z	P	W	Y	R
A	R	K	R	H	A	S	S
X	E	O	Y	E	Y	T	E
Y	T	P	V	R	X	E	B
R	J	A	Y	E	Q	M	L

SOLAR SYSTEM ORBIT EARTH
GALAXY ATMOSPHERE
UNIVERSE PLANETS MILKY WAY

The United States

What **state** do you live in? Find your state and circle it.

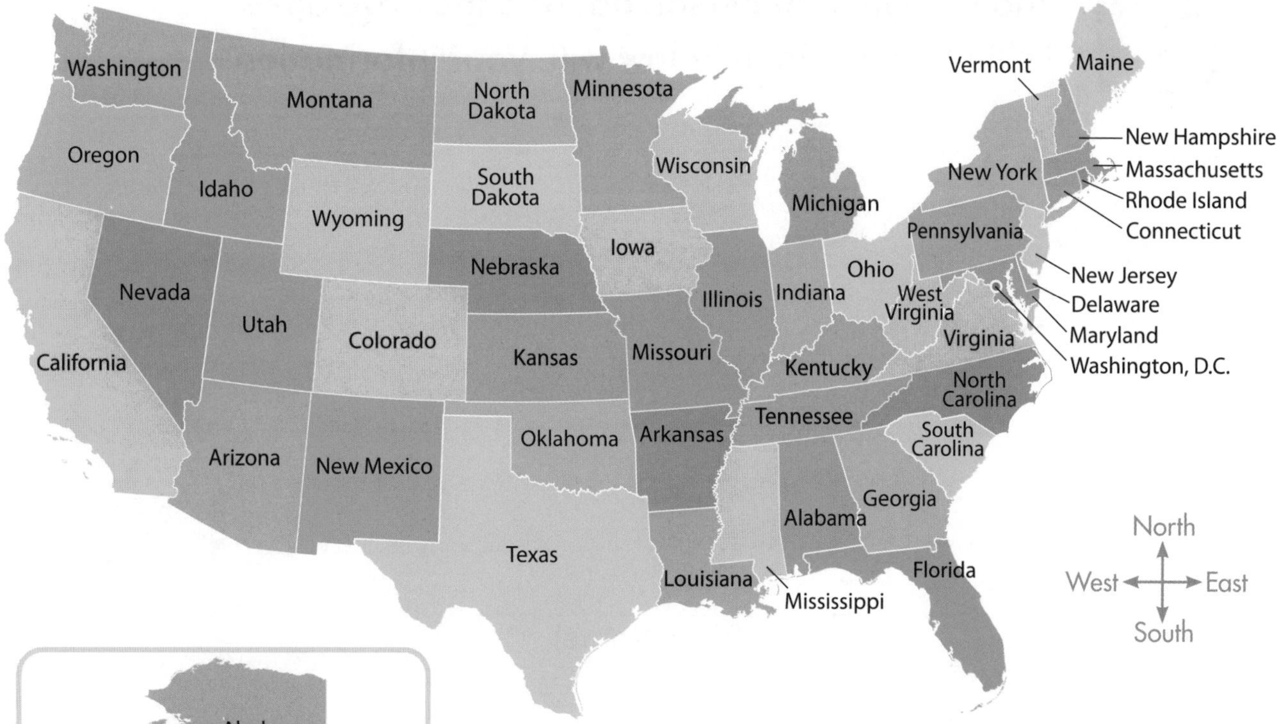

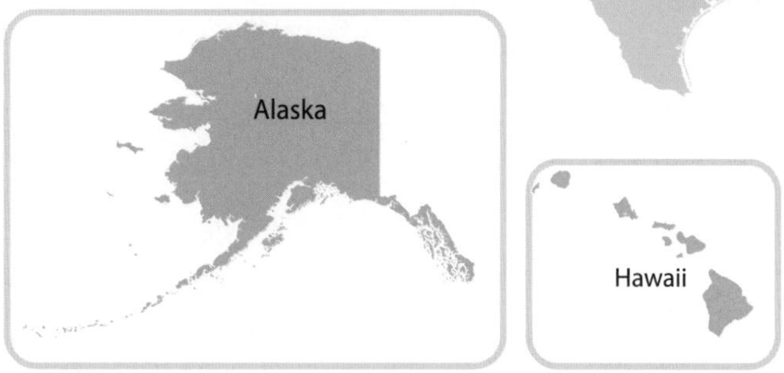

Look at the map of the United States and answer the following questions:

I live in ______________________. (state)

Is North Dakota located in the North, the South, the East, or the West? ______________________.

Name a state located in the South. ______________________.

Is your state located in the North, the South, the East, or the West? ______________________.

Where Do You Live?

If someone needed to send you a letter,
how would that person address the envelope?
Fill in the envelope below with your information.

____
(Your Name)

____
(Your Street Address)

____
(Your City, State)

____
(Your Zip Code)

Continents

There are seven **continents**. They are **Africa**, **Antarctica**, **Asia**, **Australia**, **Europe**, **North America**, and **South America**. Asia is the largest continent. Africa is the second-largest continent. Antarctica is the continent that is located around the South Pole. Europe is attached to Asia. North America has many countries, including the United States.

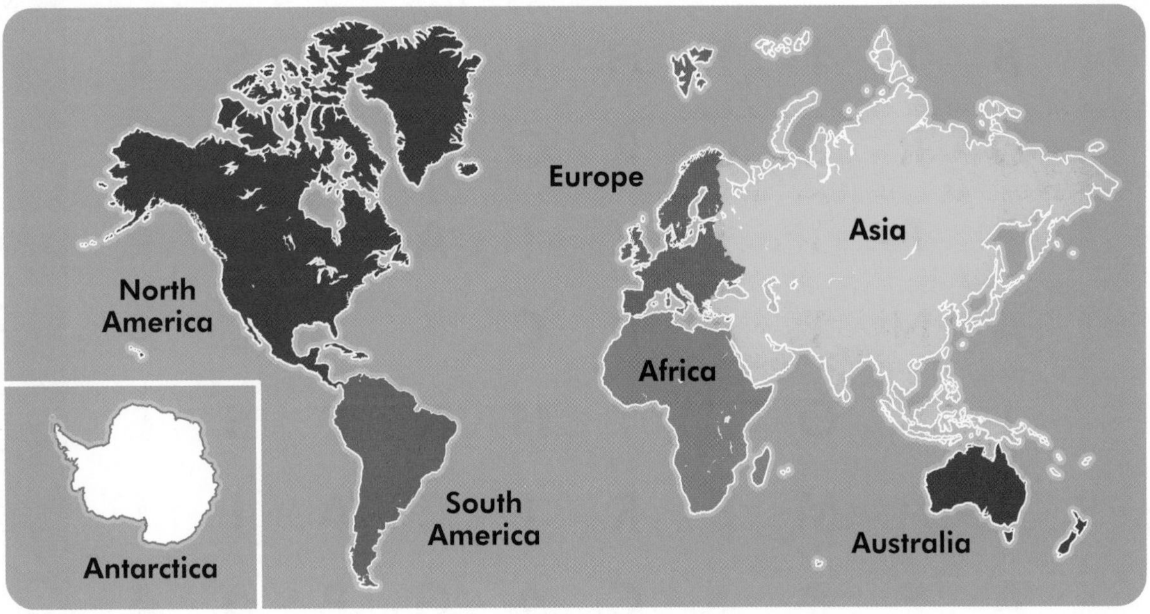

Answer the questions.

How many continents are there?

____

What continent is located around the South Pole?

____

What is the largest continent?

____

What continent is the United States located on?

____

Continents: Word Search

Find all of the **continents** in the word search below and circle them. They can be horizontal, vertical, stacked, or diagonal.

N	O	R	T	H	S	P	A	I	A
A	M	E	R	I	C	A	Q	A	U
B	I	I	P	H	R	R	I	S	S
U	R	E	U	R	O	P	E	I	T
R	P	I	I	K	I	A	S	A	R
A	N	T	A	R	C	T	I	C	A
I	S	O	U	T	H	N	P	S	L
T	A	M	E	R	I	C	A	I	I
A	F	R	I	C	A	G	P	A	A

AFRICA ANTARCTICA ASIA
AUSTRALIA EUROPE
NORTH AMERICA SOUTH AMERICA

Continents: North America

This is the continent **North America**. The **United States** and **Canada** make up the widest part while **Mexico** is the most narrow. **Greenland** is an island up top. **South America** is the continent below North America.

Color the map using a separate color for each country.

Earth's Oceans

OUR WORLD

Oceans cover about 70 percent of the Earth's surface and contain around 97 percent of the Earth's water supply. Oceans affect the Earth's temperature and weather by absorbing the Sun's heat and distributing it around the globe. The **five oceans** are the **Pacific**, the **Atlantic**, the **Indian**, the **Arctic**, and the **Southern**.

Read the names of each **ocean**. Find the matching number on the map and write the name of the ocean on the line to show where it is located.

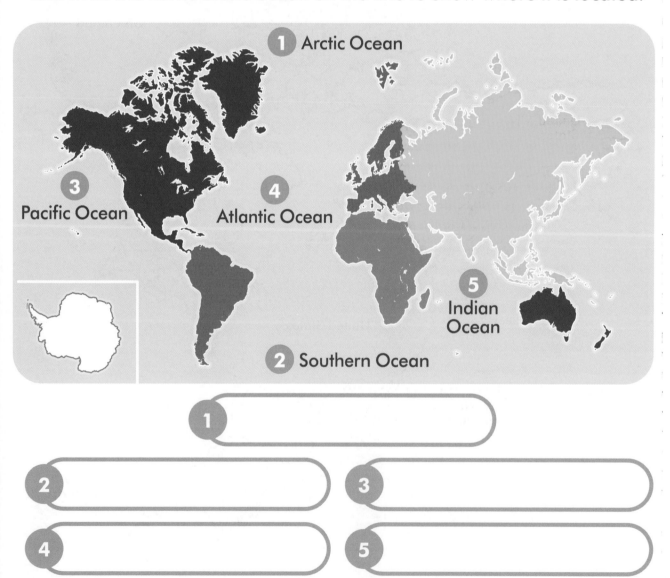

1 ____________

2 ____________

3 ____________

4 ____________

5 ____________

Animals of the Ocean

Color the **ocean animals** and label them.

fish	sea turtle	octopus
dolphin	shark	starfish

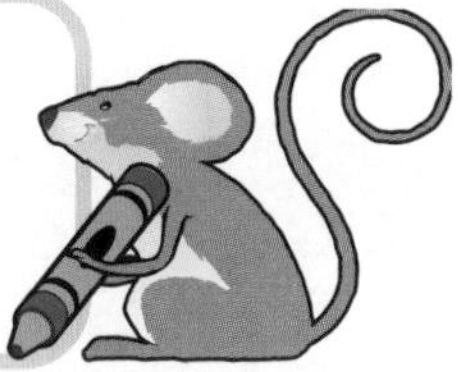

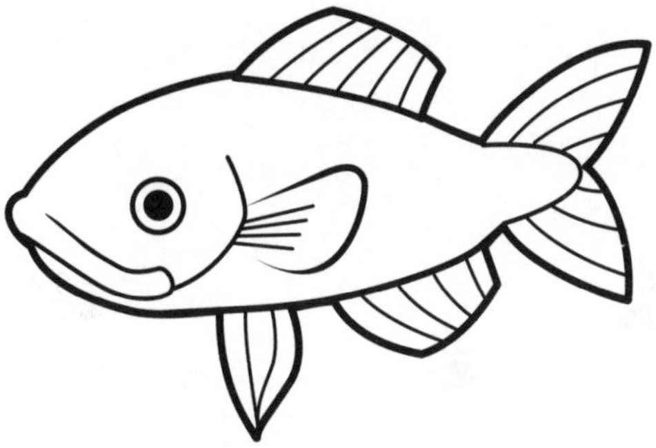

What Animal Lives in the Ocean?

Connect the dots, **skip-counting** by 2s, to find out.

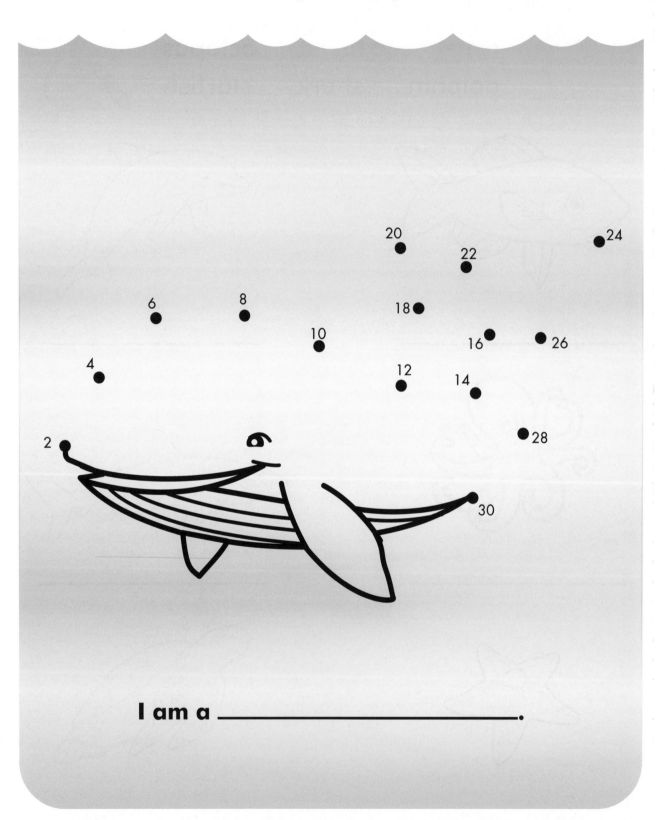

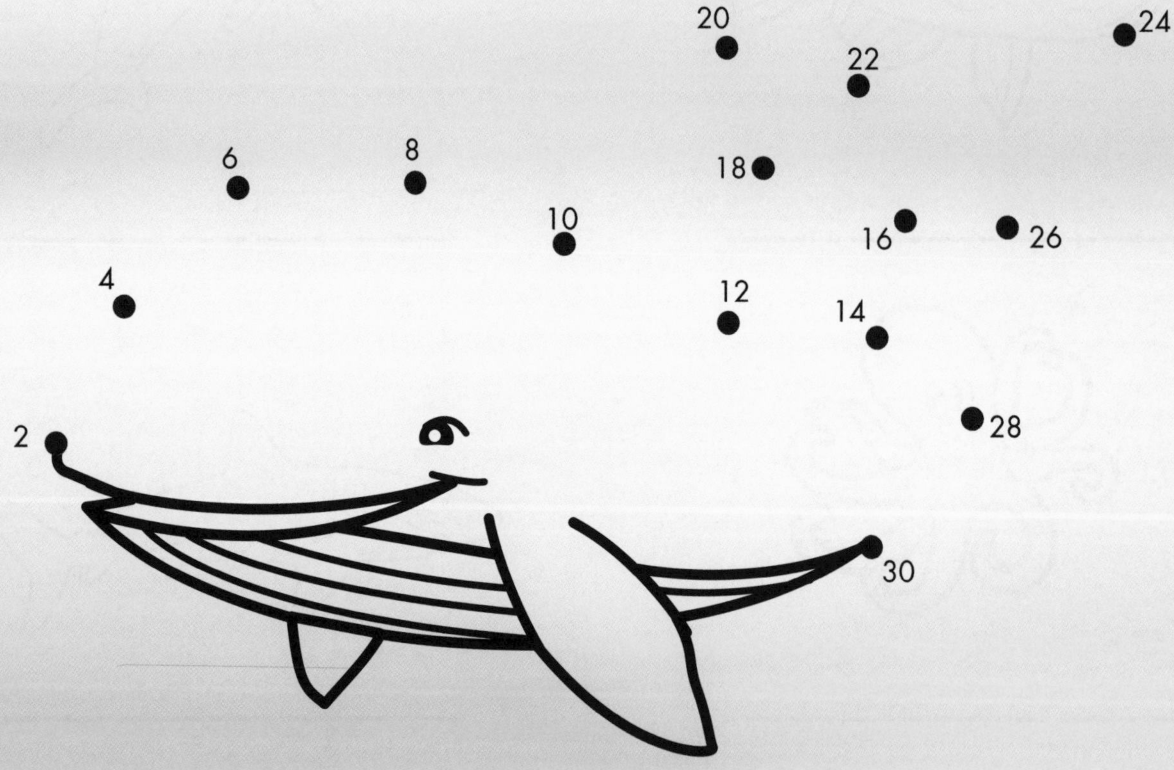

I am a ______________________________.

Hemispheres

The Earth is divided into two **hemispheres**, the **Northern Hemisphere** and the **Southern Hemisphere**. The hemispheres are divided by an imaginary line called the **equator**. The Earth also has two poles. The North Pole is at the northernmost point on the Earth. The South Pole is at the southernmost point on the Earth.

Label the two **hemispheres** and the **poles**.

north **northern** **south** **southern**

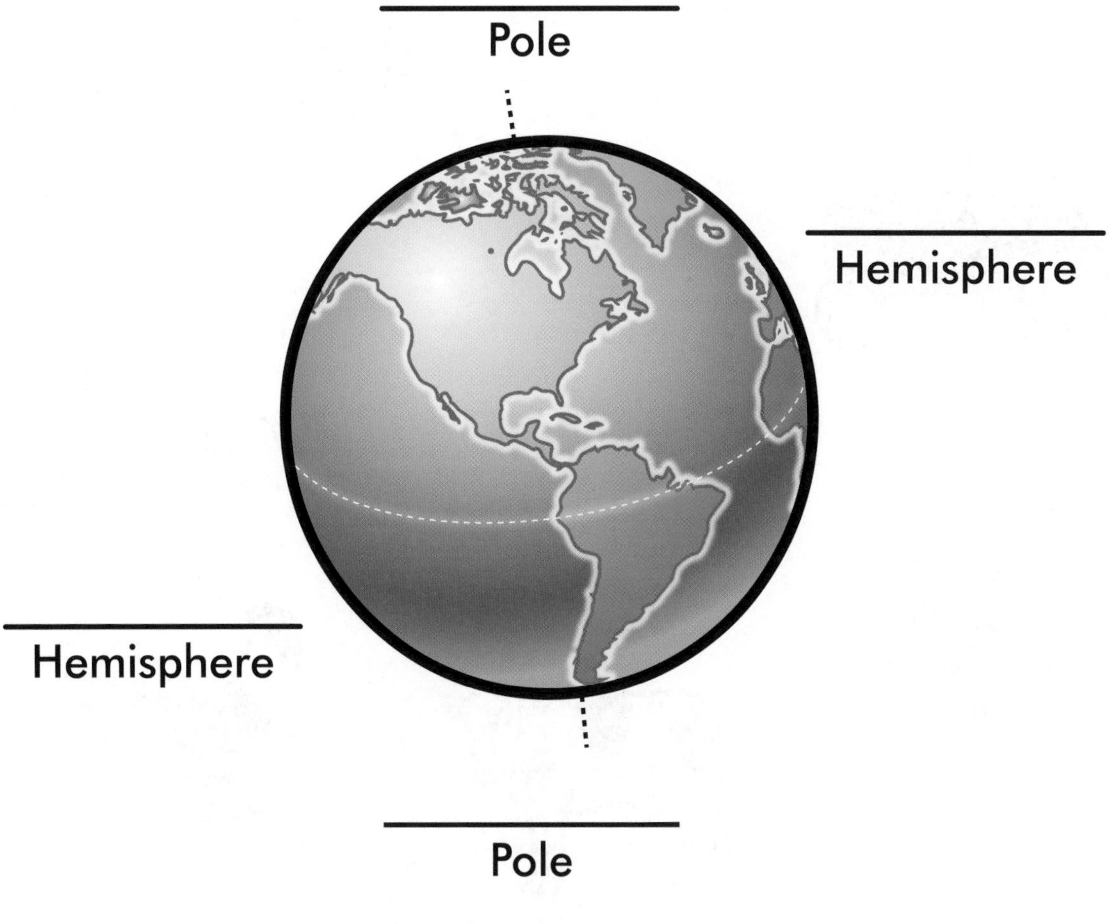

Natural Resources

Natural resources are created by nature, not by people. Natural resources are something of value people get from the environment, such as water, air, plants, animals, minerals, and rocks.

Draw a circle around the things that are **natural resources**. Put an **X** through the things that are not.

Natural Resources

Draw a line from the source to what it produces.

Natural Resources

Some **natural resources** are **renewable**.
This means that they can be replaced or can grow back.

Example: After you harvest corn,
you can plant more seeds.

Other natural resources are **nonrenewable**.
They can't be replaced or they might take a
very long time to be renewed.

Example: Gasoline takes millions of years to produce.

Look at the list below. Decide whether each item on the list is a **renewable** or a **nonrenewable** resource. Write it under the appropriate list.

air copper water soil coal wind
solar power iron oil gold trees diamonds

Renewable Natural Resources	Nonrenewable Natural Resources
____________________	____________________
____________________	____________________
____________________	____________________
____________________	____________________
____________________	____________________
____________________	____________________

Natural Resources: Wood

Wood comes from trees. Wood is used for many things.
Circle all the objects below that are made from wood.

Conservation

People are using up **natural resources** faster than they can be replaced! This causes many problems in our environment, such as pollution and loss of many plants and animals. It is important that we use our natural resources wisely so they will be here for future generations to use. **Conservation** is the careful management and preservation of natural resources and the environment. A **conservationist** is someone who works to save (conserve) things in nature. Anyone can be a conservationist . . . even you!

Brainstorm and think of five things that you can do in your home to **conserve natural resources**. Think about when you brush your teeth or use a plastic bottle.

Reduce, Reuse, and Recycle

The 3 Rs

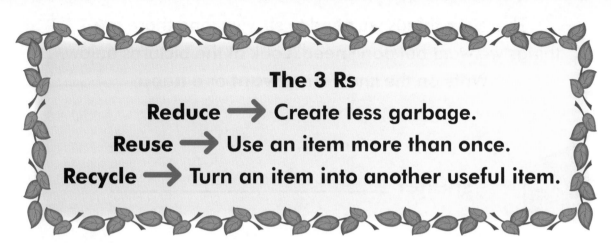

Reduce → Create less garbage.

Reuse → Use an item more than once.

Recycle → Turn an item into another useful item.

Read the following sentences. Write on the line which of the **3 Rs** the action represents.

Using cloth napkins instead of paper napkins

____

Putting your used bottles in the proper recycling bin

____

Using a plastic bag from a store for other things instead of throwing it away

____

Buying a large container of juice instead of many little containers that have to be thrown away

____

Saving scrap paper from a school project to use for a papier-mâché project

____

Using a clean, empty spaghetti sauce jar as a home for your pet worm

____

Sending newspapers you've already read to a recycling plant

____

Wants Versus Needs

There are things we need to survive, and there are things we want but don't need. Look at the pictures below. Write on the line if it is a **want** or a **need**.

shelter ______________________

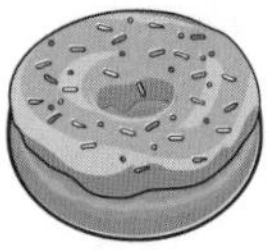

doughnut ______________________

water ______________________

medicine ______________________

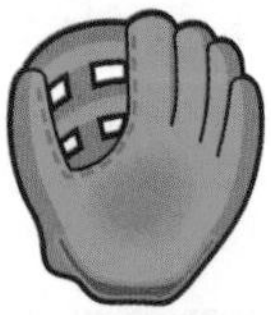

baseball mitt ______________________

food ______________________

sled ______________________

football ______________________

World Languages

Most countries have an official **language**. In Australia people speak English, but in France people speak French.

What language or languages do you speak?

____

Below are the Spanish words and their pronunciation for numbers 1–10. Answer the questions in Spanish!

1. uno (OO-noh)
2. dos (dohs)
3. tres (trehs)
4. cuatro (KWAH-troh)
5. cinco (SEEN-koh)
6. seis (sayss)
7. siete (see-EH-tay)
8. ocho (OH-choh)
9. nueve (NWEH-veh)
10. diez (dee-EHS)

____________ How many cats are there?

____________ How many dogs are there?

____________ How many mice are there?

____________ How many cats, dogs, and mice are there?

Say Hello to the World

Buon giorno. That's Italian for hello!

If you wanted to say **hello** to each of the people in the world, in their native language, you would have to learn almost 3,000 different languages! That's a lot of work. Let's learn just a few.

Look at each word and read them out loud.

Hello in Russia is **zdravstvuite**, pronounced ZzDRAST-vet-yah.

Hello in Germany is **Guten Tag**, pronounced GOOT-en Tahk.

Hello in France is **bonjour**, pronounced bohn-ZHOOR.

Hello in Japan is **konnichiwa**, pronounced Koh-NEE-chee-WAH.

Similarities in Language

A lot of words in other languages **sound very similar** to English words. See if you can match the French words on the left to their pictures on the right.

Le papier

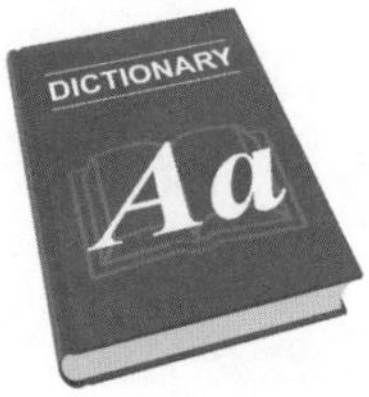

La calculatrice

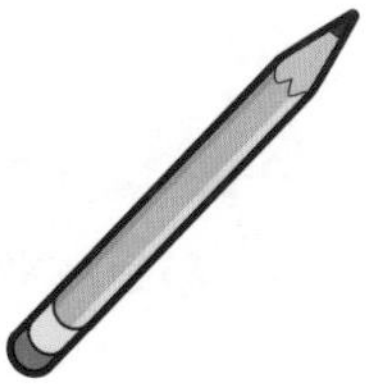

Le dictionnaire

Le crayon

Le marqueur

La regle

World Cuisine

World cuisine is a style of cooking food often related to a particular country or culture. Below is a list of cuisines from different cultures. Think of examples of a food from the different cultures mentioned. The first one has been done for you.

Culture/ Cuisine	Country	Food
Indian	India	Tandoori Chicken
Mexican	Mexico	______
Italian	Italy	______
Chinese	China	______
French	France	______

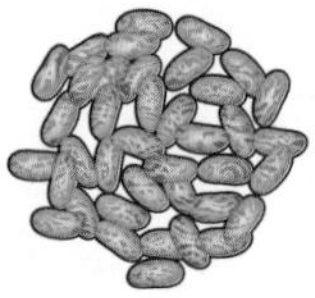

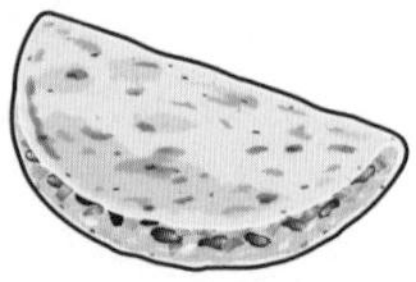

Festivals

Cinco de Mayo

Cinco de Mayo, on the fifth of May, celebrates a victory by the Mexican Army over the French Army in the Battle of Puebla in 1862. It was such a great victory because Mexican forces, consisting of about 5,000 poorly armed troops, went up against the well-equipped French army that had over 6,000 soldiers. Mexico won the battle.

Today, Cinco de Mayo is not a national holiday in Mexico, but it is a well-known celebration. There are festivals and fiestas with special music, dances, and food. People everywhere wear the colors of the Mexican flag, red and green. Not only is Cinco de Mayo a chance to honor the brave soldiers, but it is also an opportunity to celebrate Mexican culture.

Answer the questions below.

What day is Cinco de Mayo celebrated on? ____________

Cinco de Mayo celebrates the Mexican victory over the

______________________________ army.

Why is this considered such a great victory? ____________

____

How is Cinco de Mayo celebrated? ____________

____

Cinco de Mayo Word Search

Find the words below in the word search and circle them.
They can be horizontal, vertical, or diagonal.

M	E	X	I	C	O	P	Y	I	F	H
B	R	A	V	E	C	R	Q	F	E	B
A	I	I	P	H	O	R	I	T	O	P
T	F	E	S	T	I	V	A	L	S	R
T	P	I	C	P	U	E	B	L	A	I
L	N	I	A	R	C	T	I	C	Y	D
E	V	O	U	T	H	N	P	S	T	E
C	I	N	C	O	D	E	M	A	Y	O
A	F	R	I	F	I	E	S	T	A	S

CINCO DE MAYO MEXICO
BATTLE VICTORY PRIDE FESTIVALS
PUEBLA BRAVE FIESTAS

Fourth of July

The **Fourth of July** is also known as **Independence Day**. It is the birthday of the United States. On July 4, 1776, representatives of the original thirteen American colonies, meeting in Philadelphia, declared independence from Great Britain.

The **Declaration of Independence** was sent to the king of England by the Continental Congress, saying the United States wanted to be its own country, independent of England. One of the reasons the colonies broke away from Britain was they believed all people had the right to life, liberty, and the pursuit of happiness.

The first celebration of Independence Day was recorded on July 4, 1777. In 1941, Congress made Independence Day a national holiday. This means government offices are closed and mail is not delivered. Today, people get together for cookouts, parades, picnics, and fireworks on the Fourth of July to celebrate.

Answer the questions below.

The Declaration of Independence was signed in the city of

______________________________.

The colonies declared their independence from

______________________________.

Who was the Declaration of Independence sent to?

____

My World

Place these **Fourth of July** vocabulary words in alphabetical order.

parade independence liberty patriotic
England flag celebration summer

1. ____________________

2. ____________________

3. ____________________

4. ____________________

5. ____________________

6. ____________________

7. ____________________

8. ____________________

Halloween

Halloween is celebrated every year on October 31. Today it has lost most of its religious roots and is more of a fun day for children. There are many symbols for Halloween, including the colors orange and black, ghosts, orange pumpkins, and black cats.

One of the biggest Halloween activities is trick-or-treating. This is when kids knock on doors and say "trick or treat." The person at the door then gives the children a treat so as not to get tricked.

Write sentences about **Halloween**, starting with the letter at the beginning of each line.

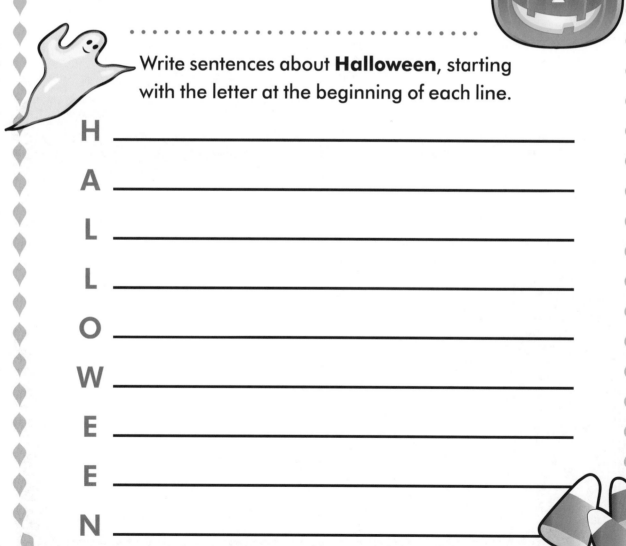

H ______________________________

A ______________________________

L ______________________________

L ______________________________

O ______________________________

W ______________________________

E ______________________________

E ______________________________

N ______________________________

The Pledge of Allegiance

How well do you know the **Pledge of Allegiance**?
Fill in the blanks below with words from the word bank.

indivisible   Republic   all   Nation
United States   liberty   allegiance

I pledge ____________ to the flag
of the ____________ of America,
and to the ____________ for
which it stands, one ____________
under God, ____________,
with ____________ and
justice for ____________.

Our Government

More than 200 years ago our Founding Fathers wrote the Constitution, a basic design for how **our government** should work. It divides the government into three branches:

Legislative
Congress is the main lawmaking, or legislative, body. Congress is made up of the House of Representatives and the Senate.

Executive
The president and vice president make sure the people follow the laws.

Judicial
The courts make decisions when people are unsure of the laws. The highest of these courts is the Supreme Court, made up of nine justices.

After reading about **our government**, answer the questions below.

Name the three branches of government.

1. ______________________ **2.** ______________________

3. ______________________

Which branch makes the laws? ______________________

Which branch makes sure people obey the law?

____

Which branch makes decisions when people have questions about the laws? ______________________

OUR WORLD

Riddle

To figure out the **riddle** below, fill in the correct letter for each number.

1 = m 2 = a 3 = o 4 = t
5 = e 6 = b 7 = h

Where was the U.S. Constitution signed?

___ ___   ___ ___ ___
2 4   4 7 5

___ ___ ___ ___ ___ ___
6 3 4 4 3 1

Symbols: Matching

Draw a line to match each word with its **symbol**.

Bald eagle	
U.S. flag	
White House	
Liberty Bell	
Statue of Liberty	

Any Citizen Can Grow Up to Be President!

To become president of the United States, a person must be born in the United States and must have been living here for at least 14 years. Each candidate must be at least 35 years of age.

When you grow up, would you like to be president of the United States? Write your answer below and the reason for your answer.

Local Government

A **local government** is the body that leads a specific community, such as a town or a city. The mayor is the elected leader of a local government. The mayor may work with a town or city council, made up of elected officials who help run the community. The local government passes laws to keep its citizens safe, and much, much more.

If you were the mayor, name one thing that you would do to improve your town or city.

ANSWER KEY

Page 10

Page 11

Page 12

Page 13

Page 14

Page 15

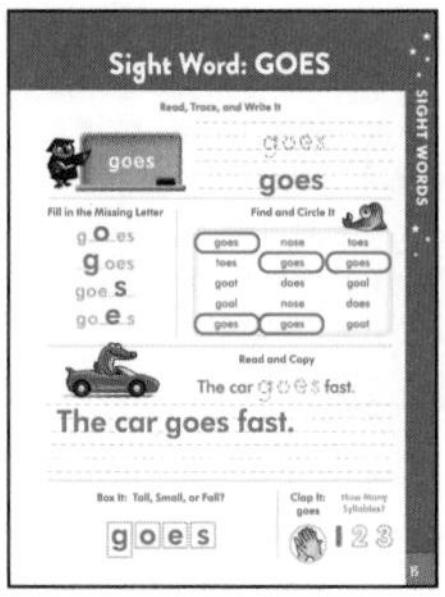

Page 16

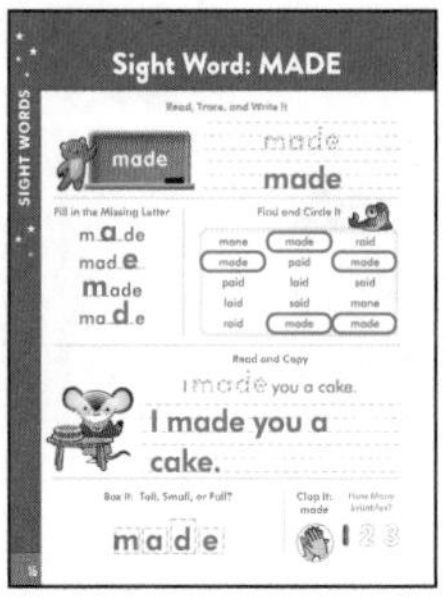

Page 17

Page 18

Page 19

Page 20

Page 21

Page 22

Page 23

Page 24

Page 25

Page 26

Page 27

Page 28

Page 29

Page 32

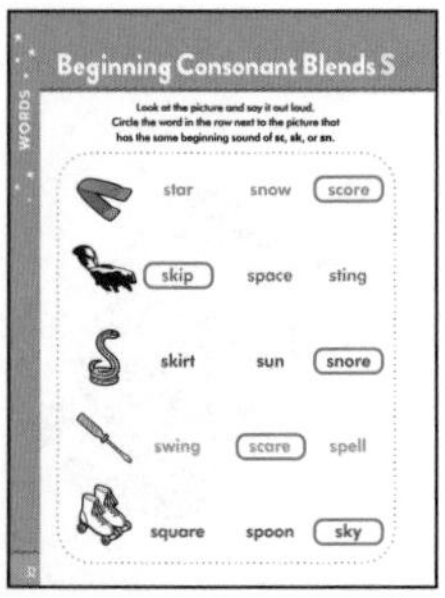

Page 33

Page 34

Page 35

Page 36

ANSWER KEY

Page 37

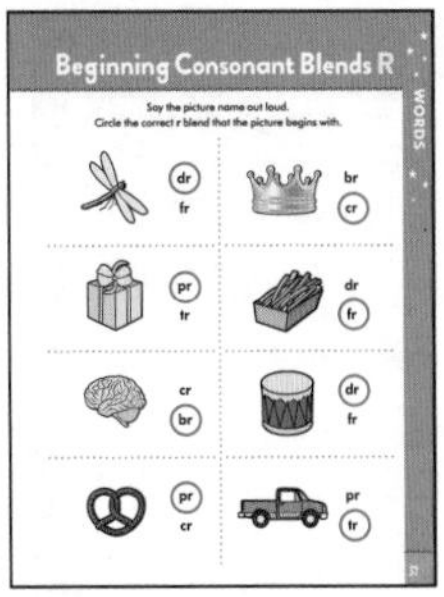

Page 38

Page 39

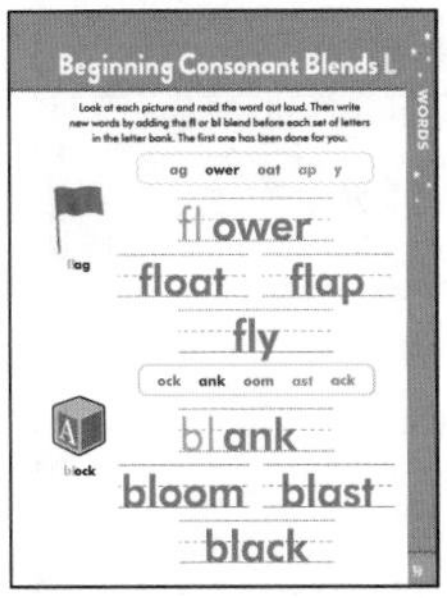

Page 40

Page 41

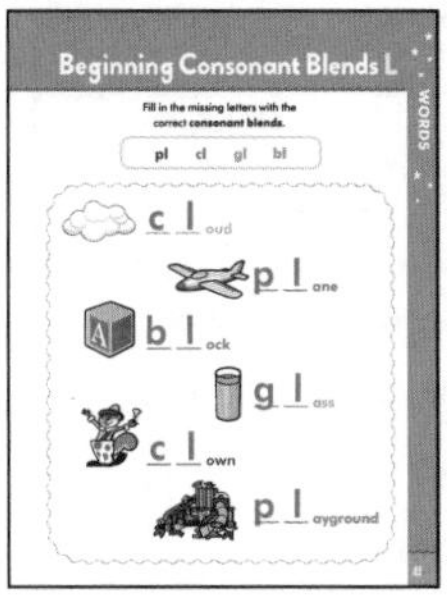

Page 42

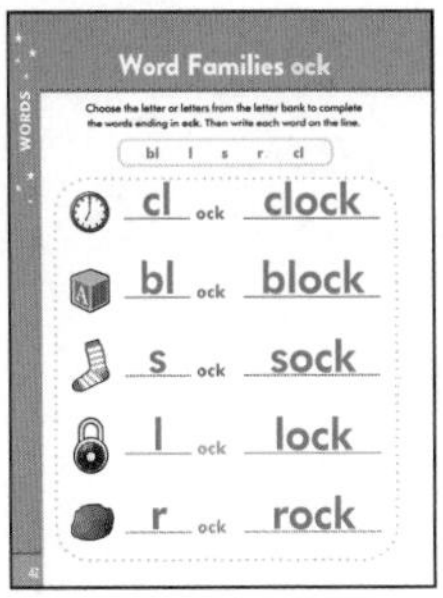

Page 43

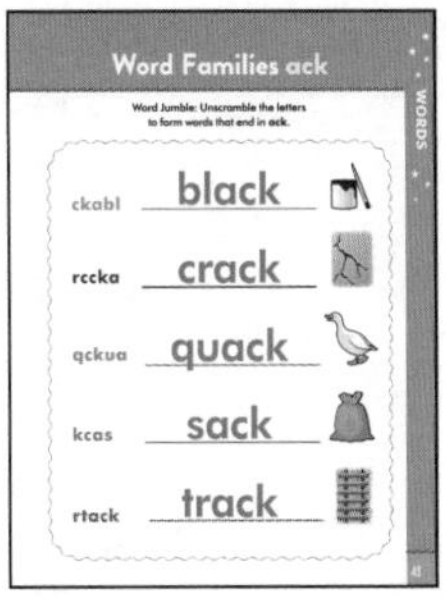

Page 44

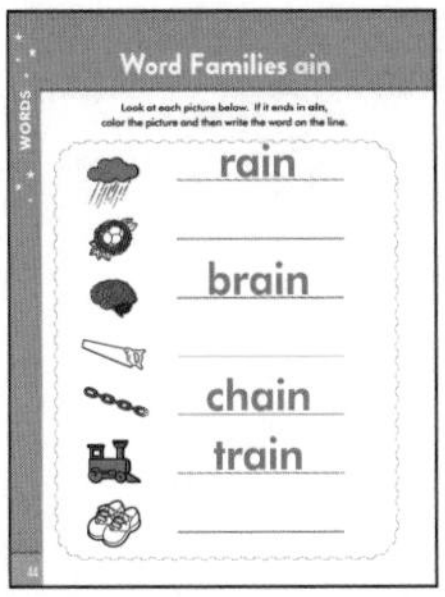

Page 45

Page 46

Page 47

Page 48

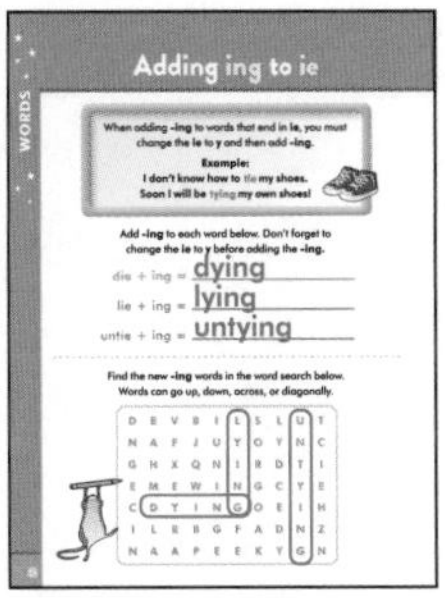

Page 49

Page 50

Page 51

Page 52

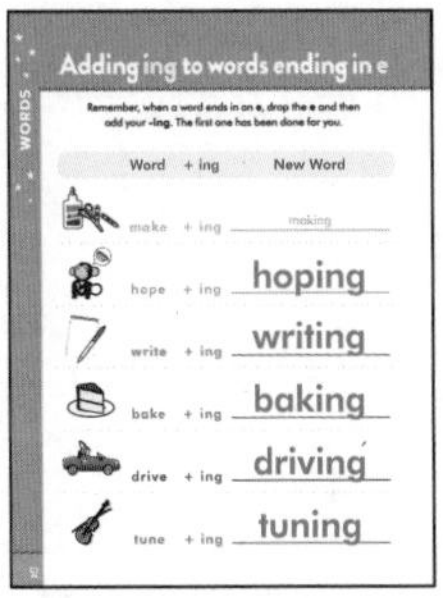

Page 53

Page 54

Past Tense Verb Sounds ed
WORDS
t d ed
dressed tied handed
talked turned greeted
rushed loved visited
looked hugged added

Page 55

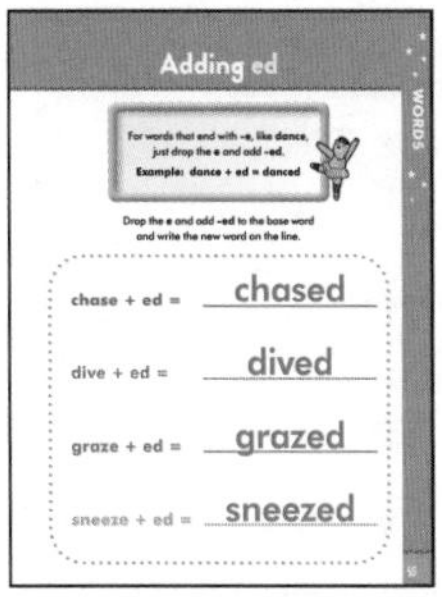

Page 56

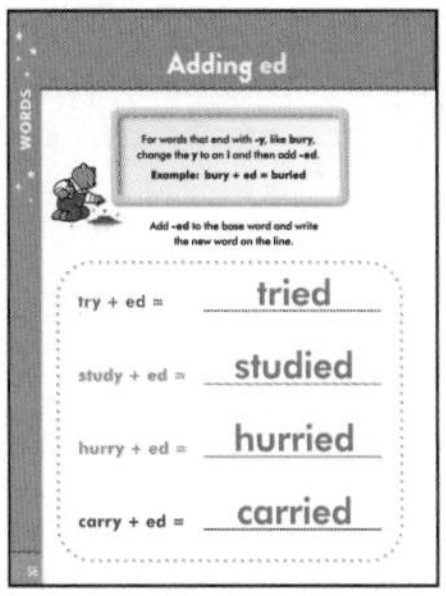

Page 57

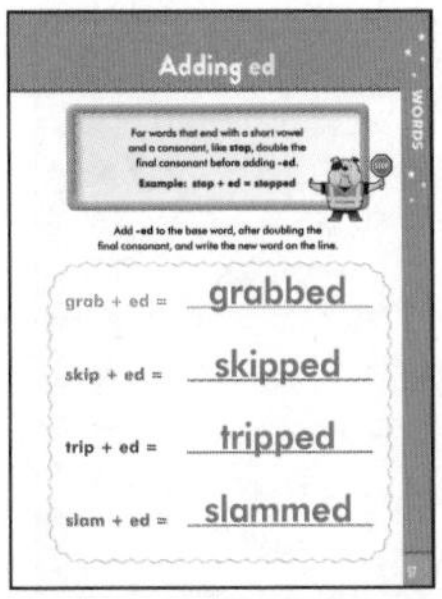

Page 58

Page 59

Contractions
WORDS
Examples:
I + will = I'll did + not = didn't she + is = she's
they + are = they're
we + are = we're
you + will = you'll
he + is = he's

Page 60

Page 61

Page 62

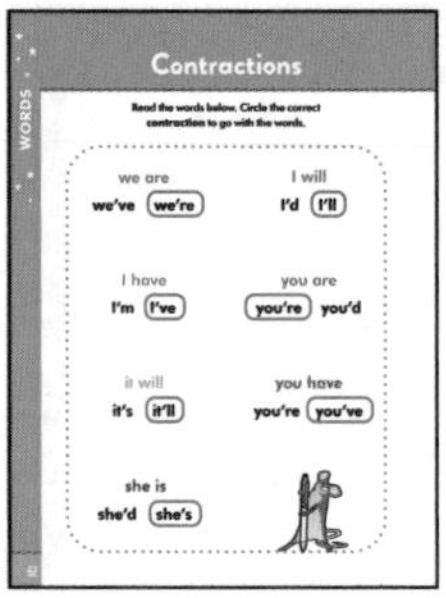
Contractions
we're, I'll, I've, you're, it'll, you've, she's

Page 63

Contractions
wouldn't, wouldn't, won't, I'm

Page 65

Compound Words
skateboard, sunshine, footprints, afternoon, airport, chalkboard

Page 66

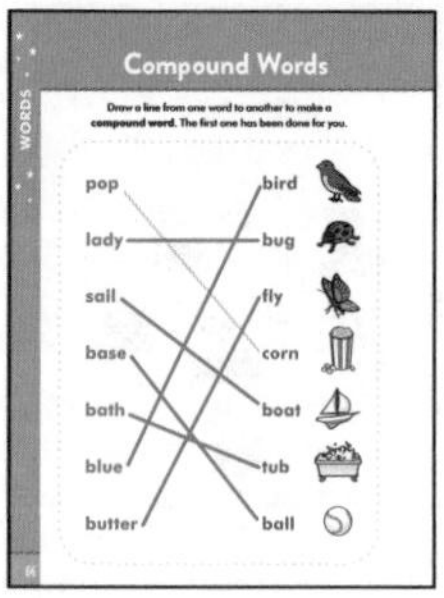
Compound Words

Page 67

Compound Words
flake, snowflake; melon, watermelon; fighter, firefighter; bowl, fishbowl; house, doghouse; snake, rattlesnake; way, highway

Page 68

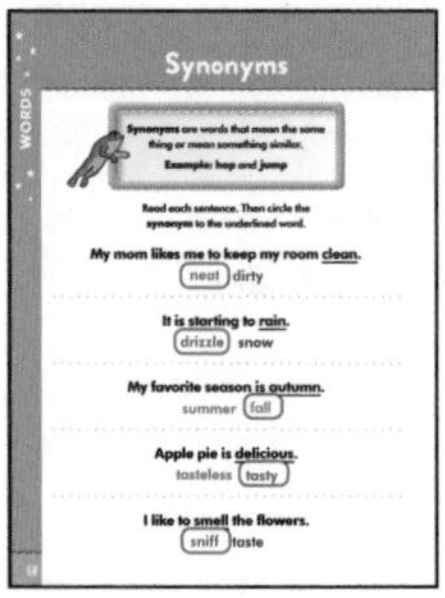
Synonyms

Page 69

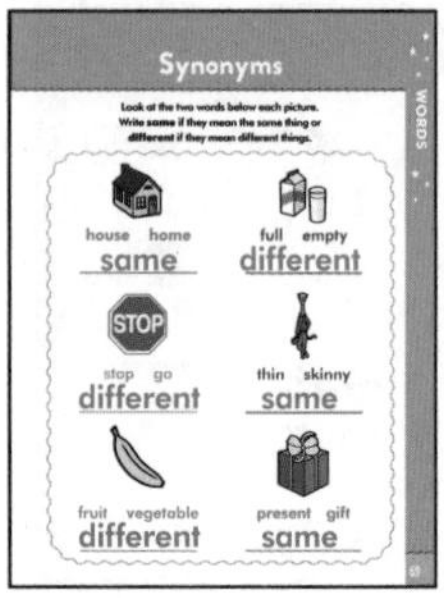
Synonyms
same, different, different, same, different, same

Page 70

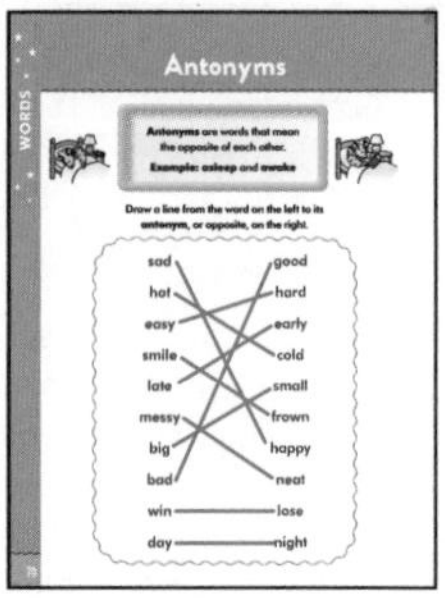
Antonyms

Page 71

Antonyms
good, hot, fast, closed, love, beautiful, stay, sweet

Page 72

Homonyms
weather, whether, tail, tale, stares, stairs, flour, flower

Page 73

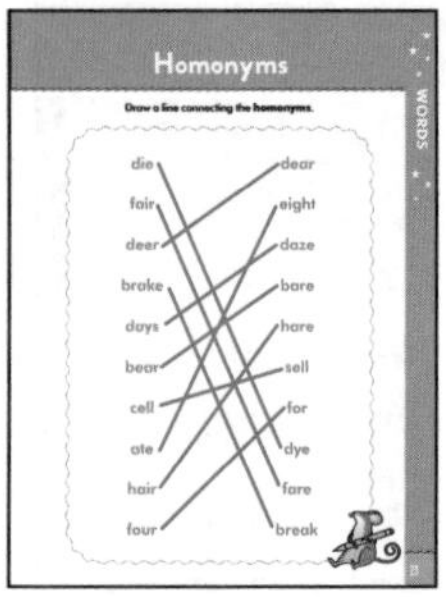
Homonyms

Page 74

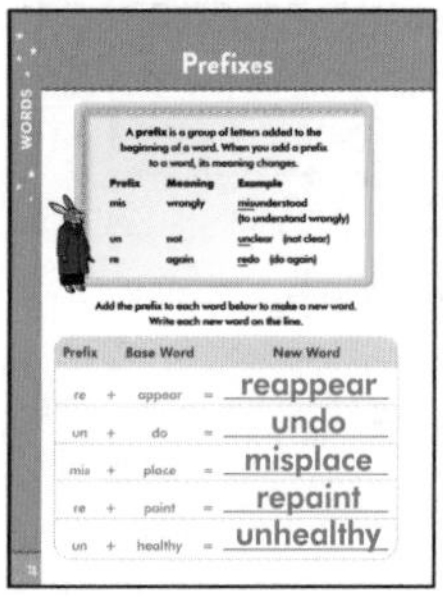
Prefixes
reappear, undo, misplace, repaint, unhealthy

Page 75

Prefixes
mis, mis, un, mis

Page 76

Prefixes
rewrite, reread, replant, rebuild, retrace, repaint

Page 77

Suffixes
taller, tallest; smaller, smallest; stronger, strongest; weaker, weakest; smarter, smartest; louder, loudest; quieter, quietest

Page 78

Suffixes
clue + less; dark + ness; forgive + ness; light + ness; grace + ful

Page 79

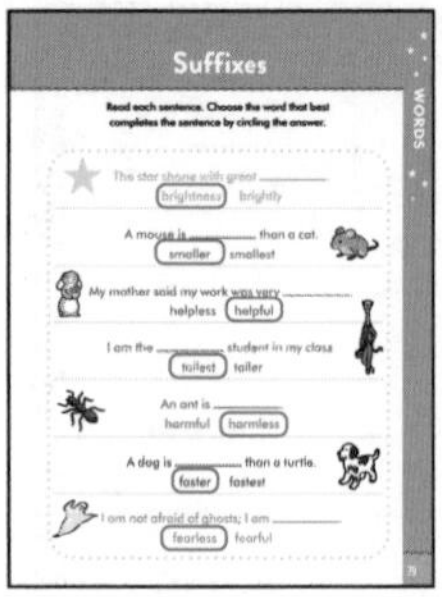
Suffixes

Page 80

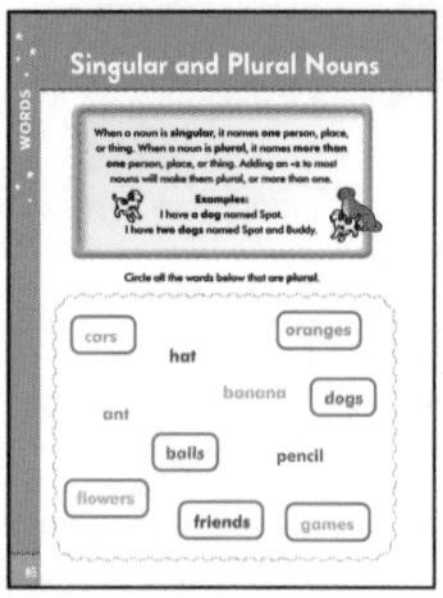
Singular and Plural Nouns

Page 81

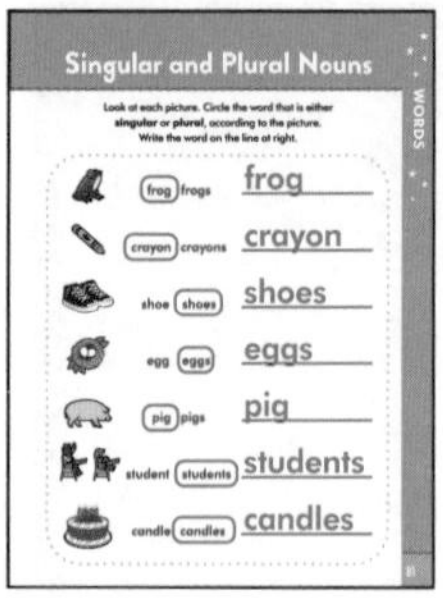
Singular and Plural Nouns
frog, crayon, shoes, eggs, pig, students, candles

Page 82

Plural Nouns
es, es, es, es, es, es

Page 83

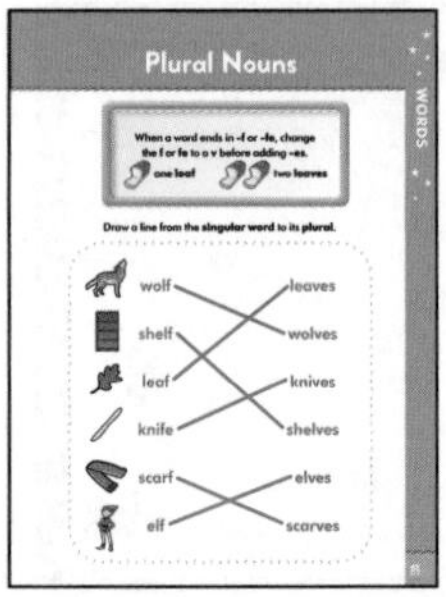
Plural Nouns

Page 84

Plural Nouns
babies, daisies, stories, parties, skies, ponies, bunnies

Page 85

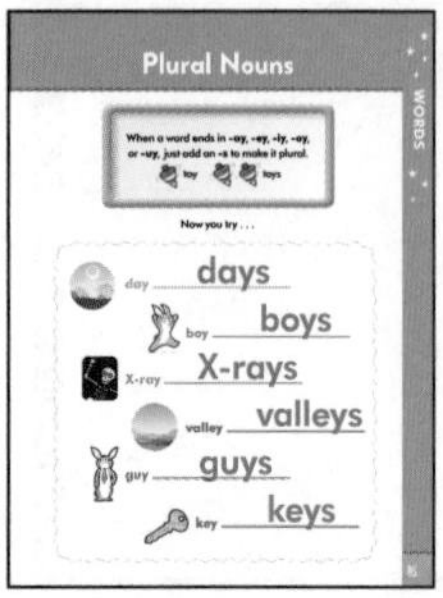
Plural Nouns
days, boys, X-rays, valleys, guys, keys

Page 86

Irregular Plural Nouns

Page 87

Irregular Plural Nouns
men, women, children, feet, teeth, Mice, people, geese

ANSWER KEY

Page 88

Page 89

Page 90

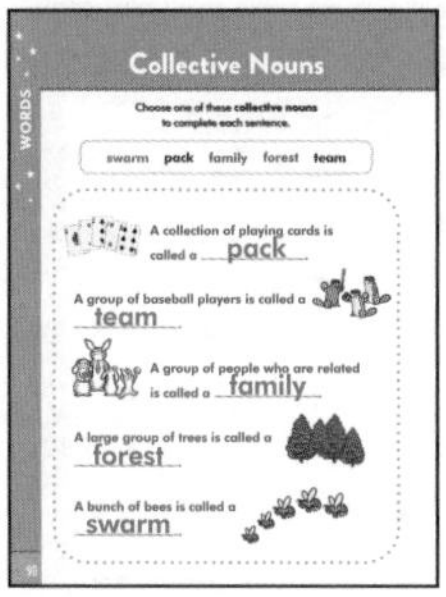

Page 91

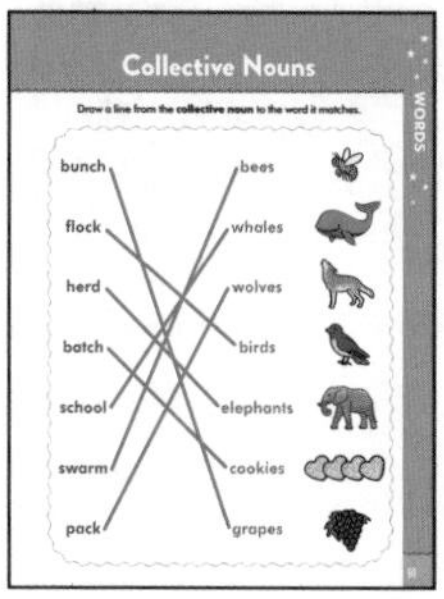

Page 92

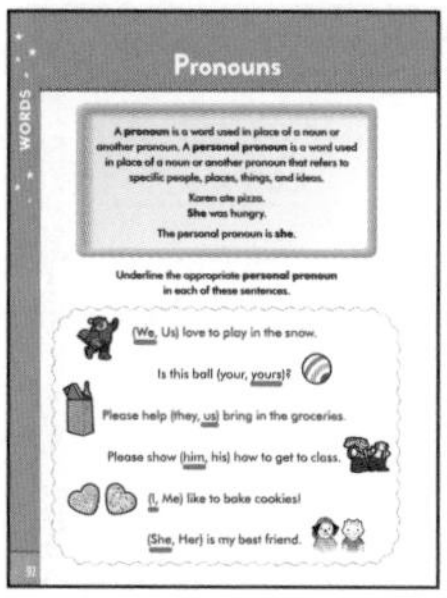

Page 93

Page 94

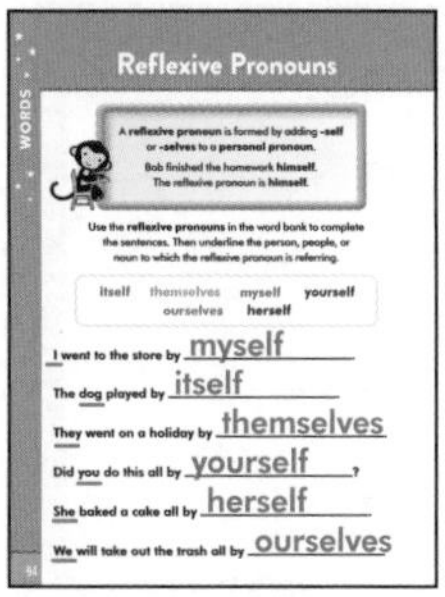

Page 95

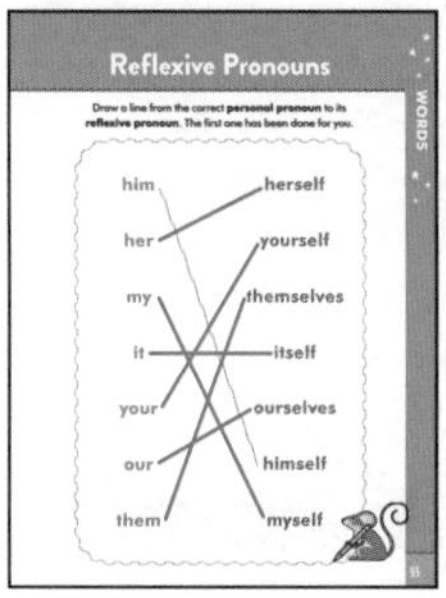

Page 96

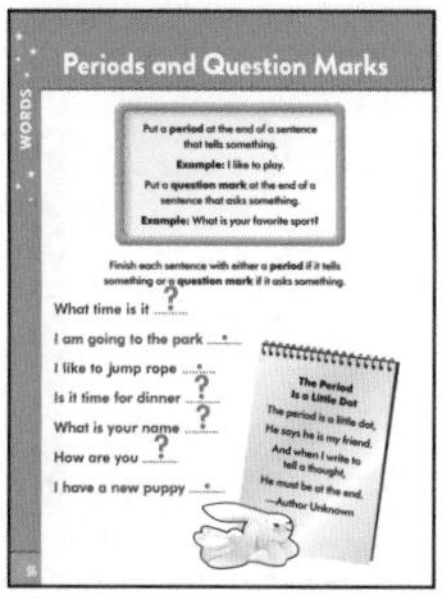

Page 97

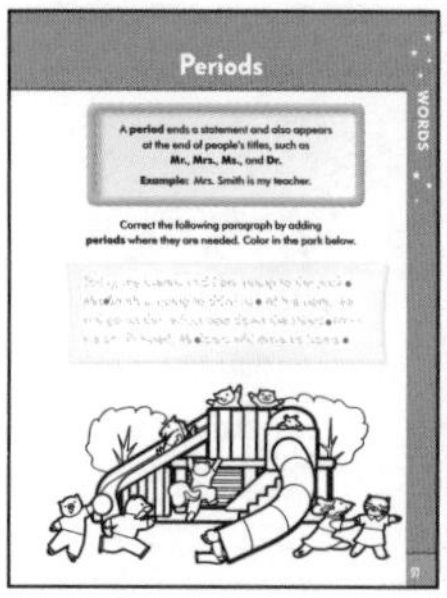

Page 98

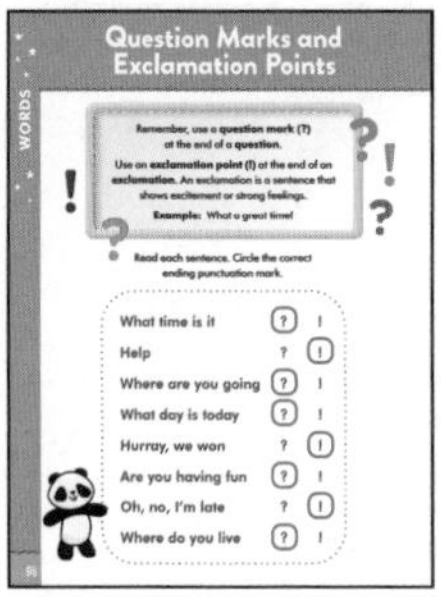

Page 99

Page 100

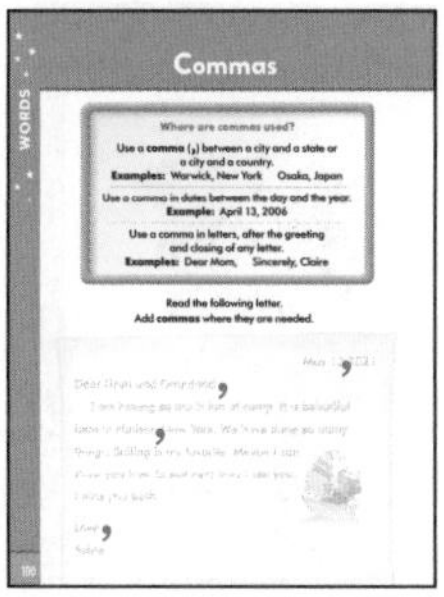

Page 102

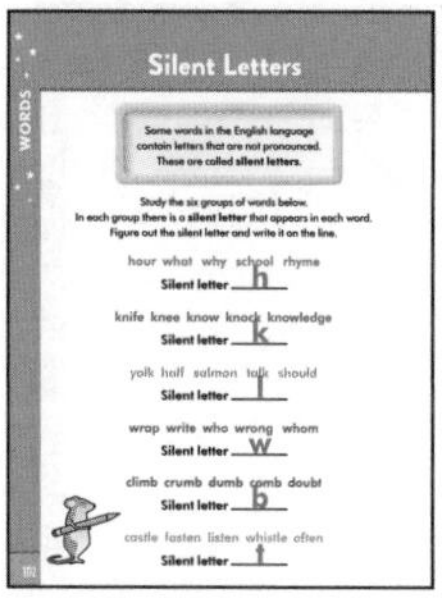

Page 103

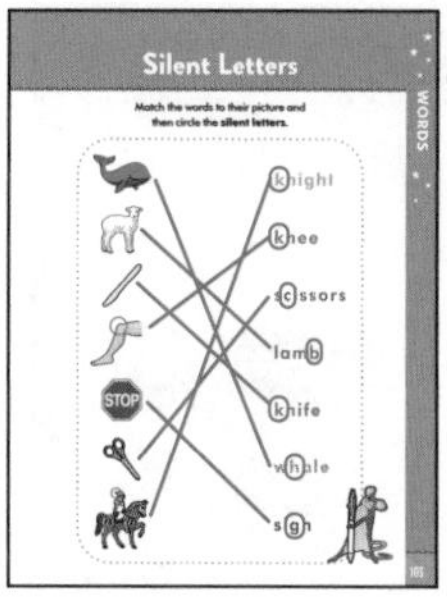

Page 104

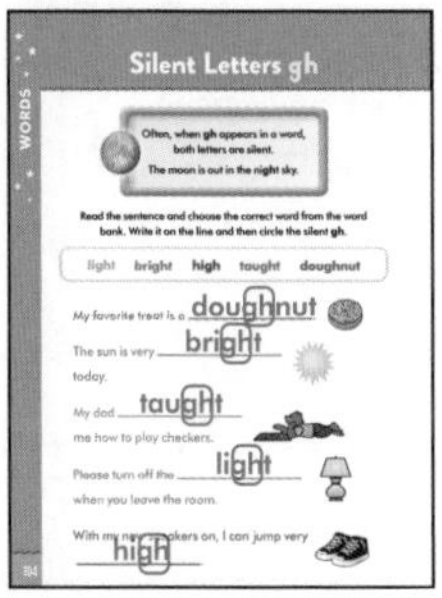

Page 105

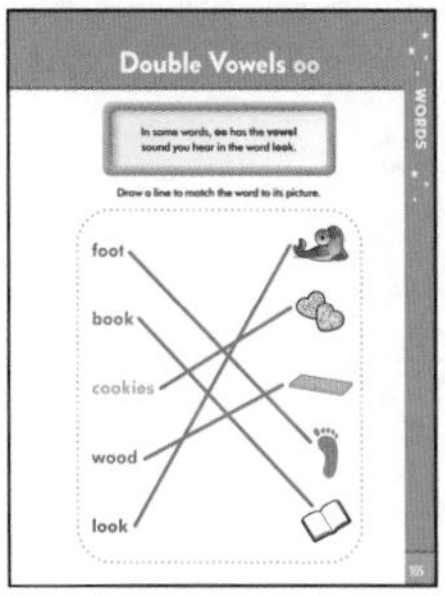

Page 106

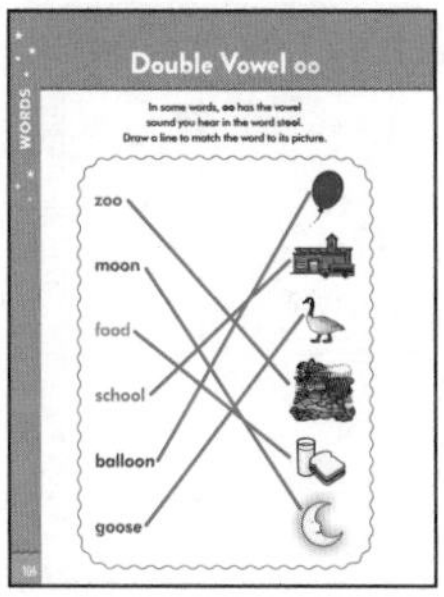

Page 107

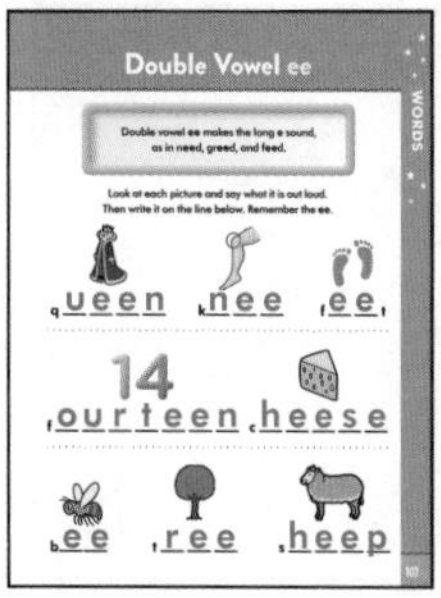

Page 108

Page 109

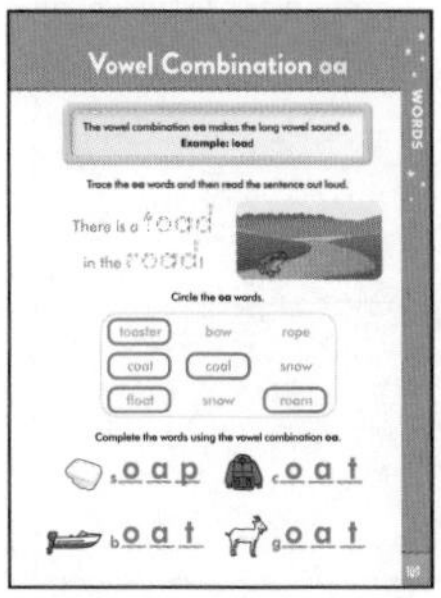

Page 110

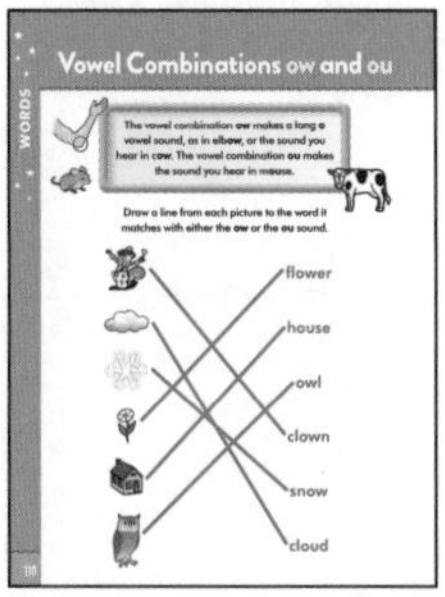

Page 112

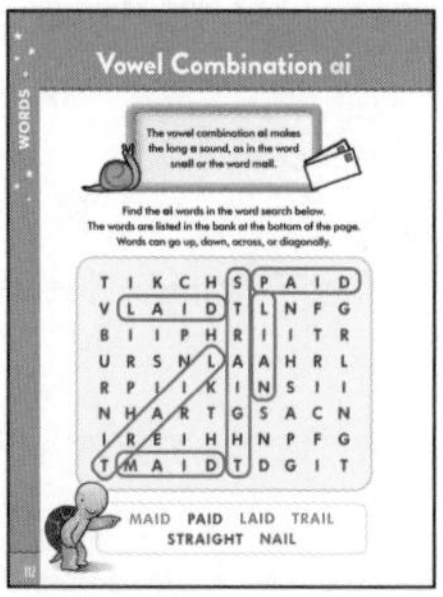

Page 113

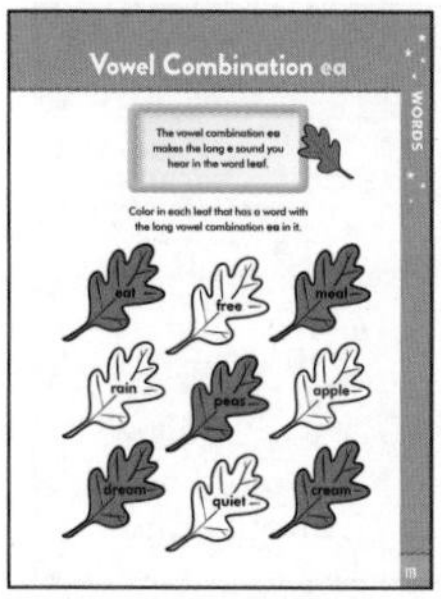

Page 114

ANSWER KEY

Page 115

Common and Proper Nouns

common November
Chicago common
Jones Street common
common America

Page 116

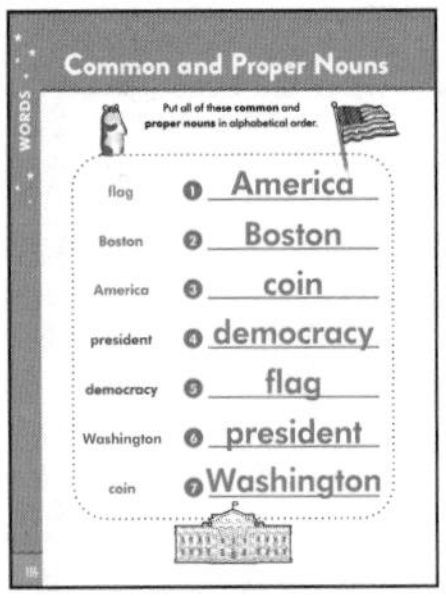
Common and Proper Nouns

1 America
2 Boston
3 coin
4 democracy
5 flag
6 president
7 Washington

Page 117

Days of the Week

Sunday Thursday
Monday Friday
Tuesday Saturday
Wednesday 7

Monday Tuesday Wednesday Thursday Friday

Saturday Sunday

Page 118

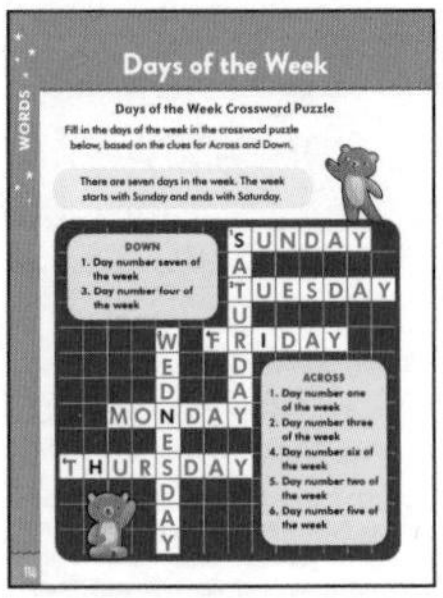
Days of the Week

SUNDAY
TUESDAY
FRIDAY
MONDAY
THURSDAY
WEDNESDAY
SATURDAY

Page 119

Proper Nouns: Months

March January
June September
November May
December July
February August
April October

Page 120

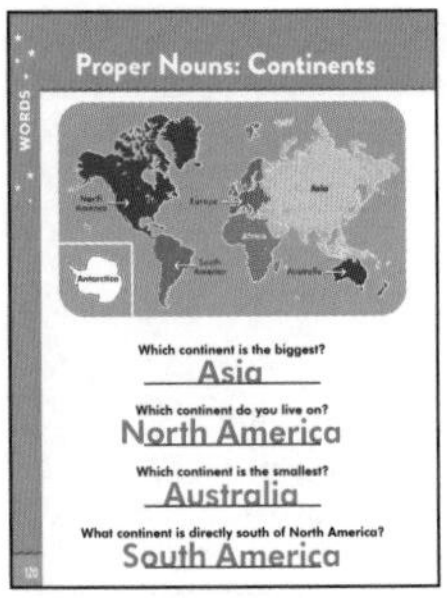
Proper Nouns: Continents

Asia
North America
Australia
South America

Page 121

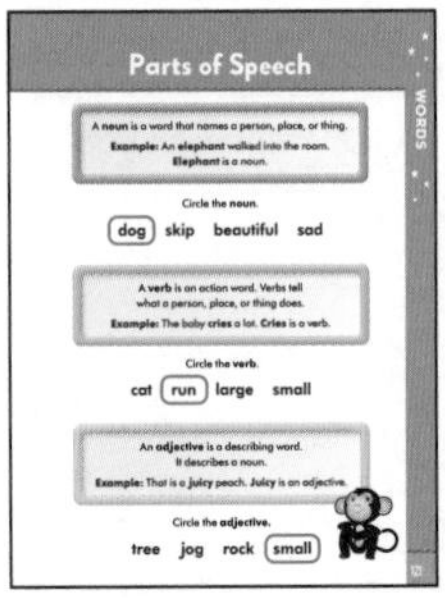
Parts of Speech

dog
run
small

Page 122

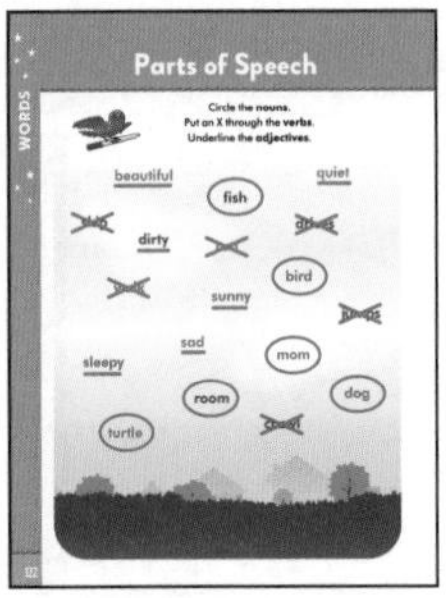
Parts of Speech

Page 123

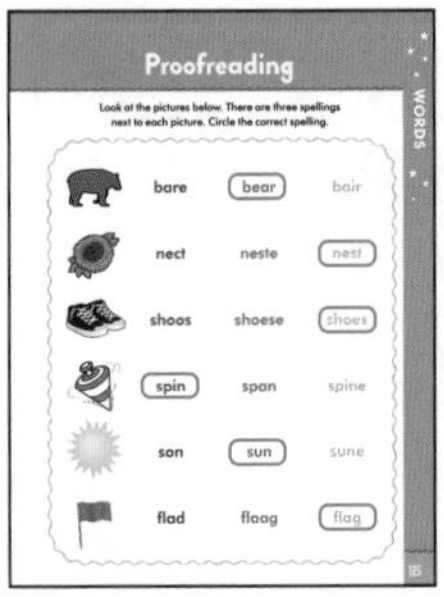
Proofreading

bear
neet
shoes
spin
sun
flag

Page 124

Proofreading

My cat's name is Fluffy.
Would you like to come over?
Mrs. Bucci is my teacher.
I live in Boston.
My birthday is in January.
How are you today?

Page 125

Proofreading

Page 127

Writing a Sentence

Page 129

Writing a Sentence

The kids play in the park.
The boy goes down the slide.
The sun is shining.
The kids run around the park.
Some kids wait in line for the slide.

Page 132

Vivid Verbs

enjoyed adored relished appreciated savored
glanced stared gawked watched peeked
sprinted raced darted rushed dashed
sobbed wailed bawled howled whined
leaped bound hopped bounced sprang

Page 134

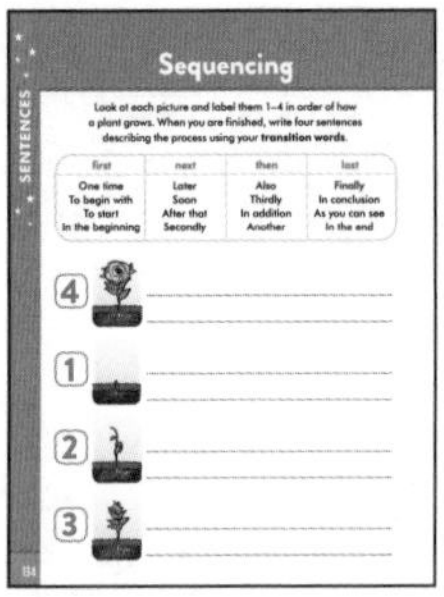
Sequencing

4
1
2
3

Page 136

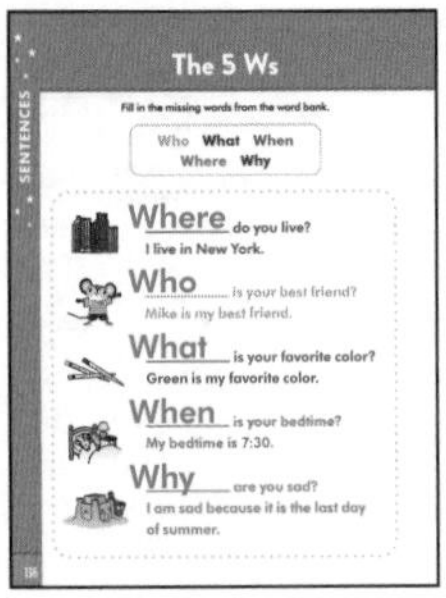
The 5 Ws

Where
Who
What
When
Why

Page 144

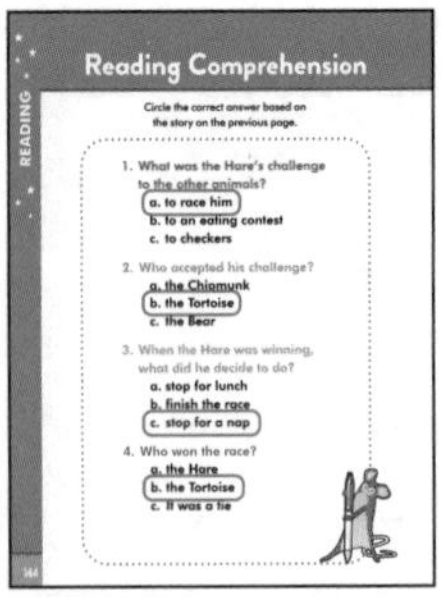
Reading Comprehension

Page 153

Counting 1 to 100

Page 154

Number Words

five
nine
three

Page 155

Number Words

eleven
fifteen
fourteen

Page 156

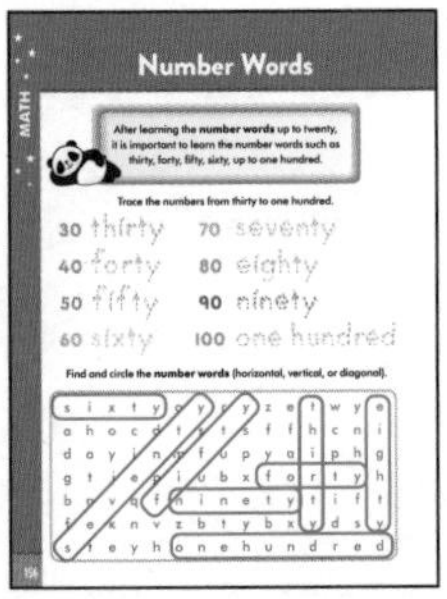
Number Words

Page 157

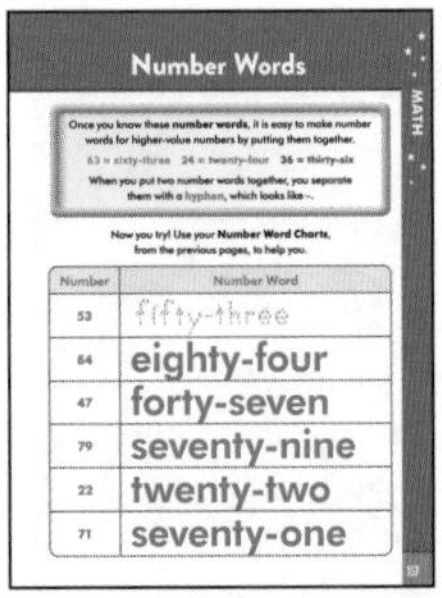
Number Words

fifty-three
eighty-four
forty-seven
seventy-nine
twenty-two
seventy-one

Page 158

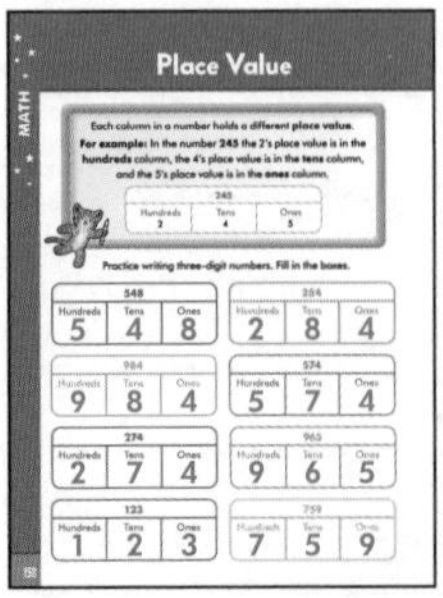
Place Value

5 4 8 | 2 8 4
9 8 4 | 5 7 4
2 7 4 | 9 6 5
1 2 3 | 7 5 9

Page 159

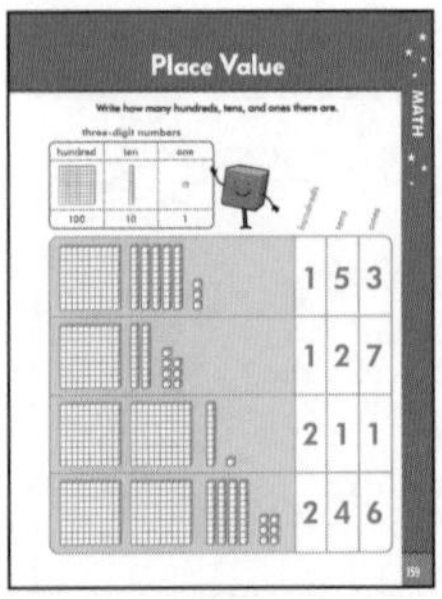
Place Value

1 5 3
1 2 7
2 1 1
2 4 6

Page 160

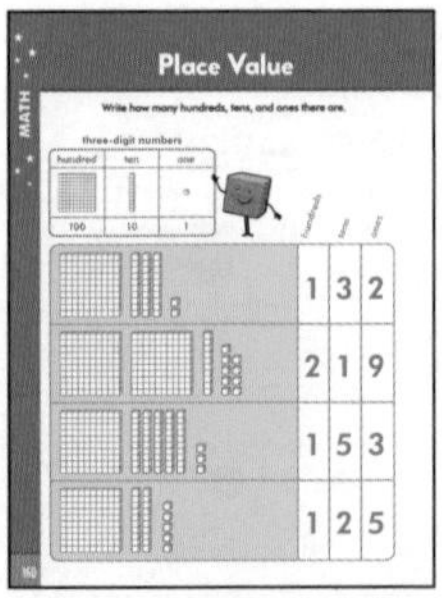
Place Value

1 3 2
2 1 9
1 5 3
1 2 5

ANSWER KEY

Page 161

Page 162

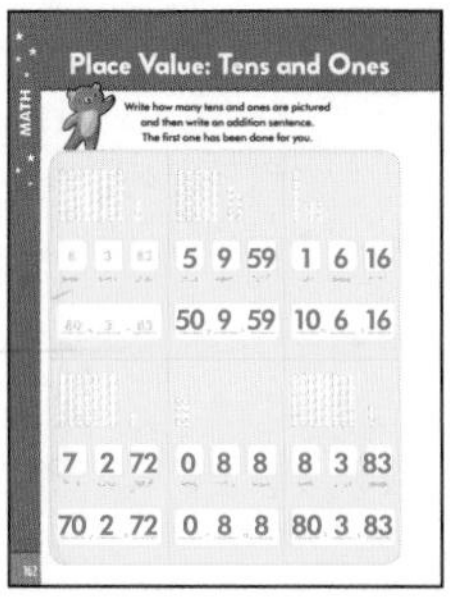

Page 163

Page 164

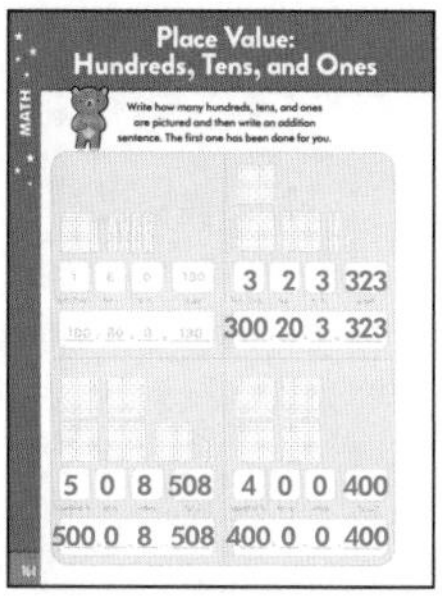

Page 165

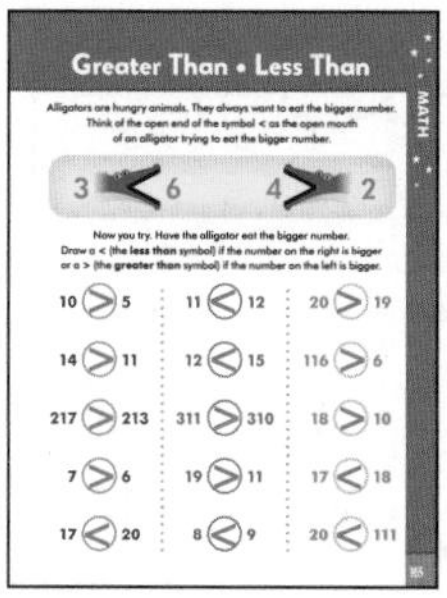

Page 166

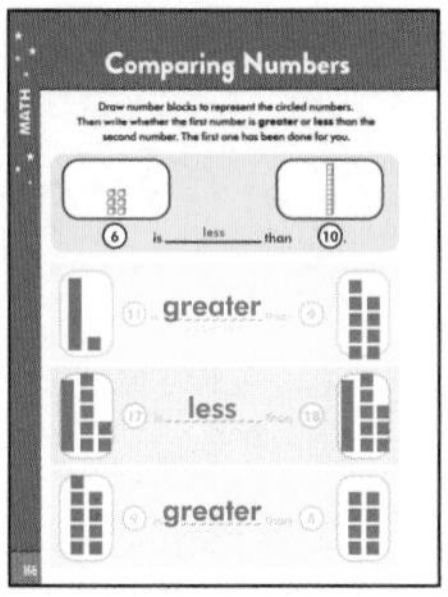

Page 167

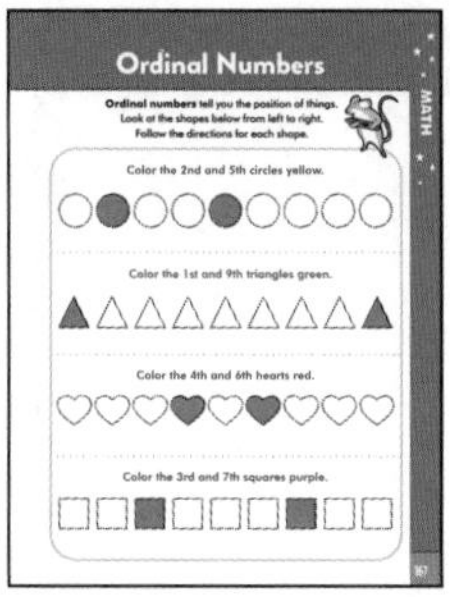

Page 168

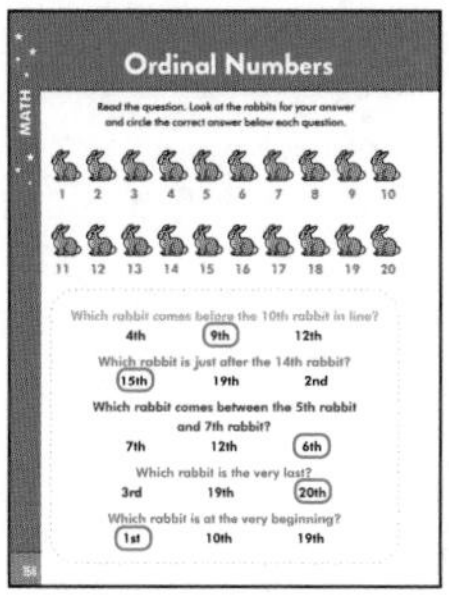

Page 169

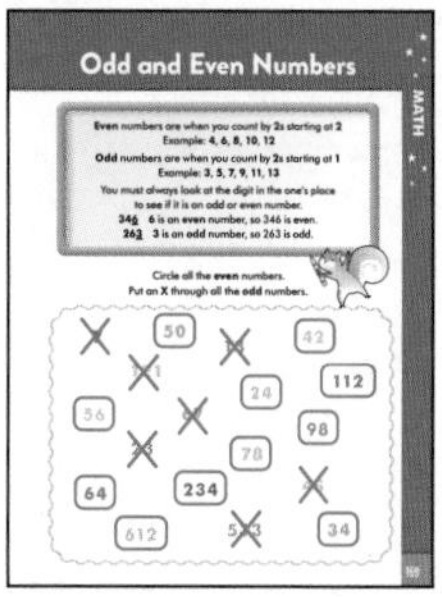

Page 170

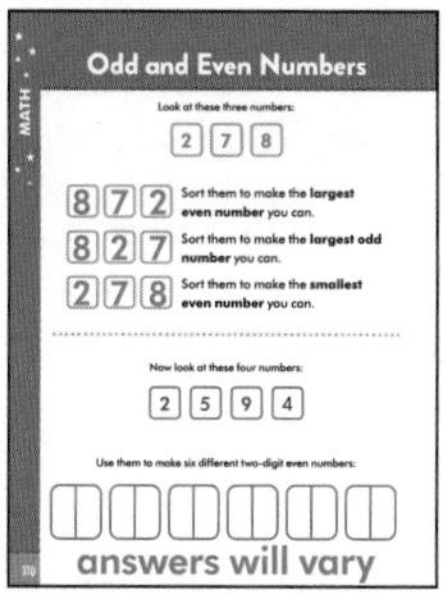

Page 171

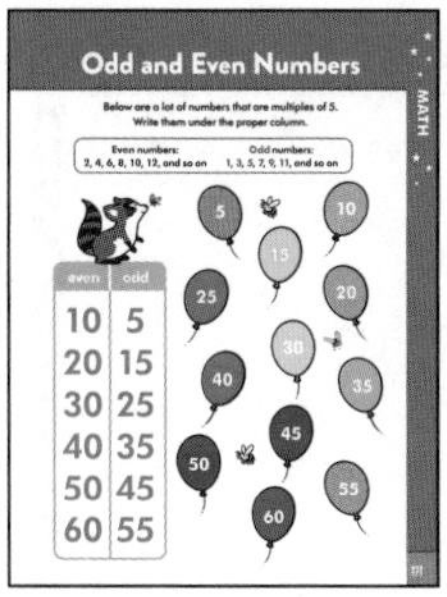

Page 172

Page 173

Page 174

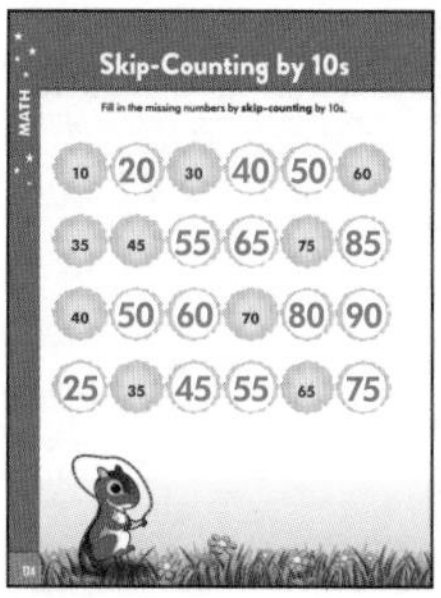

Page 175

Page 176

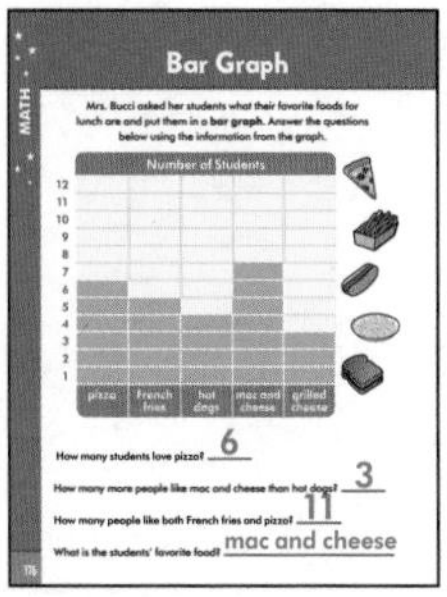

Page 177

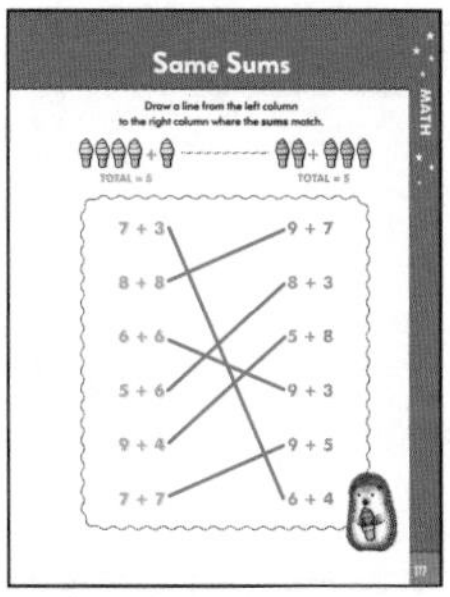

Page 178

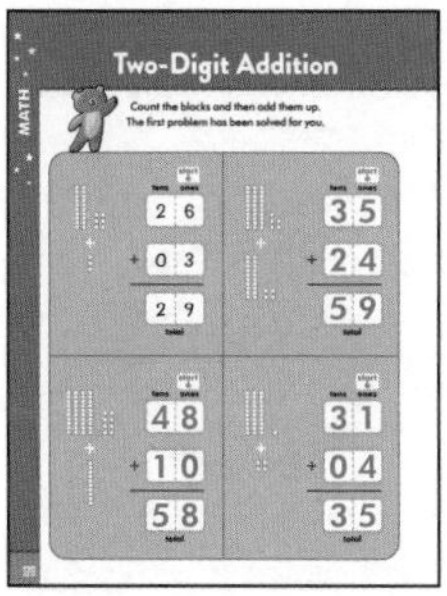

Page 179

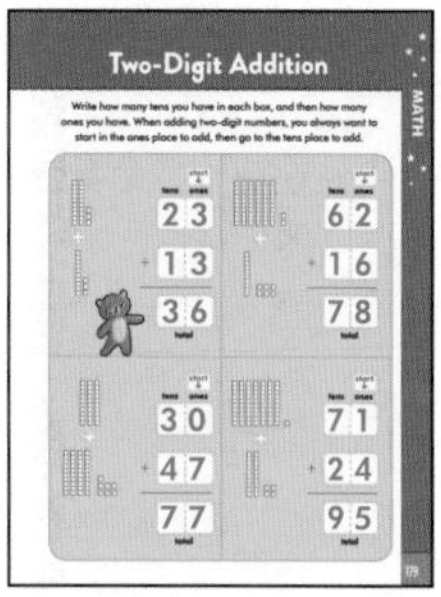

Page 180

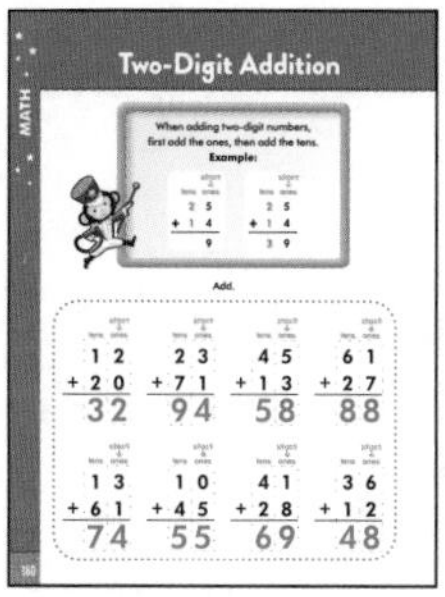

Page 181

Page 182

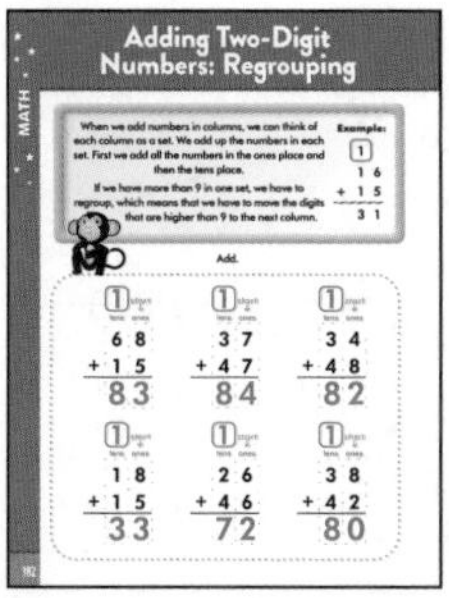

Page 183

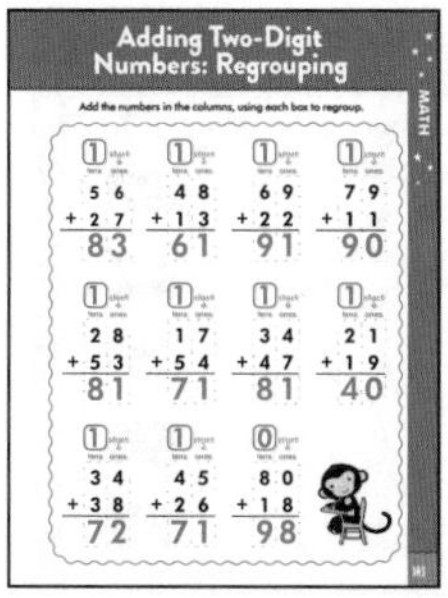

Page 184

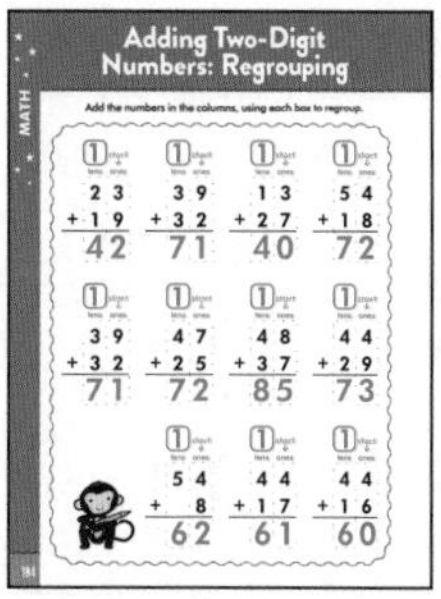

Page 185

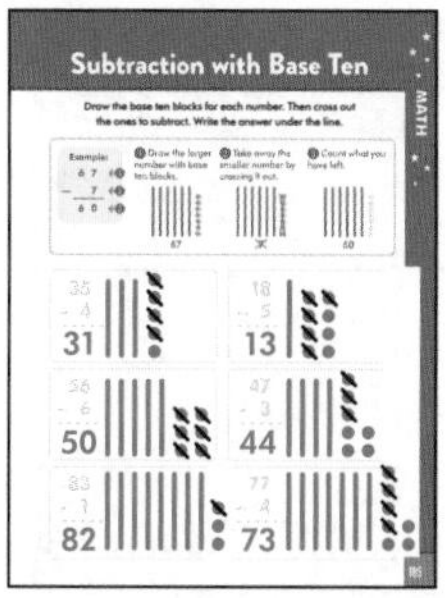

ANSWER KEY

Page 186

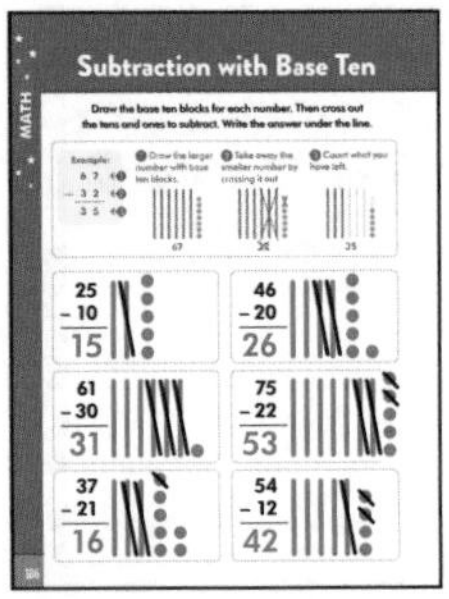

Page 187

Page 188

Page 189

Page 190

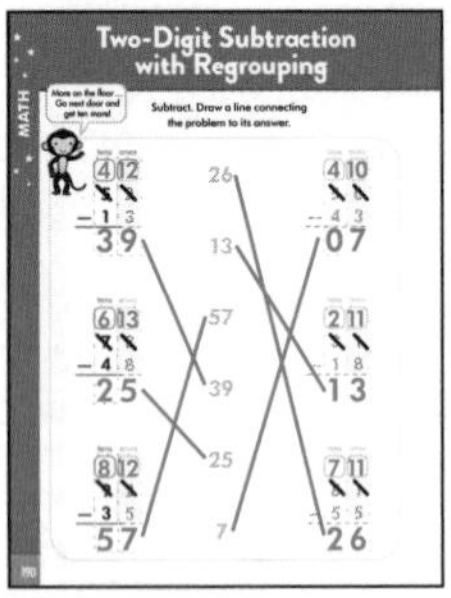

Page 192

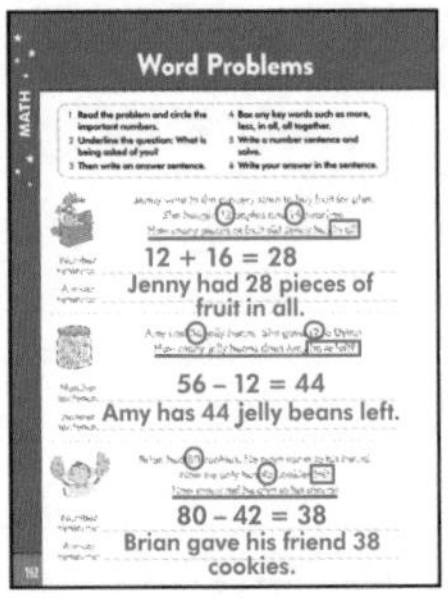

Page 193

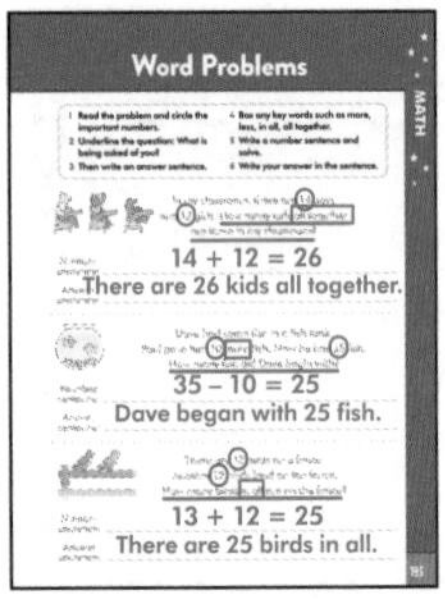

Page 196

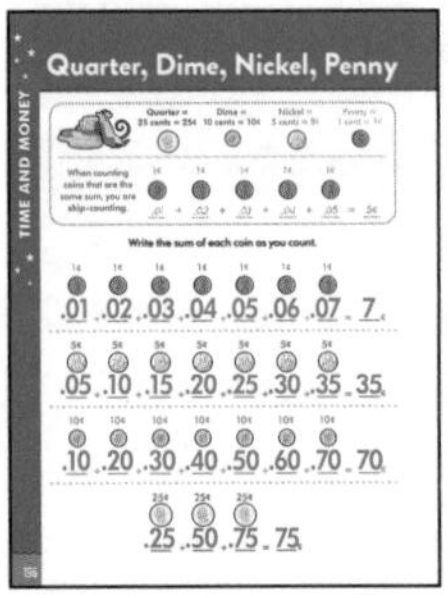

Page 197

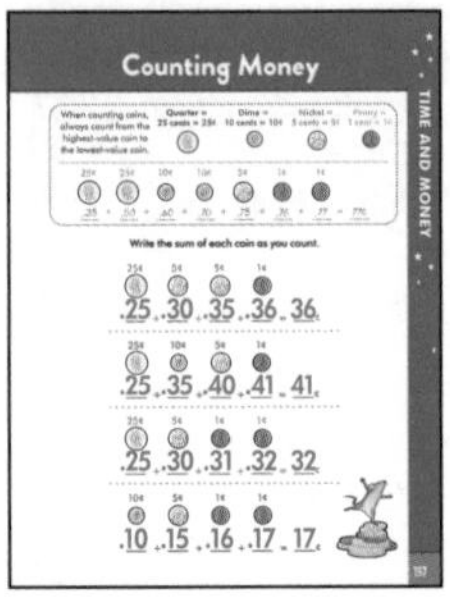

Page 198

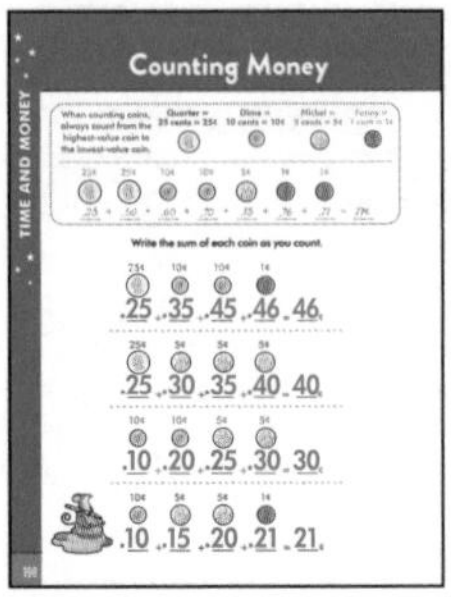

Page 199

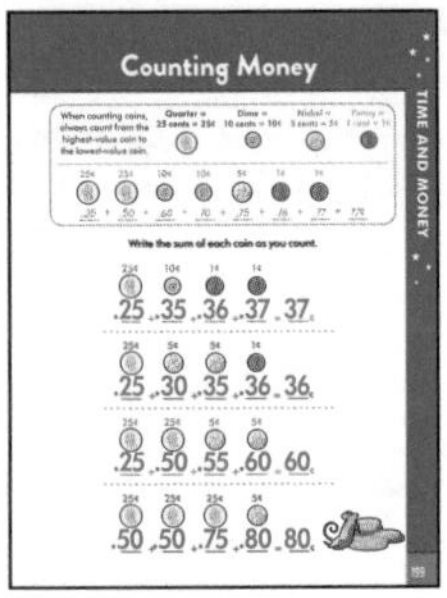

Page 200

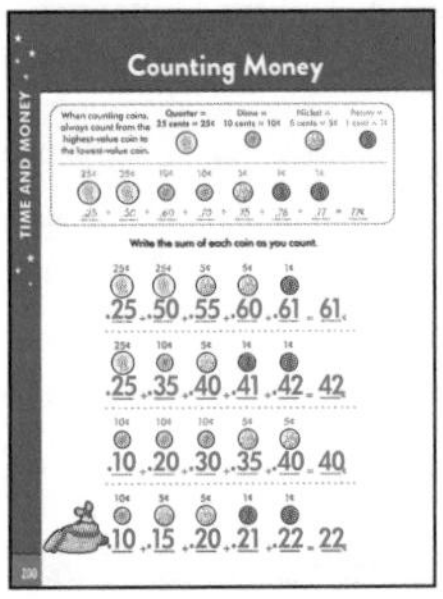

Page 201

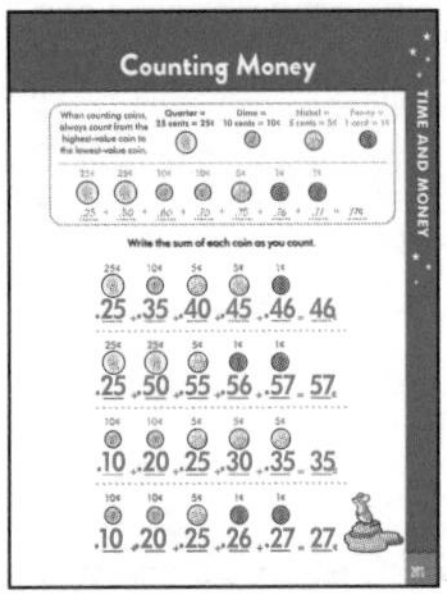

Page 202

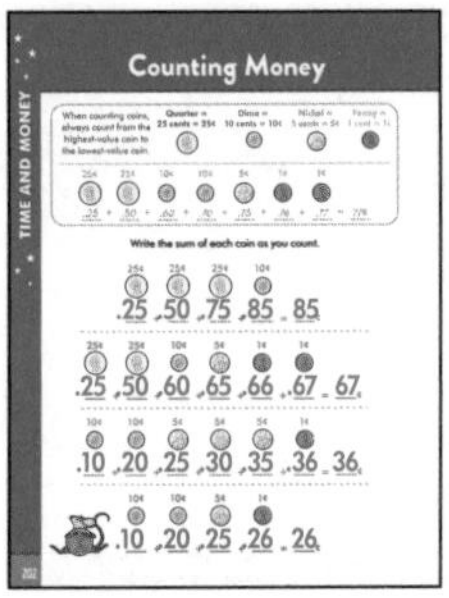

Page 203

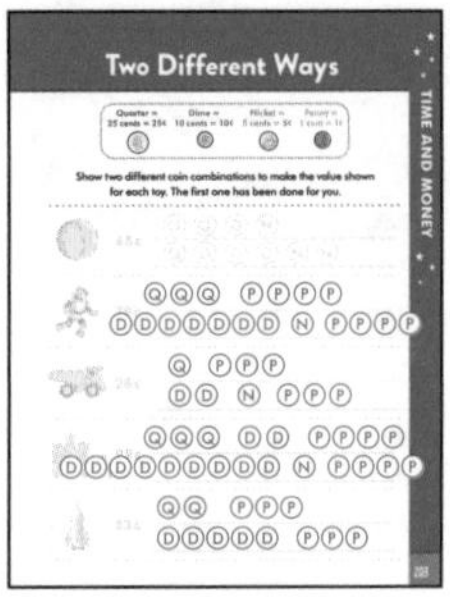

Page 204

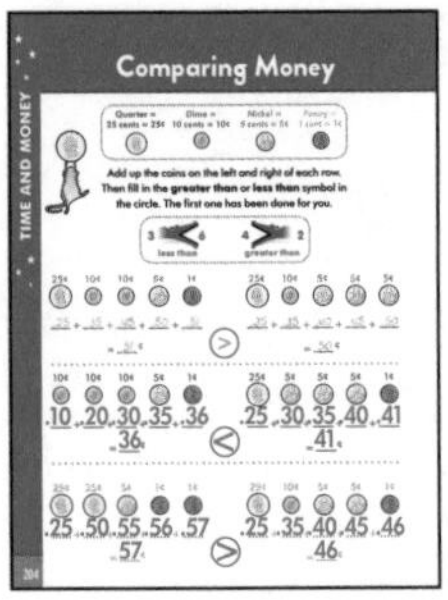

Page 205

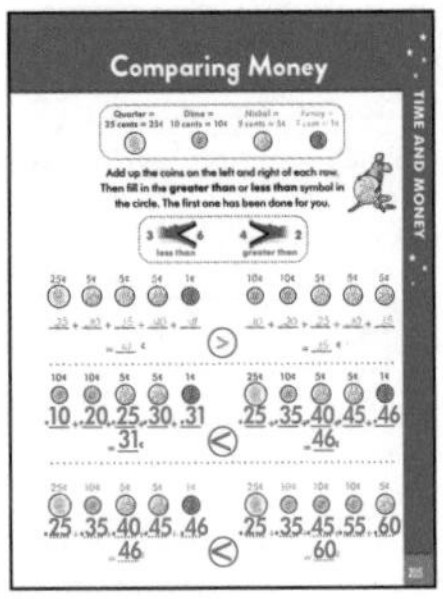

Page 206

Page 207

Page 208

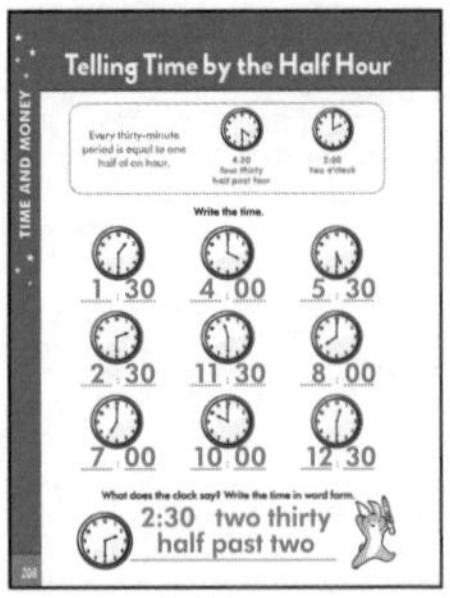

Page 209

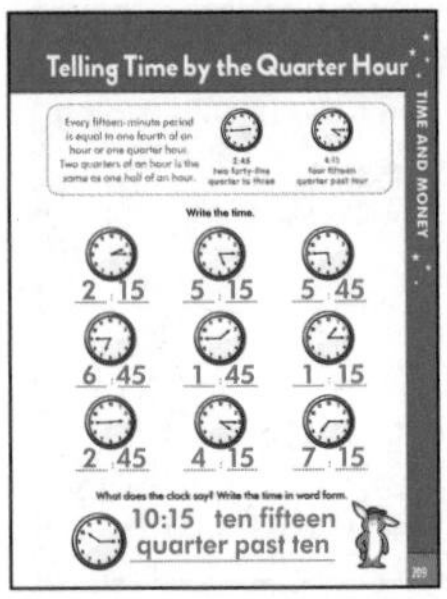

Page 210

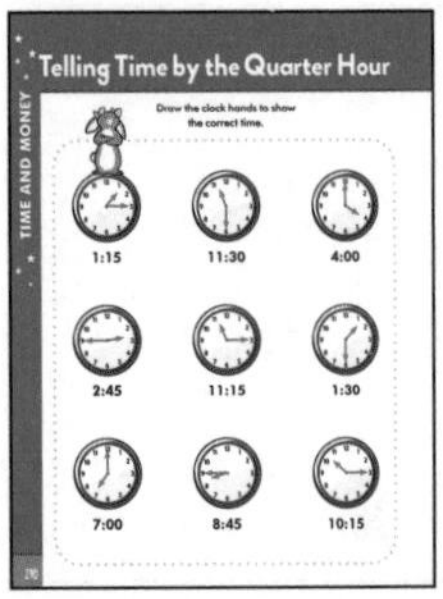

Page 211

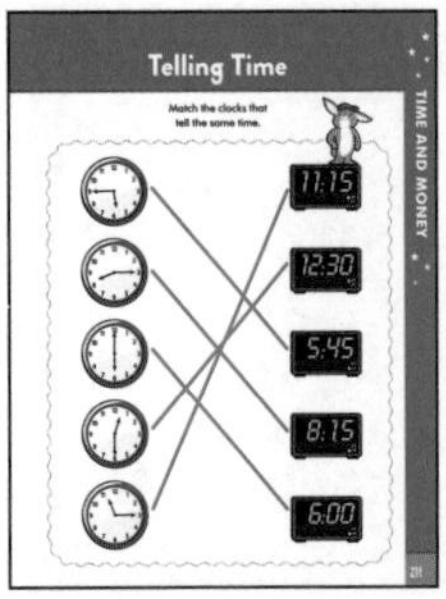

Page 212

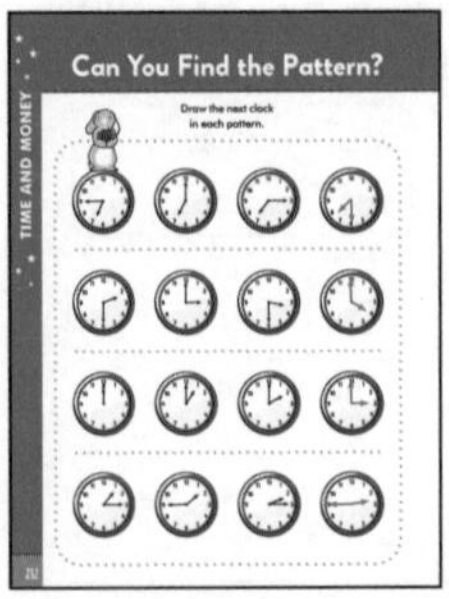

Page 215

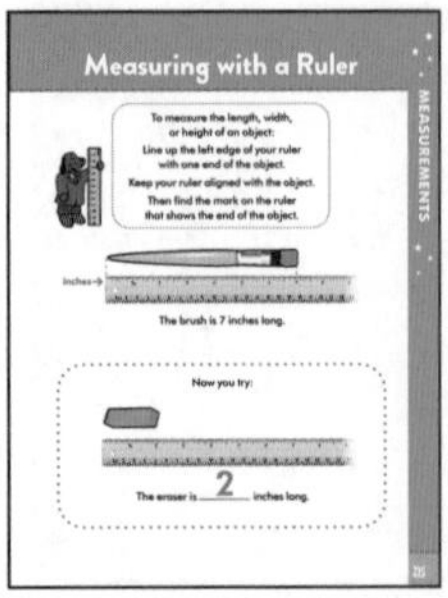

ANSWER KEY

Page 216

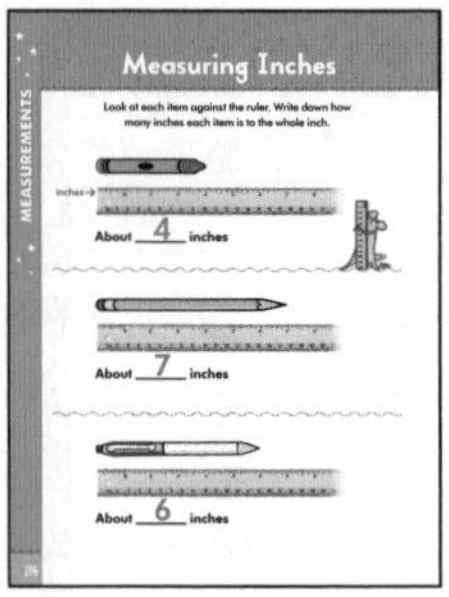

Page 217

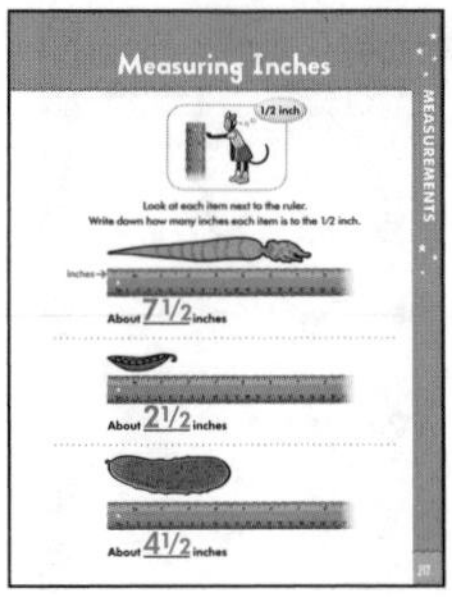

Page 218

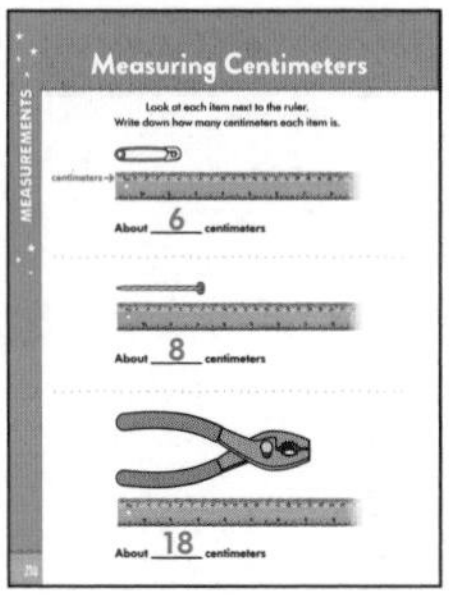

Page 219

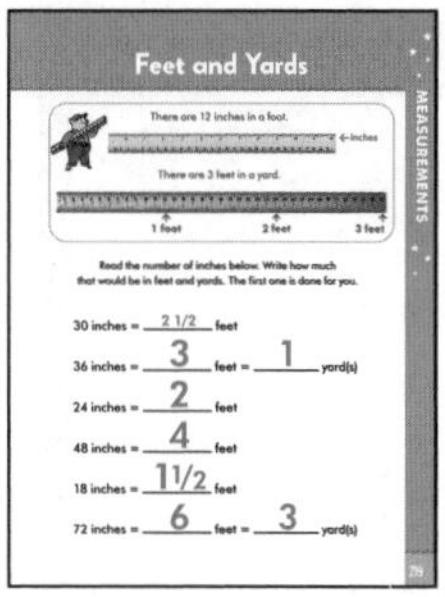

Page 220

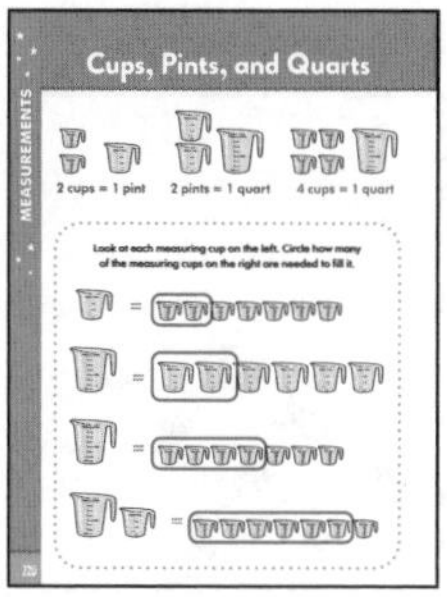

Page 221

Page 222

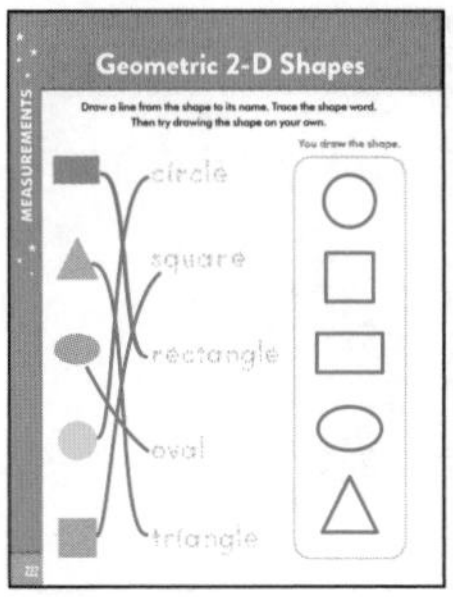

Page 223

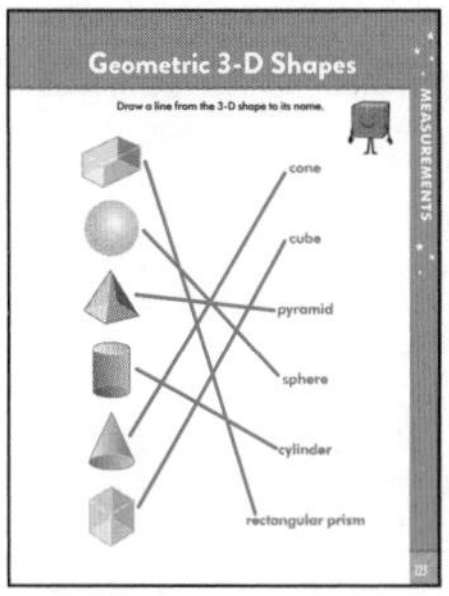

Page 224

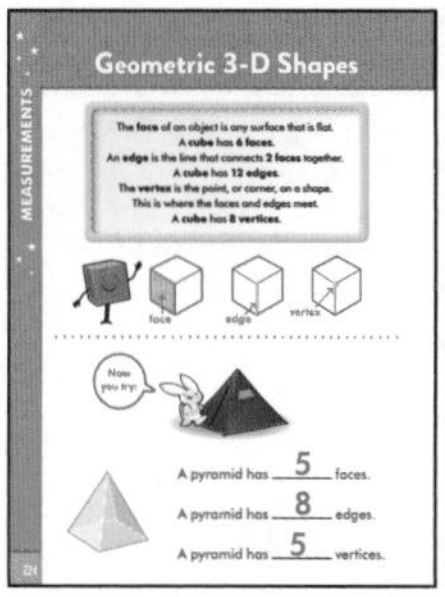

Page 225

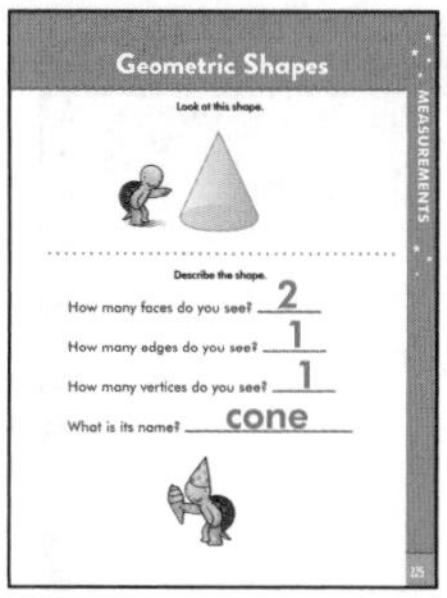

Page 226

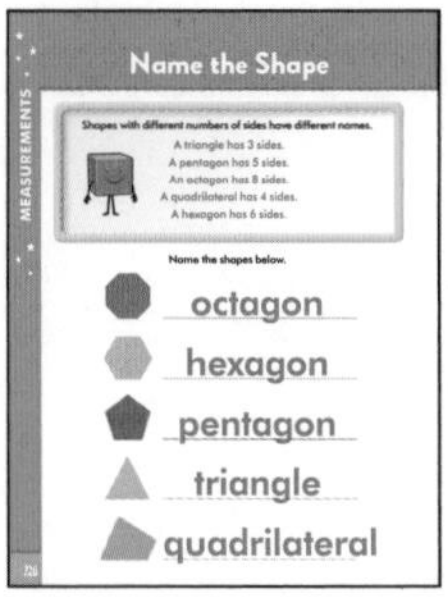

Page 227

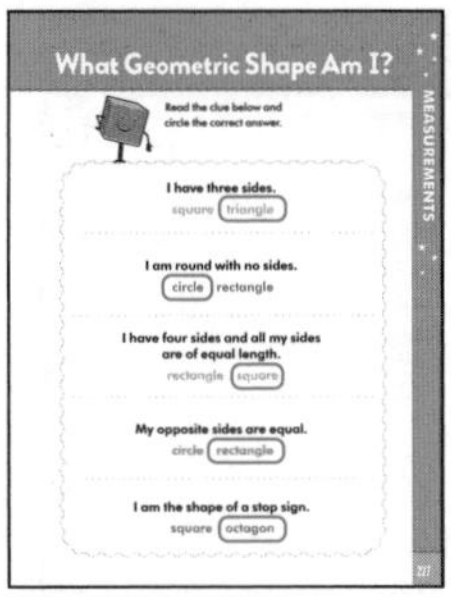

Page 228

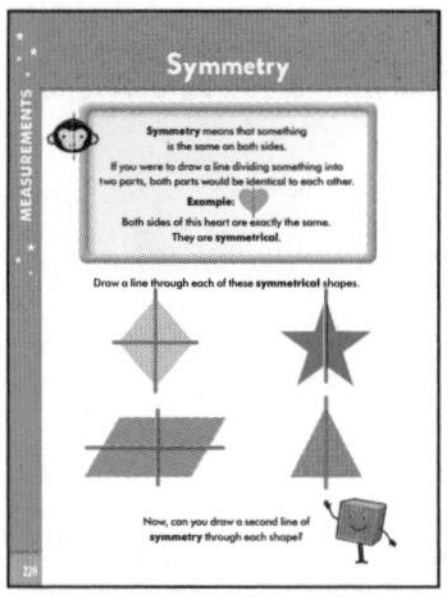

Page 229

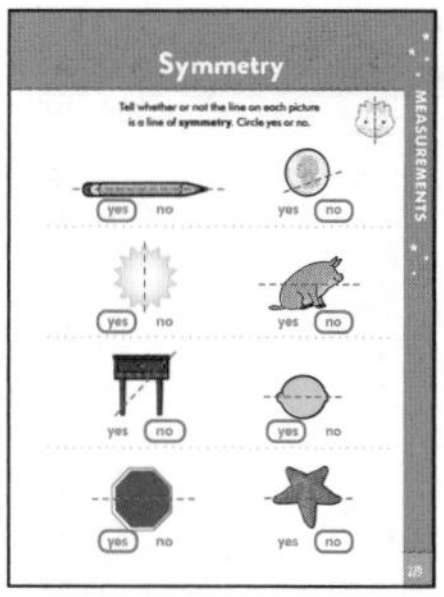

Page 230

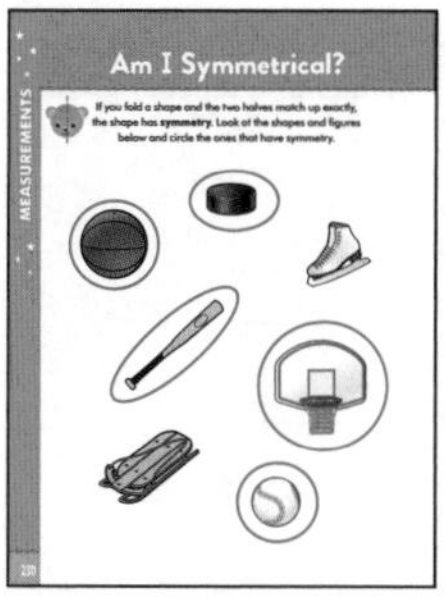

Page 231

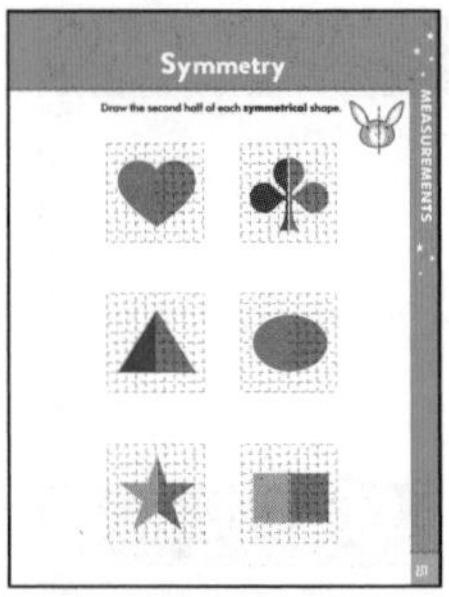

Page 233

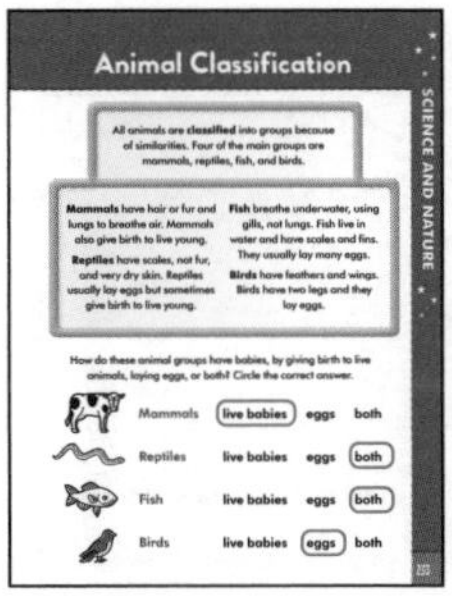

Page 234

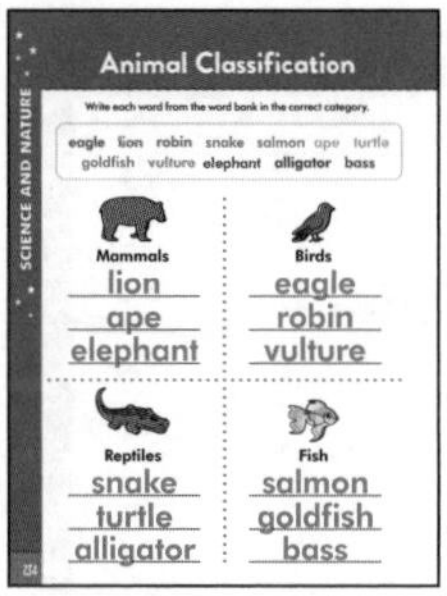

Page 235

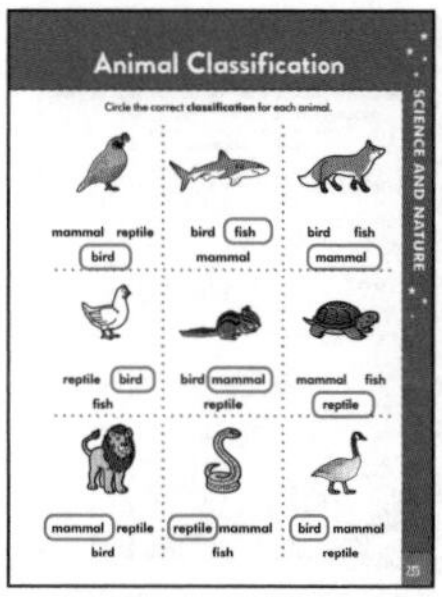

Page 236

Page 237

Page 239

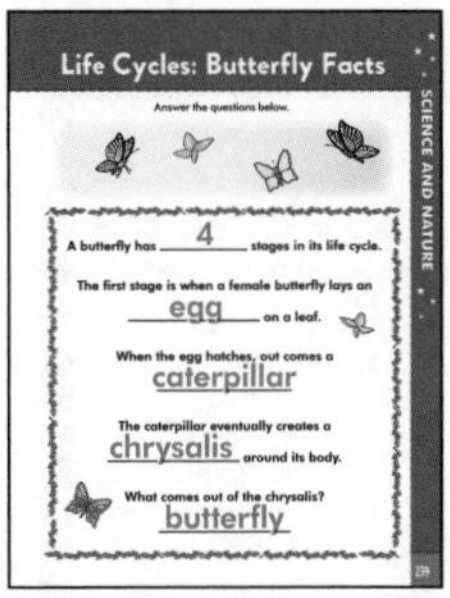

Page 240

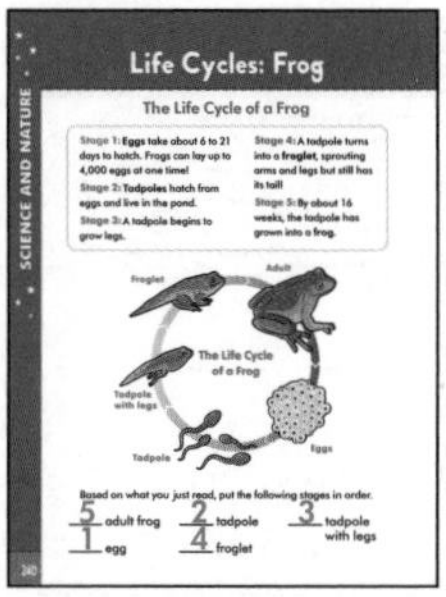

Page 242

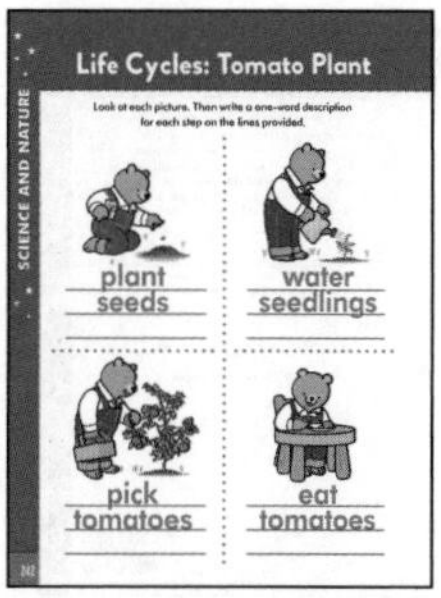

Page 244

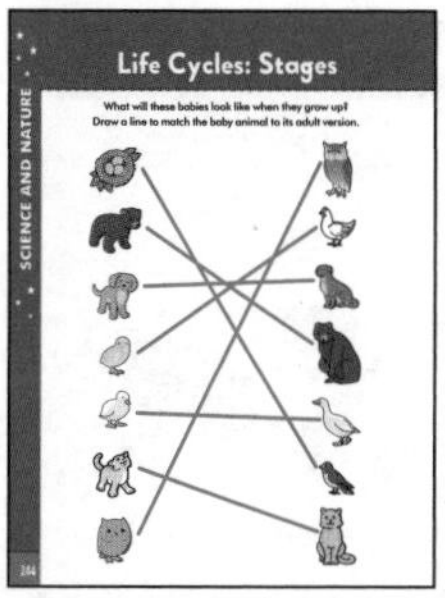

ANSWER KEY

Page 246

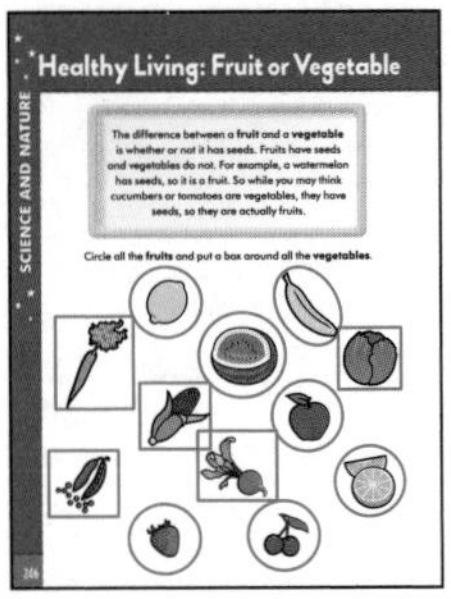

Page 247

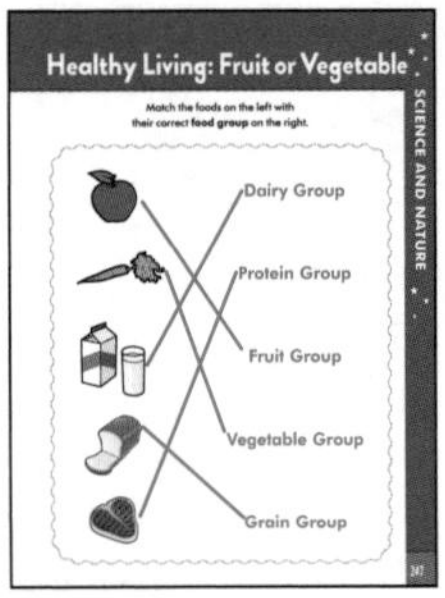

Page 248

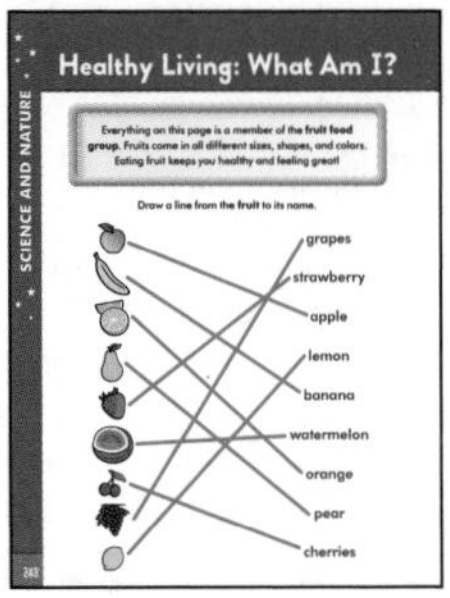

Page 249

Page 251

Page 253

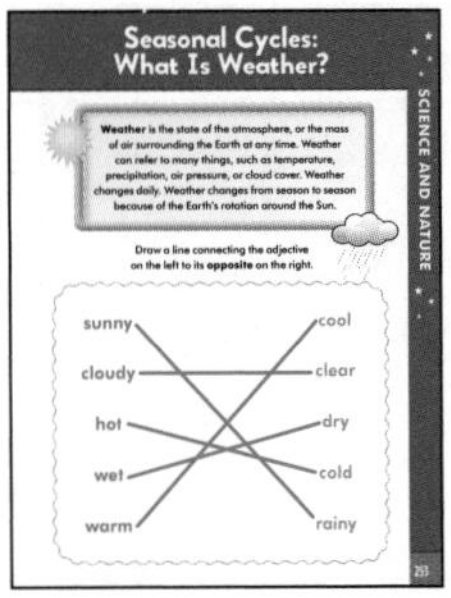

Page 254

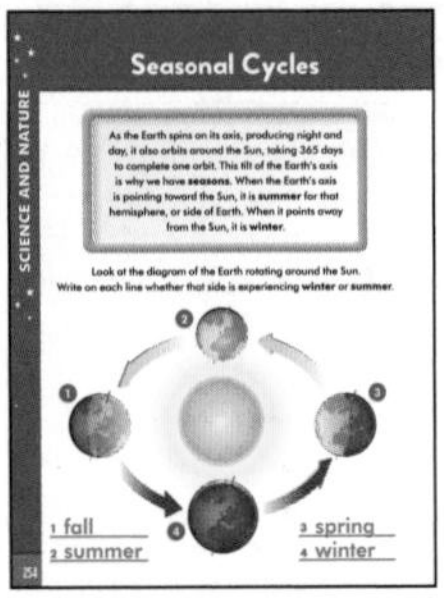

Page 256

Page 258

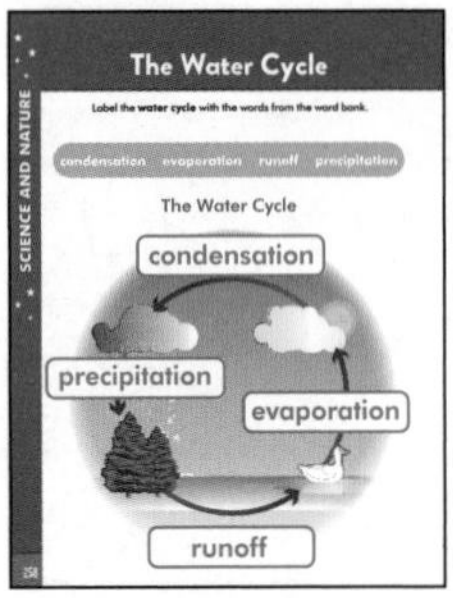

Page 259

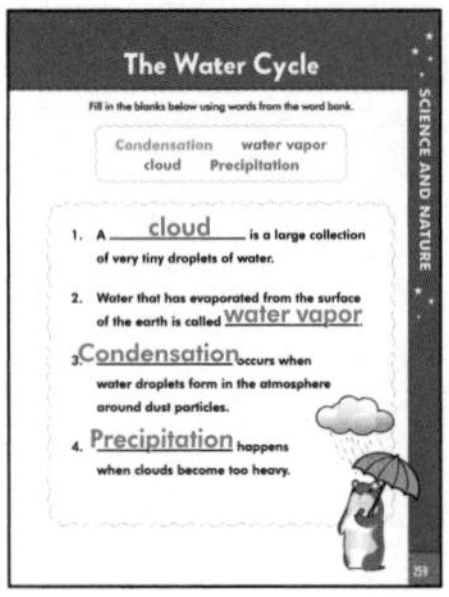

Page 260

Page 261

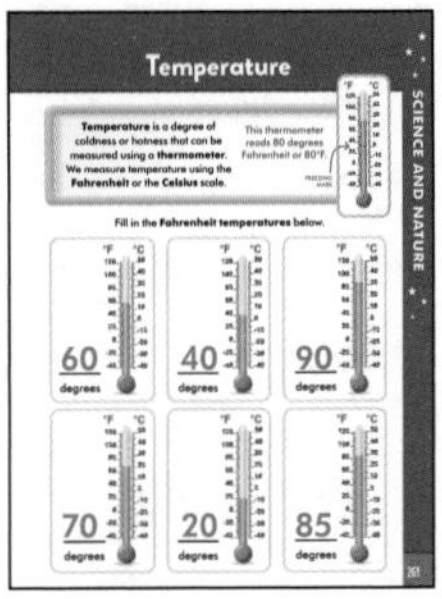

Page 262

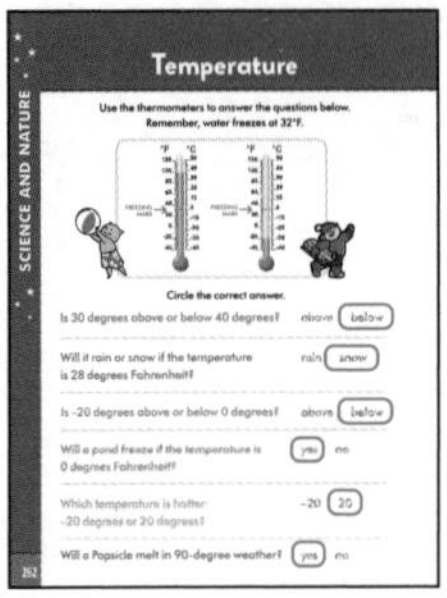

Page 263

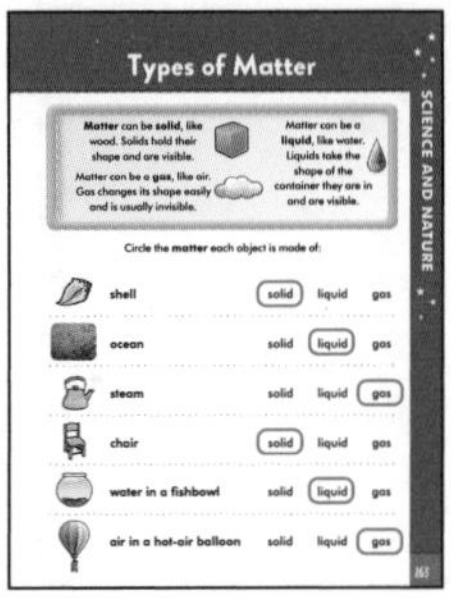

Page 264

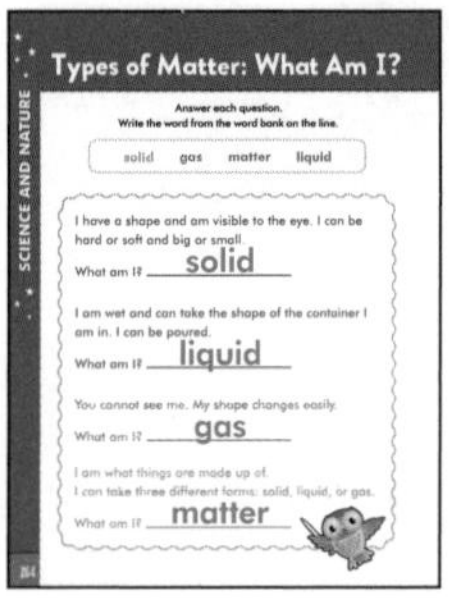

Page 265

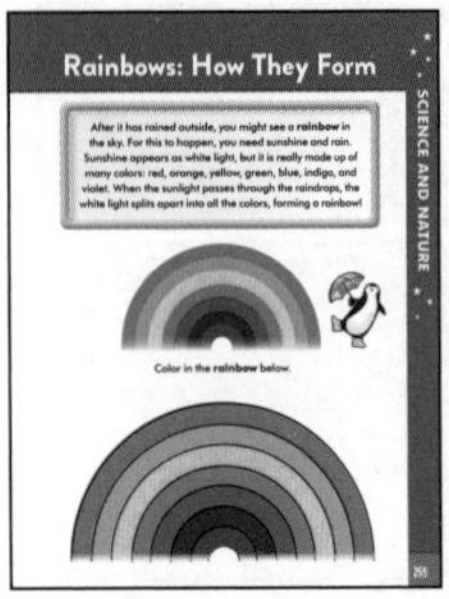

Page 266

Page 267

Page 268

Page 269

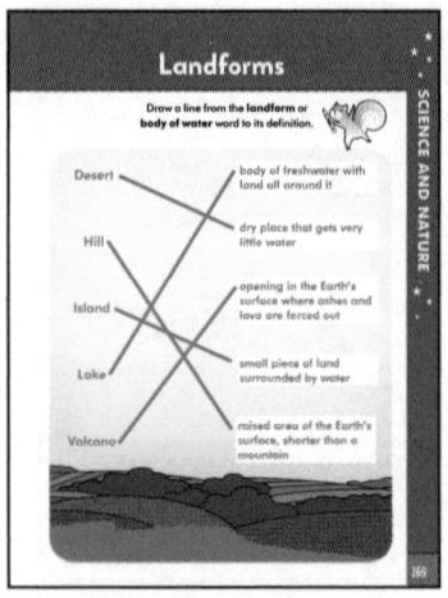

Page 272

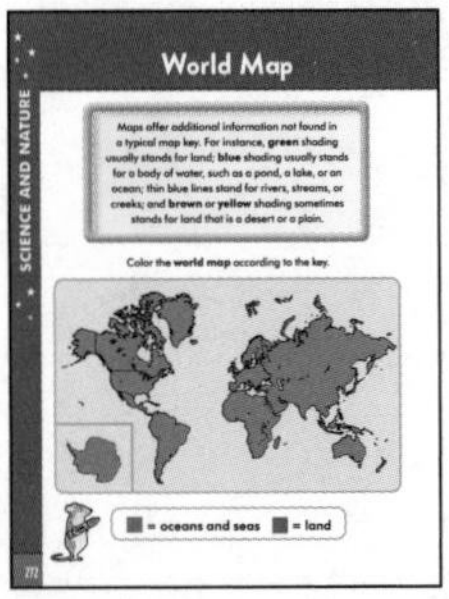

Page 273

Page 274

Page 275

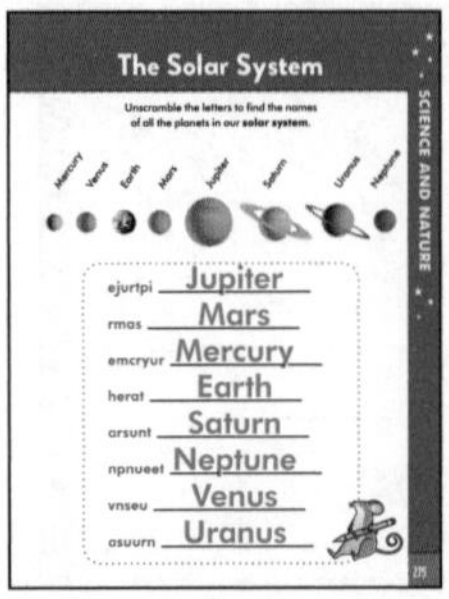

Page 276

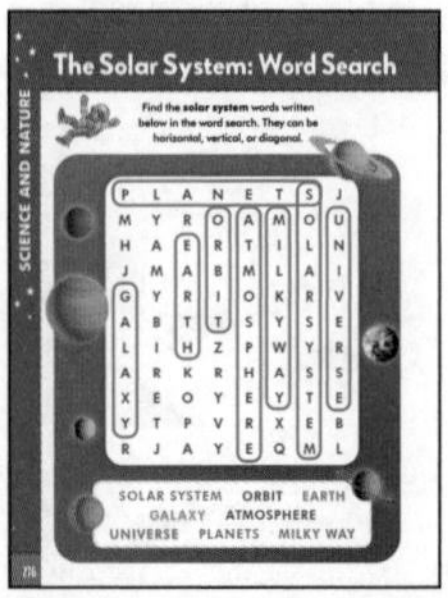

ANSWER KEY

Page 279

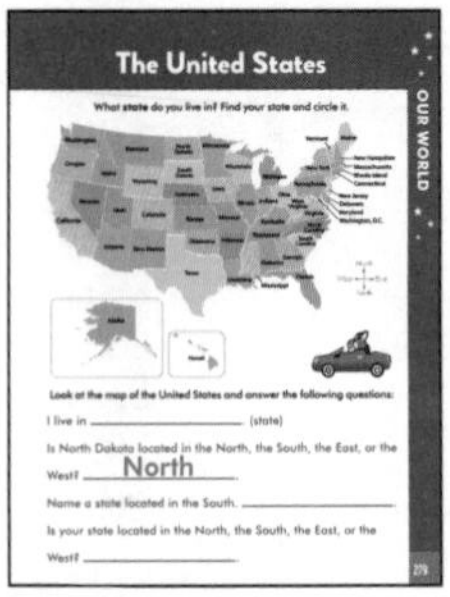

Page 281

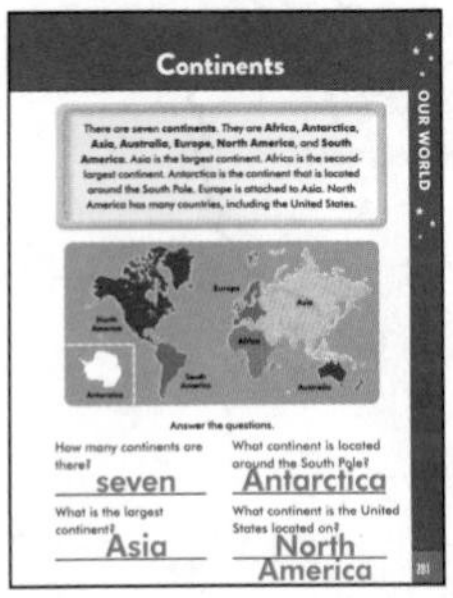

Page 282

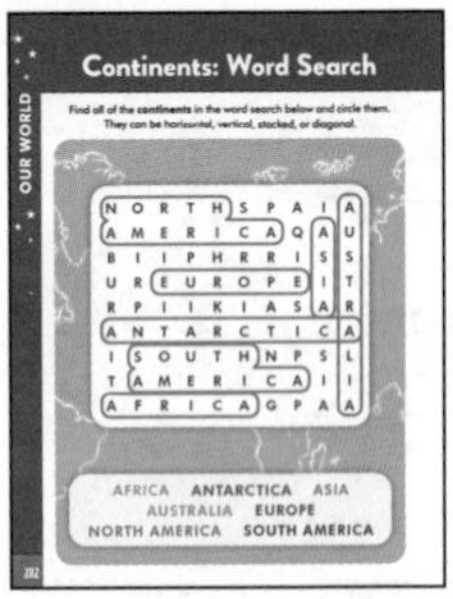

Page 284

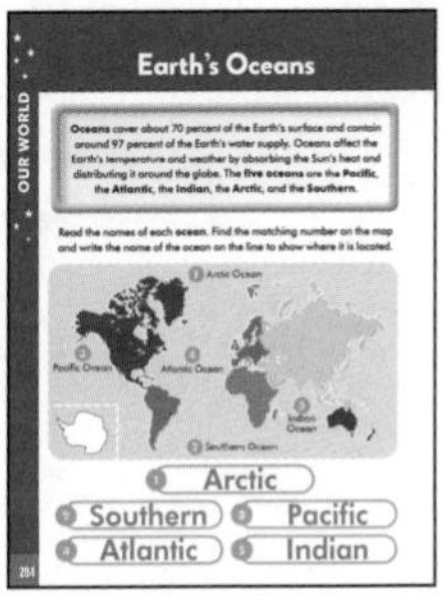

Page 285

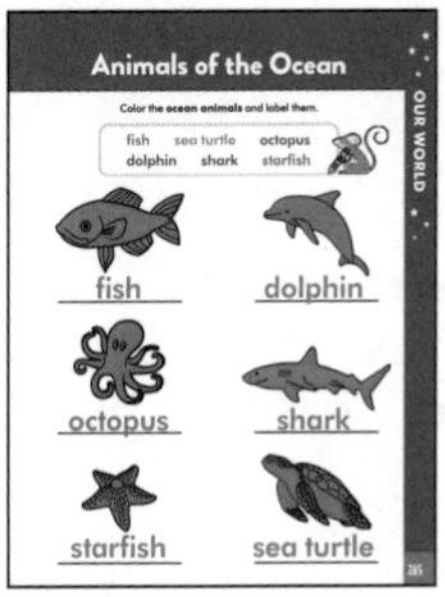

Page 286

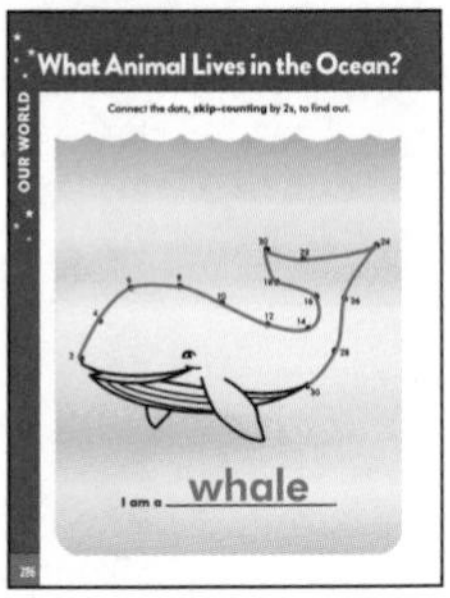

Page 287

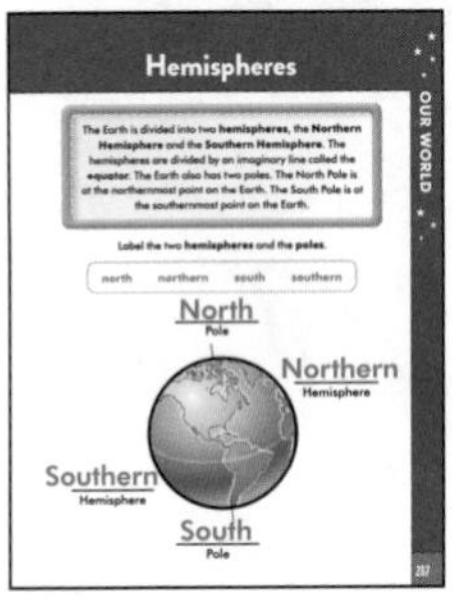

Page 288

Page 289

Page 290

Page 291

Page 293

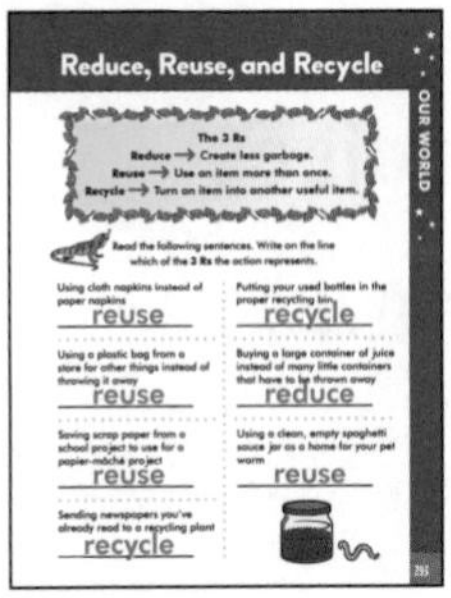

Page 294

Page 295

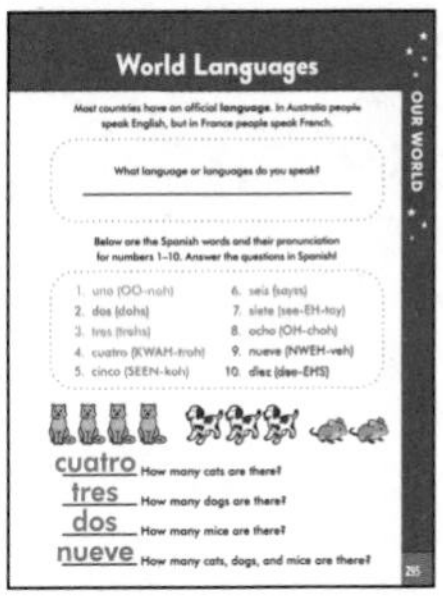

Page 297

Page 299

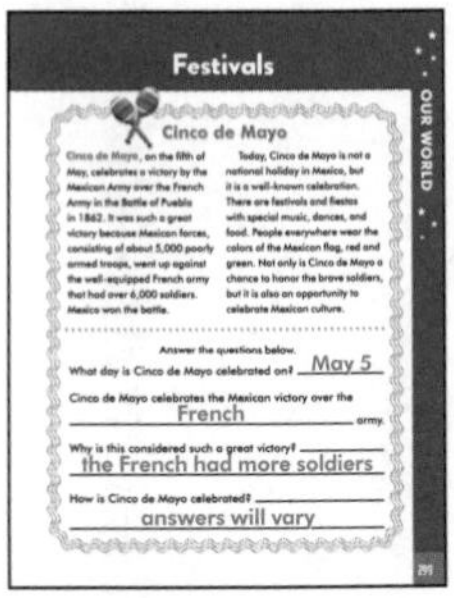

Page 300

Page 301

Page 302

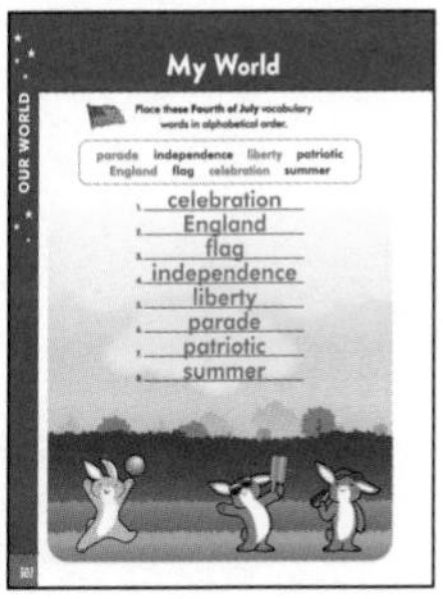

Page 304

Page 305

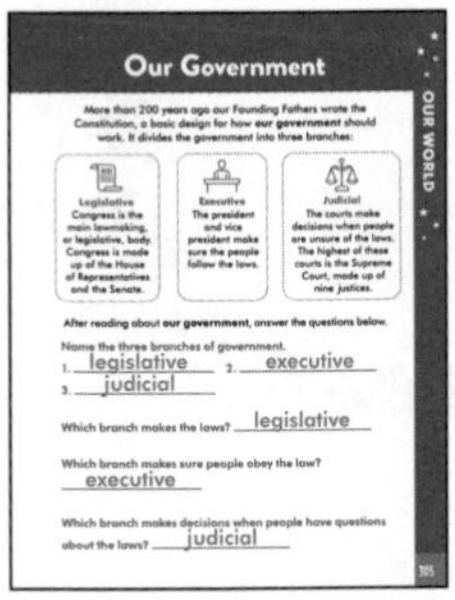

Page 306

Page 307

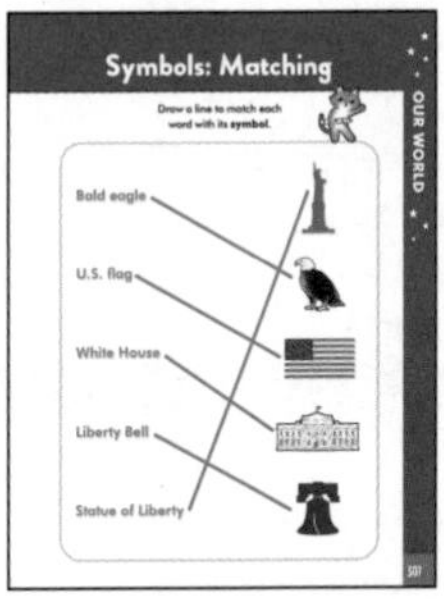

Great Job!

Quill Miles

name

has completed all the exercises in this workbook and is ready for Second Grade.

2022

date